DISABILITY, CULTURE, AND EQUITY SERIES

Alfredo J. Artiles and Elizabeth B. Kozleski, *Series Editors*

Closing the School Discipline Gap:
Equitable Remedies for Excessive Exclusion
DANIEL J. LOSEN, ED.

(Un)Learning Disability:
Recognizing and Changing Restrictive Views of Student Ability
ANNMARIE D. BAINES

Ability, Equity, and Culture:
Sustaining Inclusive Urban Education Reform
ELIZABETH B. KOZLESKI & KATHLEEN KING THORIUS, EDS.

Condition Critical—Key Principles for Equitable and Inclusive Education
DIANA LAWRENCE-BROWN & MARA SAPON-SHEVIN

Closing the School Discipline Gap

Equitable Remedies for Excessive Exclusion

EDITED BY

Daniel J. Losen

TEACHERS COLLEGE PRESS

TEACHERS COLLEGE | COLUMBIA UNIVERSITY
NEW YORK AND LONDON

Published by Teachers College Press, 1234 Amsterdam Avenue, New York, NY 10027

The editor and authors are grateful for the support of Atlantic Philanthropies and the Discipline Disparities Research to Practice Collaborative.

The chapters included in this book are an expansion of work that was initially presented during the Closing the School Discipline Gap: Research to Practice conference held on January 8, 2013, in Washington, DC. We are especially fortunate to have the collective wisdom of the members of the Discipline Disparities Research to Practice Collaborative review and approve each chapter in this book when submitted as a paper proposal for the conference.

Library of Congress Cataloging-in-Publication Data can be obtained at www.loc.gov

ISBN 978-0-8077-5613-3 (paperback)
ISBN 978-0-8077-5614-0 (hardcover)
ISBN 978-0-8077-7349-9 (ebook)

Printed on acid-free paper
Manufactured in the United States of America

22 21 20 19 18 17 16   8 7 6 5 4 3 2

To my parents,
Stuart M. Losen and Joyce E. Garskof Losen

Contents

Acknowledgments

A special thank you to members of the Discipline Disparities Research to Practice Collaborative. This group of 26 nationally known researchers, educators, policy experts, and advocates for children was formed to address the multifaceted problem of discipline disparities. Funded by Atlantic Philanthropies and Open Society Foundations, the group, under the leadership of Russell Skiba, reviewed the initial proposals, provided constructive feedback, and contributed to the decisions on the final selections. Thus it is fair to say that this book would not have been possible without the numerous contributions, guidance, and feedback from Russ and members of the Discipline Disparities Collaborative who lent their wisdom and guidance to the planning and preparation of this book. For this and many other reasons, this book should be regarded as a collaborative effort. Collaborative members include James Bell, Judith Browne-Dianis, Prudence L. Carter, Christopher Chatmon, Tanya Coke, Matt Cregor, Manuel Crillo, Jim Eichner, Edward Fergus, Michelle Fine, Phillip Atiba Goff, Paul Goren, Anne Gregory, Damon T. Hewitt, Tammy B. Luu, Kavitha Mediratta, Pedro Noguera, Blake Norton, Mica Pollock, Stephen Russell, Russell Skiba, Leticia Smith-Evans, Lisa Thomas, Michael Thompson, and Ivory Toldson. Several others supported the collaborative's review of proposals, including Cheri Hodson, Jongyeon Ee, Kareega Rausch, and Ariella Arrondondo.

Further, I am especially grateful to Carolynn Peele and Dody Riggs, who assisted with the editing of each chapter of the manuscript, and I am extraordinarily grateful to Cheri Hodson, who has been the point person for the Center for Civil Rights Remedies in all aspects of the work in preparation for this book, and to Tia E. Martinez and Jongyeon Ee for all the work they do that directly and indirectly contributed to the completion of this manuscript. A warm thank you to Laurie Russman, the administrative point person at the Civil Rights Project for the numerous ways her work supported these efforts. My acknowledgments would not be complete without a deep thank you to the directors of the Civil Rights Project, Gary Orfield and Patricia Gándara, whose enduring support and wisdom is a constant source of inspiration for the work of the Center for Civil Rights Remedies.

We'd also like to thank the Open Society Foundation for their support in disseminating many of the findings stemming from this research to policy makers, and Education Week and Gallup for cosponsoring the Closing the School Discipline Gap conference on January 8, 2013, when the initial studies and additional research were first vetted publicly. The positive and constructive feedback following that conference informed the editing process and helped shape the contents of this book.

Introduction

Daniel J. Losen

Public schools in the United States are struggling to provide the conditions for learning that our children need to be successful. Outcomes such as low rates of high school graduation and college completion and little economic upward mobility clearly indicate that students historically disadvantaged by race, ethnicity, disability status, and language-minority status are faring the worst. Hence the "achievement gap." Researchers have identified many reasons for this gap: inadequate funding; low expectations; a lack of racial and socioeconomic diversity in many schools serving historically disadvantaged children; broad inequities in housing, health, and employment; and blatant forms of injustice—including the legacy of Jim Crow.

These numerous factors likely contribute to the problem this book explores: the high frequency with which we remove students from school for disciplinary reasons, and the large disparities in disciplinary exclusion that flow along the lines of race, gender, and disability status. These disparities are also known as the "discipline gap." This book argues that the achievement gap and the discipline gap are inextricably connected.

This research volume, appearing 60 years after the U.S. Supreme Court decision in *Brown v. Board of Education*, acknowledges the depth and breadth of the issues and does not attempt to offer any simple or quick solutions. It argues instead that today's profound inequities in educational opportunity and outcomes are exacerbated by disciplinary policies and practices that schools directly control. Therefore, rather than becoming paralyzed by the overwhelming nature of entrenched inequity and pervasive injustice, in this book we focus on an area in which public schools can make improvements in a relatively short period of time—even considering that broader inequalities will not be changed in the short term.

Short-term remedies need not focus exclusively on school discipline policy per se. Solutions to disciplinary disparities seem to have certain core components in common—improving student engagement in learning, and fostering a supportive school community. Thus, even immediate more specific remedies to discipline disparities should not be regarded as distinct from deeper and broader education policy reforms. A sound approach to discipline is central to the education mission of our schools, and it is unlikely educators will close the achievement gap if they ignore the discipline gap.

The research findings and related recommendations for gap-closing nowhere suggest that to avoid suspending students, the safety of students, school personnel, or positive learning conditions should be compromised. To the contrary, the research evidence this book provides supports the argument that by eliminating excessive and unnecessary disciplinary removals schools can dramatically improve the safety and productivity of the learning environment for all children, and especially for historically disadvantaged children. Effective remedies enhance rather than curtail safety and educational opportunity.

This book focuses specifically on the decisions educators make to remove more than 3.45 million students from school annually for disciplinary reasons.[1] This 3.45 million count is the total of unduplicated students suspended out of school at least once in 2011–2012. Taken together, these students could fill every seat in every major league baseball and NFL football stadium combined (Losen & Gillespie, 2012). If we evenly divide these 3.45 million by the 182 days in a typical public school year, we see that approximately 19,000 schoolchildren are suspended out of school each school day (Office for Civil Rights, 2014).

By the time the typical student finishes high school, longitudinal studies estimate that more than one in three will have been suspended or expelled at least once (see Chapter 2). Moreover, a 1-year snapshot of all students in grade K–12 for the 2011–2012 academic year shows that schools suspend and expel children from historically disadvantaged subgroups at two and three times the rate of their nondisadvantaged peers. For example, according to OCR's Data Snapshot on School Discipline, in 2011–2012, 16.4% of Black students were suspended or expelled compared to 4.6% of White students. The following chart (Figure I.1) breaks down the out-of-school suspension rates for K–12 by race/ethnicity and gender for 2011–2012.

The K–12 disparities mask much higher suspension rates in middle and high schools. Across the nation, nearly one of every four Black students in middle and high school was suspended at least once during a single school year: 2009–2010. These rates reflect a significant rise since the early 1970s, when, by estimation, the number of students suspended was about half what it is today (Losen & Martinez, 2013). The Children's Defense Fund called attention to these troubling disparities soon after the federal government began collecting the data (Washington Research Project, 1974). For example, as Figure I.2, depicting the change in secondary school suspension rates over time, demonstrates, the percentage of students who received at least one suspension (also called the "risk for suspension") has increased most dramatically for historically disadvantaged subgroups (Losen & Martinez, 2013).

Figure I.1. Students Receiving Out-of-School Suspensions by Race/Ethnicity and Gender (K–12)

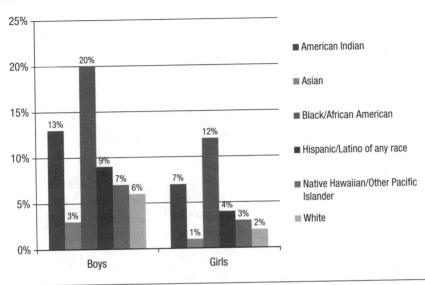

Note: Data reflect 99% of CRDC schools and a total of 290,000 American Indian/Alaska Native females, 300,000 American Indian/Alaska Native males, 1.1 million Asian males, 1.2 million Asian females, 120,000 Native Hawaiian/Other Pacific Islander males and females, 3.7 million Black females, 3.8 million Black males, 5.6 million Hispanic females, 5.9 million Hispanic males, 630,000 males of two or more races, 640,000 females of two or more races, 12 million White males, and 12 million White females.

Source: U.S. Department of Education, Office for Civil Rights, Civil Rights Data Collection, 2011–12. U.S. Department of Education Office for Civil Rights. (2014). *Civil rights data collection data snapshot: School discipline.* Retrieved from http://www2.ed.gov/about/offices/list/ocr/docs/crdc-discipline-snapshot.pdf.

Research shows deep disparities by race, English learner (EL) status, ethnicity, disability status, and gender.

Black students face the highest risk of suspension, followed by Native Americans and Latinos (U.S. Department of Education, 2013). Whites and Asians/Pacific Islanders typically have the lowest suspension rates. The disparities among subgroups are often large, even in elementary school, but the likelihood of being suspended is dramatically higher for all subgroups at the secondary level.

As depicted in Figure I.3, Black elementary school students are suspended out of school at a rate that is 5.5 percentage points higher than White elementary school students (Losen & Martinez, 2013). As the frequency of suspension rises dramatically at the secondary level, this 5-percentage point difference between Blacks and Whites expands more than threefold, becoming a 17-percentage point difference in middle school and high school.

The disparate rates for ELs and Latinos are perhaps greatly obscured when the elementary school data are joined with secondary school data. As Figure I.3

Figure I.2. Secondary School Risk for Suspension, Then and Now (2009–2010)

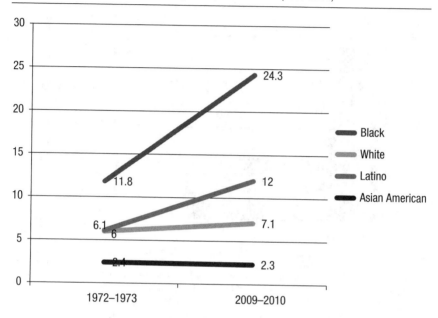

Figure I.3. Comparison of Elementary and Secondary Risk for Out-of-School Suspension by Selected Subgroup

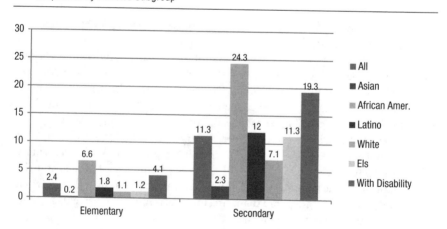

reveals, ELs at the elementary level are suspended at lower rates than most other subgroups, but the secondary school data reveal an extraordinary increase in their risk for suspension. There is a similar upward shift in Latinos' risk for suspension in secondary school, and the gap between Latinos and Whites grows eightfold, from a difference of 0.6 points to 4.9 points.

It is important to remember that 3.45 million is the count of students who were suspended out of school at least once. If we counted suspensions instead of students, we estimate the number would be over 6 million. Moreover, if each suspension averaged 2 or 3 days, the total days of lost instruction would amount to over 12 million days each year.

Despite the high frequency of disciplinary exclusion and these glaring disparities, not everyone is quick to reject the status quo. These facts often elicit three important questions for education policymakers, practitioners, civil rights advocates, and community members seeking change:

1. Don't schools need to kick out the bad kids so the good kids can learn?
2. If some historically disadvantaged groups misbehave more, *shouldn't* they be removed from school more often?
3. Are there alternatives to frequently suspending students that are more effective?

Of these three questions, the first is the most important. If the level of disciplinary exclusion we observe today were necessary to ensure the safety and efficacy of the learning environment, there would be no need for this book.

For this reason, Part I of this book starts with several chapters that demonstrate the harm caused by disciplinary exclusion. These chapters also note that the classmates who remain in the classroom do not benefit from these exclusions—a fact well established in the literature (Fabelo et al., 2011; Skiba, Poloni-Staudinger, Gallini, Simmons, & Feggins-Azziz, 2006). Thus, if removing students has serious negative repercussions for these students, and if the learning environment is not improved by frequent suspensions, then any argument for the frequent use of suspension is unsupported. If reliance on suspensions is counterproductive, then the second question about behavioral differences is moot as a matter of school discipline policy, although it is still highly relevant to questions of intentional discrimination.

Johns Hopkins researcher Bob Balfanz and his colleagues tracked the progress of nearly every 9th-grade student in the state of Florida for more than 5 years. In Chapter 1, Balfanz, Byrnes, and Fox explain that being suspended even once in 9th grade is associated with a doubling in the risk for dropping out, from 16% to 32%. Although Balfanz et al. explore many other factors that contribute to dropping out, they also find that, when controlling for the common predictors such as course failure and poor attendance, being suspended independently predicts a 20% increase in the risk for dropping out. Most important, the risks are far higher for Florida's Black and Latino students than for the White and Asian American students.

Balfanz et al.'s findings are paralleled by the first-ever nation-wide study to track self-reports of suspension, misbehavior, and long-term outcomes by thousands of individual students. This new set of findings comes from Shollenberger's research, presented in Chapter 2, in which several thousand youth, a national sample, were asked about their suspension experiences across K–12 and then followed throughout their late 20s. Her detailed analysis yields several insights that data on disciplinary actions alone could not. In addition to finding that being suspended is a strong predictor of dropping out and getting arrested, Shollenberger finds that a suspension from school often precedes any sign of seriously delinquent behavior. This pattern, true for all students, is far stronger for Black and Latino boys than for White boys. Although not offered as direct proof that suspensions increase delinquency, Shollenberger's national longitudinal findings lend support to the theory that the use of out-of-school suspensions contributes to the risk for juvenile delinquency and increases this risk more so for suspended Black and Latino youth than for White youth.

The numbers tell only part of the story. To ensure that this book does not bury the human impact of disciplinary exclusion of children within a wall of statistics, graphs, and policies, we also sought out stories of students and administrators to emphasize that human relationships are critical to the remedies described herein. The following story, told by 17-year-old Dana Alexander, was included in a report authored by Shakti Belway and published by the Southern Poverty Law Foundation as part of their efforts to draw attention to this issue.

> I've been going to school for 11 years and oh, Lord, did I used to get suspended a lot! I've been suspended for so many things: cursing, fighting, and disrespecting teachers. Suspensions are so bad for students because you miss school, you miss your education, and it's impossible to catch up. Once you get behind you may as well give up. I haven't given up because my school started doing [restorative justice] circles. Things changed for me. I haven't been suspended for a long time. Circles are like this: You sit around and talk about the root of the problems, the reasons why you do things that could get you suspended. You feel nervous, really nervous. One of the important rules is that you have to listen respectfully when the others are talking. You can't talk when someone is telling their side of the story. When you listen, you find out sometimes people aren't who you thought they were. So many times when you find out who people really are, you can avoid a fight or a conflict. (Belway, 2010, p. 5)

The empirical findings and the human realities described in this book warn that too many schools are suspending students from school unnecessarily, and that this response is often counterproductive. One reason, as illustrated in Chapter 8 by Steinberg et al's comprehensive research on the Chicago public schools, is that high-suspending schools do not improve the school community's sense of safety.

Adding high-security measures in response to safety concerns is called into question by several other authors, but most directly by Finn and Servoss in

Chapter 3. Like Chapter 2, Chapter 3 describes research findings from a national sample that includes self-reports of misbehavior. Its findings from a survey of high schools show that Black students at this level are more likely to be disciplined than their behavior ratings would predict. Equally important, Chapter 3 demonstrates that efforts to make schools safer—such as installing metal detectors and having school police on campus—after controlling for teacher and student behavior ratings, poverty, and many other factors, fail to make members of the school community feel safer. What's more, after controlling for these other variables, employing high-security measures predicts higher suspension rates for Black high school students.

The findings in Chapter 3 not only raise serious doubts about the efficacy of suspension, they also raise questions about the wisdom of adding high-security measures as a way to encourage better behavior. Given the high cost of these security measures, the possibility that they are counterproductive, and the fact that they contribute to more frequent suspension and inequities in school exclusion, should cause education policymakers to pause before they expend scarce resources on unproven strategies.

Chapter 4 takes a closer look at the costs of disciplinary removal from the classroom. As authors Marchbanks, Blake, Booth, Carmichael, Seibert, and Fabelo describe, taxpayers incur the hidden costs of disciplinary exclusion that result from the increased likelihood that students who are suspended will be retained in grade, drop out, or become embroiled in the juvenile justice system.

Marchbanks et al. provide a range of cost estimates that build on their highly regarded study of school discipline in Texas, which tracked over 1 million middle school students for more than 6 years (Fabelo et al., 2011). For example, after controlling for many other contributing factors, suspensions in Texas were associated with a 14% increase in the risk of dropping out and a twofold increase in the risk of being retained in grade. The former could translate into $750 million for each cohort of potential graduates in lifetime costs. The latter, by adding extra years of schooling and delaying entry into the workforce, could cost $178 million additional a year. These are rough estimates, but their findings introduce an important "bottom line" economic perspective that often is missing from policy debates about school discipline. As the data from 2009–2010 indicate, these costs are not borne equally and burden some groups of students and communities far more than others.

One group who bears the burden is students with disabilities, who tend to be suspended at more than twice the rate of their nondisabled peers (U.S. Department of Education, 2013). Like other groups, the discipline gap between students with disabilities and those without rises from a difference of 2.3 points at the elementary level to 12.7 points at the secondary level. Moreover, schools typically suspend male students at two or three times the rate they do females (U.S. Department of Education, 2013), and this male/female gap is much larger at the secondary level than at the elementary level (Losen & Martinez, 2013).

A cross-sectional analysis shows that the highest risk of suspension is experienced by students who belong to two or more disadvantaged subgroups. For example, a nationwide analysis of the 2009–2010 data, as illustrated in Figure I.4, shows that 36% of all Black males with disabilities enrolled at the secondary level were suspended at least once (Losen & Martinez, 2013). These disparities are even greater in Chicago, where three out of every four (75%) Black middle school male students with disabilities were suspended out of school (Losen & Martinez, 2013).

The importance of these cross-sectional data cannot be overstated, and further disaggregation reveals other profound disparities. Black females, for example, are at equal or greater risk of suspension than White and Latino males.

The disparities described thus far are explored more deeply in the remaining chapters, beginning with the focus in Chapter 5 on the suspension rates of Black females. Blake, Butler, and Smith, whose analyses of suspension among Black females are further broken down by type of offense, drive home the importance of examining disciplinary disparities for what they might reveal—not just about the experiences of certain racial groups, and not just by gender or disability, but with these characteristics across the racial spectrum. Similarly, in Chapter 6, Losen Ee, Hodson, and Martinez use data from over 72,000 schools across the nation to explore relationships among race, gender, and disability, including Black and White males with disabilities.

Chapter 6 also raises questions about the impact of novice teachers on the risk for suspension and the quality of behavioral supports and services provided

Figure I.4. Students With Disabilities Secondary Level Suspension Risk

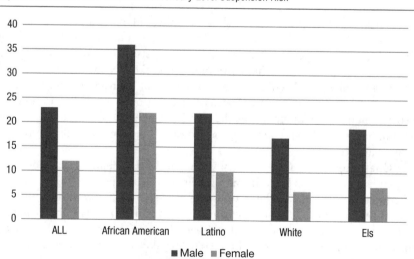

Source: Losen & Martinez, 2013

to students with disabilities. The findings in Chapter 6 suggest there might be a relationship between high suspension rates, schools' tendencies to identify students as having emotional disturbance or a specific learning disability, and exposure to a higher than average number of novice teachers.

Most but not all chapters in this book look at suspension disparities by race and include analyses that control for poverty. However, it is important to note that there is no research to suggest that disciplinary exclusion is an appropriate response to most forms of misbehavior. To the contrary, the Centers for Disease Control have criticized the frequent use of suspension for being especially harmful to children from poor families because of the additional stress that having a child sent home might cause (Losen, 2011). The Academy of American Pediatrics' recent statement put it bluntly when they concluded, "out-of-school suspension and expulsion are counterproductive to the intended goals, rarely if ever are necessary, and should not be considered as appropriate discipline in any but the most extreme and dangerous circumstances, as determined on an individual basis rather than as a blanket policy . . ." (Council on School Health, 2013, p. 1005).

Part I continues with a deeper exploration of the contributing factors and suggestions for remedies. Chapters 7, 8, and 9 describe the robust use of individuals' and teachers' ratings of student behavior, combined with other data, to understand more fully what factors contribute to these racial disparities in the use of suspension. Each of these chapters concludes with the finding that schools can control some of these factors. In Chapter 7, Toldson, McGee, and Lemmons look at one of the subgroups suspended most frequently—Black males. They track the school factors associated with behavioral issues and conclude that improving academic engagement, though beneficial to all, would be particularly effective in reducing suspensions for Black males. In Chapter 8, Steinberg, Allensworth, and Johnson take a close look at the sense of safety in the Chicago public schools and find—after controlling for many variables, including the poverty level and dangerousness of the neighborhood served—that a school community's sense of safety is profoundly influenced by the level of student engagement and by the level of trust between teachers and students and teachers and parents. Furthermore, when Steinberg et al. compare schools serving similar populations, all other things being equal, lower suspending schools are safer schools.

Finally, in Chapter 9, research by Skiba, Chung, Trachok, Baker, Sheya, and Hughes shines new light on several important issues relevant to policymakers. First, they find that student and teacher behavior ratings do not explain the higher frequency of punishment meted out to Black students, especially Black males. They also find that the attitude of school leaders is among the strongest predictors of both frequency of suspension and racial disproportionality in punishment. The findings in Part I, and most pointedly Skiba et al.'s research, highlight how factors that are under the schools' control drive both the frequency and the racial disparity observed in the use of school suspension.

The chapters in Part I discuss research on contributing factors and suggest policy solutions. The chapters in Part II provide a concrete analysis of a wide array of potential remedies. The first three chapters in Part II describe remedies with the strongest base of evidence in terms of reducing disciplinary exclusion and closing the racial discipline gap. The first of these three, Chapter 10, focuses exclusively on restorative practices.

A central goal of the restorative practices approach is to change the mindset of students who display challenging behavior and help them to gain greater respect for individuals in their community, including themselves, and more accountability to the community at large. Restorative practices aim to replace a punitive approach to discipline with a more constructive, collaborative, and humane approach that embraces all members of the community, including those who break the rules. Restorative practices thus entail systemic changes in how educators think about the role of the adults, the purpose of school discipline, and how disciplinary responses are meted out. Central to the concept of accountability are repairing any harm caused to victims and making the community whole, and doing so in a manner that addresses the needs of the offenders so they are less likely to misbehave in the future.

Notably, the benefits of restorative practices are not limited to reductions in suspensions. In Denver, González reports that during a period of 5 years the risk for suspensions dropped 5 points, from 10.58% to 5.63%. For African Americans, the risk dropped even more, from 17.6% to 10.42%; for Latinos it dropped from 10.18% to 4.74%, and for Whites from 5.88% to 2.28%. As a result, the Black/White gap was reduced in absolute terms from a difference of nearly 12 points to just over 8 points. During this same period, test scores for all subgroups steadily improved. Although the racial disparities remain substantial, these findings demonstrate that systemic improvement is possible, thereby busting as myth the theory that you have to kick out the bad kids so the good kids can learn.

Equally impressive are the findings presented in Chapter 11 from a randomized control study of a sustained and rigorous teacher-training program in a large school district. Randomized controls are often considered the "gold standard" among researchers. This first-of-its-kind study found that teachers who sought to improve the learning environment in their classrooms and focused on improving student engagement, through a training program called My Teaching Partner–Secondary, not only dramatically reduced their use of disciplinary exclusion but eliminated racial disparities. The control group made no such progress. It should be noted that this training program had already been proven effective for improving teaching and raising student achievement.

Given its broad focus on improving conditions for learning in the classroom, this training program might be just the kind of remedy Balfanz et al. recommended at the conclusion of their study (see Chapter 1), also supported by findings in Chapter 7 and Chapter 13, and elsewhere throughout this book. Namely, the most effective approaches to addressing concerns about the inequitable impact disciplinary disparities have on students' academics and lives are those that consider the multiple predictors of dropping out—low attendance, course failure, and discipline—and regard them as intertwined rather than separate reform initiatives.

On the other hand, highly specific remedies that undo far-too-common harsh responses to student misbehavior can certainly help. An example of such a remedy is found in Chapter 12, in which Cornell and Lovegrove suggest that— even in difficult cases in which students exhibit threatening behavior—there are alternatives to disciplinary exclusion that are better for both the child and the school community.

Cornell and Lovegrove's study of the implementation of Virginia's "threat assessment guidelines" (see Chapter 12) suggests that there are effective state-level policy changes that can reduce the frequency of disciplinary exclusion as a response to threatening behavior, while also narrowing the racial discipline gap. Specifically, responding to students' threats of violence in schools using systematic nonpunitive protocols, rather than resorting to zero-tolerance suspensions, is shown to reduce suspensions across the state of Virginia for both Black and White students. When students threaten violence, the Virginia Student Threat Assessment Guidelines help teachers and administrators select appropriate responses that do not primarily rely on long- or short-term suspensions. As a result, suspensions (as a response to threats) decreased by 19% (long term) and 8% (short term). A follow-up analysis demonstrates that the guidelines significantly benefit Black males and helped narrow the race/gender discipline gap in schools that adopted them (see Chapter 11).

Part II also explores two potential remedies that show great promise. The first is Osher et al.'s study of the implementation of social and emotional learning strategies in Cleveland, Ohio. In Chapter 13 they describe how districtwide investment in social and emotional learning strategies pay greater dividends than adding security measures and produce noteworthy improvements even where resources are limited. Following a school shooting, the Cleveland school district initially invested in stringent security measures such as metal detectors and school police, but these efforts did not increase the school community's perceptions of safety or achievement.

However, when the city's majority-minority schools invested in social and emotional learning, student support teams, and planning centers, they shifted the punitive system toward a learner-centered approach (this occurred between 2008 and 2011) and experienced a drastic reduction in reported behavioral incidents. Reported incidents decreased from 233 to 132 per school, with the greatest benefits occurring in schools with the highest fidelity of implementation. Although all students benefited, it's unclear whether the groups most often suspended and expelled benefited as much as groups that had lower rates of exclusion to begin with.

Similarly, mixed benefits are reported by Vincent, Sprague, CHiXapkaid, Tobin, and Gau in Chapter 14, which closely examines the implementation of schoolwide positive behavior interventions and supports (SWPBIS), a well-established systemic and data-driven approach to improving school learning environments. This approach emphasizes changing the underlying attitudes and policies of school staff in terms of how student behavior is addressed (Sugai & Horner, 2002). The expectation is that, as disciplinary referrals to the office are reduced for all students—which is a common result for schools implementing SWPBIS with integrity—those most often referred might see a somewhat greater reduction. The findings do not show a narrowing of the racial gap, but additional analysis and review of the relevant research led to two critically important policy suggestions: First, that schools and districts adapt the PBIS framework to pay specific attention to the data on race and ethnicity and seek community involvement; and second, citing research by Fenning, that schools and districts revise their school codes to align with the positive and constructive framework of PBIS (Fenning et al., 2013). Together, Vincent et al. suggest that such measures will make PBIS more effective in reducing both suspensions and racial disparities.

In Chapter 15, Vanderhaar, Petrosko, and Muñoz present a cautionary tale about disciplinary alternative schools as a remedy. Sending chronically misbehaving students to alternative schools as an alternative to out-of-school suspension and expulsion might seem like an obvious solution, but it could be counterproductive.

Vanderhaar et al.'s longitudinal investigation in a large southern school district finds strong relationships among out-of-school suspension, placement in disciplinary alternative schools, and subsequent juvenile detention. Of the children entering 3rd grade, nearly 1 in 10 experiences placement in a disciplinary alternative school by 12th grade. Racial gaps in alternative school placement are pronounced: 13% of all African American students in the cohort experienced alternative school placement, compared to 4% of White students. Half of the students placed in alternative schools while in elementary school experienced subsequent juvenile detention within less than 4 years, whereas 43% of students placed in alternative schools while in middle school were detained as juveniles within less than 2 years.

Although, like the use of alternative schools examined in Chapter 15, some remedies may falter, this book is a call for action, and it ends on an optimistic note. First, we present a personal narrative in the form of an interview with Karen Webber-Ndour, the executive director for student safety and support for Baltimore City Schools, where ongoing efforts, including training of school principals, designed to improve conditions for learning have led to thousands of fewer suspensions while graduation rates continue to improve. Webber-Ndour's narrative provides a transition to our conclusion, which notes that in many states where disciplinary removals are acknowledged as excessive the risk for suspension is coming down, and the racial gap is narrowing, too. We also point out that, although the number of schools suspending excessive numbers of students is still high, there are many others that appear to use disciplinary exclusion sparingly. Finally, we conclude by drawing from each chapter's policy-relevant findings and provide a clear set of policy recommendations to promote the most effective remedies. The good news is that many of these are not mere suggestions but are embodied in recent policy changes at the federal and state levels, and they often have implications for improving our public schools that go well beyond discipline policy.

NOTE

1. The Department of Education's release of the data on March 21 included the summary called *Civil Rights Data Collection Data Snapshot: School Discipline*. The note on page two states that 1.9 million students were suspended out of school once, and 1.55 million were suspended multiple times. A total of 3.45 million is the count of unduplicated students suspended out of school at least once in 2011–2012.

REFERENCES

Belway, S. (2010). *Access denied: New Orleans students and parents identify barriers to public education.* New Orleans, LA: Southern Poverty Law Center.

Council on School Health. (2013). Out-of-school suspension and expulsion. *Pediatrics, 131*(3), e1000–e1007. doi:10.1542/peds.2012–3932

Fabelo, T., Thompson, M. D., Plotkin, M., Carmichael, D., Marchbanks, M. P. III, & Booth E. A. (2011). *Breaking schools' rules: A statewide study of how school discipline relates to students' success and juvenile justice involvement.* New York, NY, and College Station, TX: Council of State Governments Justice Center and Texas A&M University Public Policy Research Institute. Retrieved from http://www2.mysanantonio.com/PDFs/Breaking_Schools_Rules_embargo_final_report.pdf

Fenning, P., Pigott, T., Engler, E., Bradshaw, K., Gamboney, E., Grunewald, S., . . . McGrath Kato, M. (2013). *A mixed methods approach examining disproportionality in school discipline.* Paper presented at Closing the School Discipline Gap: Research to Practice, Washington, DC.

Losen, D. (2011). *Discipline policies, successful schools, and racial justice.* Retrieved from http://nepc.colorado.edu/publication/discipline-policies

Losen, D. J., & Gillespie, J. (2012). *Opportunities suspended: The disparate impact of disciplinary exclusion from school.* Los Angeles, CA: University of California, Los Angeles.

Losen, D. J., & Martinez, T. E. (2013). *Out of school and off track: The overuse of suspension in American middle and high schools.* Los Angeles, CA: The Civil Rights Project at UCLA, the Center for Civil Rights Remedies.

Skiba, R. J., Poloni-Staudinger, L., Gallini, S., Simmons, A. B., & Feggins-Azziz, R. (2006). Disparate access: The disproportionality of African American students with disabilities across educational environments. *Exceptional Children, 72*(4), 411–424.

Sugai, G., & Horner, R. (2002). The evolution of discipline practices: School-wide positive behavior supports. *Child & Family Behavior Therapy, 24*(1–2), 23–50. doi:10.1300/J019v24n01_03

U.S. Department of Education. (2013). *The transformed civil rights data collection.* Retrieved from http://www2.ed.gov/about/offices/list/ocr/docs/crdc-2012-data-summary.pdf

U.S. Department of Education Office for Civil Rights. (2014). *Civil rights data collection data snapshot: School discipline.* Retrieved from http://www2.ed.gov/about/offices/list/ocr/docs/crdc-discipline-snapshot.pdf

Washington Research Project. (1974). *Children out of school in America.* Washington, DC: Children's Defense Fund. Retrieved from http://diglib.lib.utk.edu/cdf/data/0116_000050_000207/0116_000050_000207.pdf.

DIRECTIONS FOR
BROAD POLICY CHANGE

We count what we care about. The research presented in the 9 chapters that comprise Part I help explain why we all should care about disparities in exclusionary discipline. Once policymakers realize the importance of the issue to improving the academic and life outcomes of students, to school climate, to delinquency protection, to avoiding the waste of tax dollars, and to protecting children against discrimination, they will understand the need to make policy changes. Thus each chapter in Part I directly or indirectly supports an argument that we need to count discipline data more carefully, aggregated as well as disaggregated, including cross-sections by race, gender, and disability status. Most important, these chapters empirically analyze data in new ways and yield new findings that should inform improvements to policy and practice.

Each chapter in Part I could easily conclude with a call for more research to deepen our understanding of the problem, but the findings-based advice to policymakers contained within are also calls for broad policy action. The research findings are relevant to improving civil rights law-enforcement policy, making more equitable decisions about education resource distribution, and improving access to experienced teachers. The findings might help policymakers use discipline data to more effectively flag and then target areas of need for earlier interventions to prevent dropouts and delinquency or to identify potential shortcomings in special education services.

The message in Part I is that policymakers can and should make better use of the knowledge and information we have because many of the factors that drive up disciplinary exclusion and contribute to large disparities are factors that schools and policymakers control. Finally, these chapters share a theme: that attention to discipline, when combined with other information, can help evaluate the equity of educational opportunity. It can also be used to better target resources and other forms of assistance to schools as well as individual students who need support. Altogether, the chapters in Part I provide a deeper and broader understanding of the nature of the problem and the need to reject the status quo, as well as suggest important actions that policymakers should pursue instead.

## CHAPTER 1

Sent Home and Put Off Track

The Antecedents, Disproportionalities, and
Consequences of Being Suspended in the 9th Grade

Robert Balfanz, Vaughan Byrnes, and Joanna Hornig Fox

Over the past several years, research from several states (Arkansas, Colorado, Florida, Tennessee) and several large U.S. city school districts (Indianapolis, Nashville, Philadelphia) has identified out-of-school suspensions as one of the primary indicators of high school dropout (Balfanz, Herzog, & MacIver, 2007; Center for Social Organization of Schools, 2007; Everyone Graduates Center, 2010a, 2010b, 2010c, 2011; MacIver, Balfanz, & Byrnes, 2009). Excluding students from school for disciplinary reasons is directly related to lower attendance rates and increased course failures, and can set students on a path of disengagement from school that will keep them from receiving a high school diploma. This will diminish their chances of enrolling in postsecondary education and of realizing many lifelong career opportunities. Aside from these consequences for individual students, policies that increase student exclusion from school are also likely to be detrimental to the efforts and resources that district and school administrators invest in raising achievement levels and increasing their graduation rates.

Recent research also has suggested that there are clear and evident demographic disparities in the use of out-of-school suspensions as a disciplinary measure and that certain subgroups of students, particularly those from minority and high-poverty backgrounds, are more likely than their counterparts to be suspended at least once, as well as more often, for longer periods of time, and often for minor offenses (Fabelo et al., 2011; Georgia Appleseed, 2011; Losen & Martinez, 2013). Given the impact suspensions have on student academic outcomes, any racial disparities in the application of such disciplinary practices will also increase the achievement gap between White and non-White students in the United States (Harris & Herrington, 2006).

Following this research, we analyze data from a cohort of students from the state of Florida and find that out-of-school suspensions have significant negative impacts on students' chances of graduating from high school and enrolling in postsecondary school. We further find that out-of-school suspensions are disproportionately high amongst Black, economically disadvantaged, and special education students, thereby exacerbating inequality levels between these and other student groups by limiting lifelong opportunities. We examine the connection between out-of-school suspensions in the 9th grade and high school and postsecondary outcomes, as well as the interplay between school suspensions and two primary indicators that students are off track and will likely not graduate high school: poor attendance and course failures. The chapter also explores demographic disparities in school suspensions, their relationship to poverty, and the extent to which demographic disparities in school suspension contribute to gaps in high school graduation and postsecondary attainment.

OVERVIEW OF THE RESEARCH

The following analyses are based on a longitudinal study of data for a cohort of 181,897 Florida students who were first-time 9th-graders in the 2000–2001 school year. The full cohort included 205,337 students, but longitudinal analyses excluded students who transferred out of the state system in subsequent years, as their ultimate high school and postsecondary outcomes cannot be known. The data follow the cohort forward to 2005–2006 for high school outcomes (2 years past the expected time of graduation, 2003–2004) and through 2007–2008 for postsecondary outcomes (4 years past the expected time of graduation). Outcomes focus on high school graduation and dropout events and postsecondary enrollment at 2- and 4-year degree-granting institutions.

There are several student measures available as controls and correlates of high school and postsecondary outcomes, such as demographic characteristics (ethnicity, special education status, limited English proficiency, being over age for grade), academic behaviors (attendance, disciplinary incidents, low course marks, and course failure), student mobility (enrollment, withdrawal, and transfer data), and achievement test scores. We obtained this data sample from the Florida K–20 Education Data Warehouse so we could examine the early-warning indicators of high school dropout and postsecondary enrollment. In this chapter, we examine in greater depth the role of school suspensions in students falling off the path to high school graduation and postsecondary attainment.

Specifically, we use the data to address the following research questions:

- To what extent are suspensions connected to lower academic outcomes, both immediate (poor attendance, course failures) and long term (high school graduation and postsecondary persistence)?
- Are different demographic subgroups of students suspended at higher rates and/or for longer periods than others? If so, do these differences persist even after controlling for poverty level? Do these disparities contribute to high school graduation and postsecondary attainment gaps?

We conclude the chapter by addressing the policy and practice implications of our findings.

Our sample consisted of 181,897 Florida 9th-grade students from the 2000–2001 school year. Whereas just over half the students were White (54%), there also were sizeable minorities: One quarter of the students were Black (24%), and one fifth were Hispanic (19%). The majority of students (59%) were eligible for the federal free/reduced-price lunch program during their 9th-grade year, one quarter (26%) had special education status, and 16% were of limited English proficiency. Finally, about one quarter (26%) were over age for their grade (a year or more older than the typical 9th-grader).

The 23,440 students who transferred out of the cohort were similarly distributed across subgroups, but they were disproportionately over age, suggesting they had repeated a grade, and were disproportionately new to the Florida public school system, suggesting their families were highly mobile. Similarly, the 2,472 students from our analytic sample who were missing attendance data and the 19,515 who were missing course data were also disproportionately over age and new to the Florida public schools. However, the majority of the students in the cohort were neither over age nor new to Florida. Students who transferred out of the cohort and those missing data largely resembled those who remained part of our analyses. Most of the analyses were based on complete case data of 181,897 students, with reduced samples for analyses that included attendance or course marks data.

Students who are mobile and over age and/or who have missing data are likely to have lower academic outcomes, such as poor attendance and low achievement. Thus, by removing "transfers out," our sample is likely to be representative of students with somewhat higher outcomes than the Florida student population has on average. However, we would not expect these differences to alter the relationships or significantly influence our results for any theoretical reasons.

WHO GETS SUSPENDED IN THE 9TH GRADE?

Overall, of our cohort of 181,897 students—more than one in four (27%)—received an out-of-school suspension at least once in the 9th grade. Those suspended were suspended twice on average during the school year, and each missed an average of 7 school days due to suspension. Whereas the cohort's average days lost due to suspension is increased by the small number of students suspended for lengthy periods of time, half of all students suspended missed up to 3 days of school, another quarter missed from 4 to 7 days, and one in seven missed from 8 to 13 days of school. Forty percent of all students who were suspended during the 9th grade missed at least 5 days because of suspension.

Looking at the average 9th-grade suspension rates for students by demographic background in Table 1.1, we can see a wide variation among subgroups. Thirty-nine percent of Black students were suspended at least once, followed by

Hispanics (22%) White and Native American (22%), and Asian students (10%). Those eligible for the free/reduced-price lunch program (34%), students eligible for special education (31%), and students who were over age for their grade (40%) were suspended at higher rates than the cohort average (27%). Black students received twice as many suspensions as White students and almost twice as many as Hispanic students.

The results of our cohort analysis are similar to those found at the national level in a study conducted by the Center for Civil Rights Remedies that was based on K–12 data from the 2009–2010 school year. That study, which included nearly half the nation's school districts and roughly 85% of all public school students, found that Black students and students with disabilities had the highest suspension rates and were the two subgroups most likely to be suspended multiple times the same year (Losen & Gillespie, 2012).

Table 1.1. 9th-Grade Suspension Rates for Cohort Examined by Demographic Background[a]

	Percentage Suspended at Least Once	Average Number of Suspensions	Average Number of Days Suspended	Average Number of Suspensions (for Those Suspended)	Average Number of Days Suspended (for Those Suspended)
White	22%	0.4	1.5	1.8	6.6
Asian	10%	0.2	0.7	1.6	6.8
Black	39%	0.8	2.9	1.9	7.4
Hispanic	26%	0.5	1.7	1.8	6.2
Native	22%	0.5	1.5	2.0	6.3
Free/reduced-price lunch	34%	0.7	2.5	2.0	7.1
Special education	31%	0.7	2.4	2.1	7.4
Limited English Proficiency	27%	0.5	1.7	1.8	6.1
Over age	40%	0.8	3.0	2.1	7.6
ALL	27%	0.5	1.9	1.9	6.8

[a]Eligible for free/reduced-price lunch

A survey of school administrators in California found that over 66% were concerned that their school discipline policies were having a differential impact on students from different racial and ethnic backgrounds (Freedberg & Chavez, 2012). This study also found that Black, economically disadvantaged, and students with disabilities were often disproportionately suspended for minor and nonviolent offences that do not require out-of-school suspension by any state mandates but are applied at the discretion of school or district administrators. This means that alternatives to out-of-school suspension could be employed, a result found consistently among the other studies in this book (see Chapters 3, 7, and 9).

In our cohort of Florida students, 39% of Black students were suspended one or more times, compared to 22% of White students. The difference of 17 percentage points in Black and White suspension rates is identical to the national average for secondary school students (Losen & Martinez, 2013).

Although the suspension rates in our Florida sample is higher due to the focus on 9th-grade students alone, the differential rates among subgroups are similar to those of the aforementioned studies. The most recent data available from the Florida Department of Education website show similar outcomes.

For this study, we conducted additional analyses using multiple regression models to control for the interaction among different students' characteristics (see online draft for full results, http://tinyurl.com/JanCRPconference). Although we found that race (i.e., being Black) and poverty status are highly correlated and interrelated, the individual relationships among suspension rates and ethnicity, being eligible for free/reduced-price lunch, special education, and over-age status remain statistically significant, even when controlling for this interaction. Poverty is the student factor most strongly related to higher suspension rates, but even when controlling for poverty status, Black students have significantly higher suspension rates than White students and other minority groups, which tells us that economic disadvantages do not account for all of the racial disparities in rates of discipline.

We also conducted analyses using multilevel models that controlled for district-level factors, such as student enrollment, percentage of students eligible for free/reduced-price lunch, and the percentage of students in each minority group (see online draft, http://tinyurl.com/JanCRPconference). However, these district-level factors were not predictive of either overall suspension rates or suspension rates for certain student subgroups, after controlling for individual student-level factors. In other words, across Florida, there was no evidence that larger school districts and districts serving predominantly minority or high-poverty students were suspending students more often or for longer periods of time, beyond the fact that they served students who were suspended at higher rates individually.

Similarly, individual students from various subgroups (eligible for free/reduced-price lunch, Black, students with disabilities) were not suspended at higher rates in some districts than others because of the district's size or student population. The results did find significant variations in suspension rates among school districts, but these differences are likely explained by other factors, such as leadership and policy, which we were not able to account for with our available data (Georgia Appleseed, 2011). We found similar results for analyses conducted at the school level. Some high-poverty high schools are suspending many Black students and students eligible for special education, whereas others are suspending only a few, which suggests that how schools are organized and operated plays a significant role in determining suspension rates, echoing results found in Chapters 8 and 9 of this book.

THE IMPACT OF SUSPENSIONS ON HIGH SCHOOL AND POSTSECONDARY OUTCOMES

The consequences and implications of any demographic disparities are illustrated in Figures 1.1 and 1.2 and Table 1.2, all of which show the high school and postsecondary outcomes for students relative to the number of suspensions they received in 9th grade.[1] Figure 1.1 shows that the chances of graduating decrease with each suspension in 9th grade, as do the chances of enrolling and persisting in postsecondary schooling. Students' chances of succeeding academically are quite sensitive to even one suspension in 9th grade, as the greatest change in a student's odds of success occurs with that first suspension. With only one suspension in 9th grade, the associated chances of graduating drop from 3 in 4 to only half, and the chances of enrolling in postsecondary education from 58% to 39% or less.

As seen in Figure 1.2, the odds of dropping out of high school double (from 16% to 32%) with the first suspension in 9th grade and increase in smaller increments with each subsequent suspension. This point has important implications for the use of out-of-school suspension as a disciplinary policy, as the risks it imposes on a student's chances of high school and postsecondary success are a threat not only to students who are repeat or habitual offenders but also to students who receive one isolated suspension.

When regression modeling is used to examine the impact of suspensions in conjunction with demographics and other indicators that a student is off track, the number of 9th-grade suspensions remains significantly related to both high school and postsecondary outcomes. We created a logistic regression model and controlled for demographics, attendance, and course performance (see online draft for full results, http://tinyurl.com/JanCRPconference) and found that each suspension decreases a student's odds of graduating high school by an additional 20% and decreases their odds of enrolling in postsecondary school by 12%. It should be noted that the apparent lesser impact on postsecondary schooling does not account for the indirect effects suspension has on postsecondary enrollment, such as lowering a student's chances of graduating from high school.

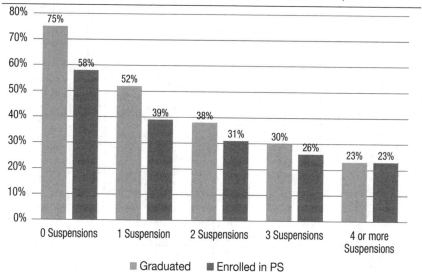

Figure 1.1. High School and Postsecondary Outcomes by Number of 9th-Grade Suspensions

■ Graduated   ■ Enrolled in PS

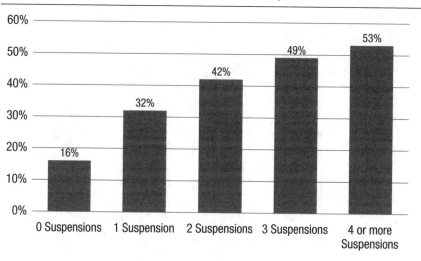

Figure 1.2. High School Dropout Rates by Number of 9th-Grade Suspensions

■ Dropped Out

23

Table 1.2. High School and Postsecondary Outcomes by 9th-Grade Behavioral Indicators[a]

	Characteristic	Number of Students With Characteristic	Percentage of Students Who Dropped Out	Percentage of Students Who Graduated	Percentage who Enrolled in Postsecondary School	Average Postsecondary Terms Completed
Behavior	0 suspensions	133,044	16%	75%	58%	4.0
	1 suspension	25,821	32%	52%	39%	1.9
	2 suspensions	11,693	42%	38%	31%	1.2
	3 suspensions	5,833	49%	30%	26%	0.9
	4 or more suspensions	5,506	53%	23%	23%	0.7
Attendance	Attendance >/= 95%	101,296	11%	81%	62%	4.3
	Attendance 90–94%	34,601	25%	63%	47%	2.7
	Attendance 85–89%	16,210	39%	44%	35%	1.6
	Attendance 80–84%	7,307	47%	31%	26%	1.1
	Attendance <80%	14,386	57%	15%	19%	0.6
Course marks	0 failures	93,626	8%	85%	67%	4.9
	1 failure	18,500	23%	66%	44%	2.3
	2 failures	14,909	29%	56%	40%	2.0
	3 failures	7,482	38%	45%	31%	1.2
	4 or more failures	27,865	51%	26%	25%	0.9
	Entire cohort	181,897	22%	66%	51%	3.3

[a]Attendance data were missing for 2,472 students and course marks for 19,515. For these categories, percentages are calculated for those students with data. Students with missing data were somewhat more likely to be new to the Florida public school system and over age for grade; however, this was not the case for the majority of students with missing data who otherwise resembled the sample as a whole.

INTERACTION AMONG SUSPENSIONS
AND OTHER ACADEMIC FACTORS

As seen in Table 1.2, students' 9th-grade course marks and attendance are also key factors determining their odds of graduating from high school and enrolling in postsecondary school. Both attendance and passing courses are intermediate academic outcomes that are themselves mediated by students' suspensions. Studies conducted in five Massachusetts school districts and in Austin, Texas (Everyone Graduates Center, 2010d, 2010e), tracked high school dropouts back through the 3 school years preceding their dropping out and found that, on average, behavior that warned of their disengagement from school was the first problem to emerge, before attendance or course failure issues.

In our sample of Florida data, it is not possible to know the extent to which being suspended in the 9th grade preceded or followed poor attendance and course performance in that grade. We do know, however, that suspended students missed an average of 7 days of school. Among students who were suspended at least once in the 9th grade, the number of days lost due to suspension, on average, accounted for 40% of their total absences. Although this average is skewed by extreme cases in which students received long suspensions, the number of days lost to suspension was still equivalent to at least 30% or more of their total days absent for half the students who received a suspension, and equivalent to 60% or more of their total days absent for a quarter of the students suspended.

Perhaps the most important point those contemplating policy and intervention remedies should consider is that behavioral and disciplinary issues affect students in several complex and interconnected ways. More detailed analysis of the interrelationships among suspension, attendance, and course performance shows two clear groups of students. We looked at how frequently suspension co-occurs with attendance and course failure, and found that almost half the students suspended in 9th grade also had attendance rates under 90% (42%) and nearly three quarters (73%) failed a course. These rates are triple and double those for students who were not suspended in the 9th-grade year (13% had low attendance; 36% failed a course). Thus districts and schools need to focus on more than just decreasing suspension rates alone, as the performance of students suspended in 9th grade indicates their broad disengagement from and lack of success in school (see Chapter 7).

There is a second set of students suspended in the 9th grade (about 1 in 5 in our sample) whose only 9th-grade off-track indicator was behavioral. This is clear evidence that, for 9th-grade students who are otherwise regularly attending school and passing their courses, being suspended can lead to more suspensions, lower attendance, and course failure in later years. As such, suspension is the trigger that puts them on the path to dropping out. Most of the students whose only off-track indicator in 9th grade was being suspended exhibited other academic or behavioral issues throughout their later high school years, primarily additional suspensions, but also in course failure and chronic absenteeism. From 10th to 12th grade, 42% of students whose only off-track indicator in 9th grade was being suspended became chronically absent, and 59% experienced course failure (66% were also suspended again in a later grade). This suggests that for about 20% of the students suspended in 9th grade, finding alternatives to suspension could have a significant payoff in terms of reducing dropout rates and increasing postsecondary attainment rates.

Conversely, for many students suspended in 9th grade, this is not their first behavioral incident in school. Thus a key factor in terms of policy and practice is that, for many students, being suspended in 9th grade is the continuation of an experience that goes back to 6th grade or even earlier. Over two thirds (69%) were suspended at least once in the middle grades: One third were suspended as early as 6th grade (39%), and roughly half were suspended in either 7th or 8th grade (47% and 51%, respectively). Moreover, nearly half the students who were suspended in 9th grade (48%) were also chronically absent during at least one of their middle grade years, indicating they entered high school already significantly disengaged from school. Whereas students who had several off-track indicators in 9th grade were most likely to exhibit an indicator in the middle grades, the majority of those who received only a suspension in 9th grade had previously exhibited some kind of indicator in the middle grades.

Finally, of all 9th-graders who had an off-track indicator (suspension, poor attendance, or course failure) and were either suspended or chronically absent in the middle grades, roughly half had been suspended before they became chronically absent. In other words, being suspended was among their first off-track indicators. (Course marks were not available for the middle grades in our data sample.) Other recent studies also have tied the effects of suspension to socioemotional indicators (see Chapter 8), correlating the use of suspensions with weaker student-teacher bonds and with school climates that have lower perceived levels of safety.

The Florida data thus suggest that, for half to two thirds of students, suspension in 9th grade is the continuation of a multiyear experience with behavioral sanctions and/or attendance issues. Some students might be suspended for the first time in 9th grade, but this also co-occurs with other off-track academic indicators. For still others (perhaps about one in five of suspended students [20%]), 9th-grade suspension might be their first and only indicator of dropping out, but for many it leads to other indicators in the upper grades. These relationships between disciplinary incidents and other academic and behavioral measures such as attendance and course failure are similar and consistent for the demographic subgroups, including Black students, economically disadvantaged students, and students eligible for special education, who are all suspended at higher rates than their counterparts.

Because our analysis examined only those students who were not missing data, and students with missing data typically exhibit the academic indicators examined above more frequently, we thus expect our estimates of both the frequency with which these indicators occur and the frequency with which they appear in tandem to be conservative. For all groups of students experiencing 9th-grade suspension, the interaction of behavioral issues with other academic indicators, and with past, present, and future patterns, emphasizes that keeping all students on track to high school and postsecondary success will be more complex than just finding disciplinary alternatives to suspension. On the other hand, the data do suggest that, for a significant number of students, being suspended from school is a triggering event that leads to poor attendance and course failure and, ultimately, to dropping out. As a result, efforts to reduce the number of suspensions in the middle grades and in high school might help keep more students on track to high school graduation and postsecondary attainment. Some policy and practice alternatives, such as early-warning indicator systems, professional development to improve classroom management (see Chapter 11), social-emotional learning, positive schoolwide behavioral interventions and supports, and restorative justice practices (see Chapter 10), target reductions in suspensions but also are part of broader efforts to improve student engagement and achievement.

POLICY AND PRACTICE IMPLICATIONS

The Florida cohort data indicate that being suspended in the 9th grade is experienced by more than one in four students. The data further show that suspension rates and the number of days suspended are disproportionately high among Black students, economically disadvantaged students, and students with disabilities. The data demonstrate that suspensions are not only common but that they have significant negative consequences for students' educational success. Suspension in 9th grade is directly related to students' high school and postsecondary outcomes, putting certain student subgroups at an even greater disadvantage. Through their relationship to student attendance and passing courses, suspensions are a key influence on the odds that students will graduate high school and enroll in postsecondary schooling. Consequently, even a single suspension in the 9th grade considerably lowers the odds that a student will graduate from high school or enroll in college. Being suspended even once in 9th grade is associated with a twofold increase in the risk for dropping out, from 16% to 32%.

Most students who were suspended in the 9th grade were suspended and/or experienced at least 1 year of chronic absenteeism in the middle grades. Most also were either chronically absent or experienced course failure in the 9th grade, and continued to do so in the upper high school grades. For many students suspended in the 9th grade, the suspension was part of an array of indicators that the student had fallen off the path to high school graduation and postsecondary success, indicating that efforts to improve educational outcomes will need to be more comprehensive than just attempting to limit suspensions during high school. For a significant subset of students, however, the data do indicate that being suspended in middle or high school is the triggering event, which then leads to broader dis-engagement from schooling and eventually dropping out.

Policies intended to reduce disciplinary disparities among groups of students and to close the racial gaps on other academic outcomes need to adopt a strategy of working to reduce suspensions while also working in a more comprehensive and systematic manner to address student attendance and passing courses as interrelated key indicators of student high school and postsecondary outcomes. Conversely, interventions that seek to improve student engagement or passing courses but ignore disciplinary exclusion are failing to address a major factor that contributes to these problems.

The swell of predictor research has led directly to recent policy changes and to states' and districts' systematic application of this knowledge in an attempt to slow the dropout crisis and increase their local graduation rates. The knowledge that suspensions, attendance, and passing courses are highly interrelated, and that students' behavior in 9th grade can identify their future outcomes, has led to the development and implementation of early warning systems that identify those students most at risk of dropping out, based on their 9th-grade records and data.

Support from the U.S. Department of Education for its High School Graduation Initiative projects, from the National Governors Association Center for Best Practices, and for independent state and local efforts has allowed some states and an increasing number of districts to establish early-warning systems. Schools implementing such systems must first determine which indicators are most useful for their students and generate reports for school staff that are based on student information and performance management systems and that identify the students most at risk; this will help school personnel intervene successfully before students become totally disengaged from school and keep them on track to graduation.

This work needs to be taken a step further by integrating early-warning systems, including data on school discipline, into the nation's ongoing efforts to turn around its lowest-performing schools. In particular, when states are given waivers from the No Child Left Behind Act, they should be required to provide technical assistance to districts with low-performing schools to increase their capacity to implement and monitor the effectiveness of comprehensive reforms that not only provide better instruction to students but enable them to avoid being suspended, to attend school regularly, and to succeed in their courses.

Bipartisan awareness of the importance of raising graduation rates and, increasingly, of combating chronic absenteeism has broadened and deepened understanding of the multiple elements that need to be addressed to increase educational achievement in the United States. To this we need to add a deeper understanding of the role school discipline and its disproportionalities play in the nation's educational success. States and districts need to review their discipline policies to be aligned with an educational purpose. Although schools should hold students accountable for misbehavior, they should avoid unnecessarily or excessively punishing students. Specifically, out-of-school suspensions should be measures of last resort, given what we have learned about their contribution to the likelihood that students will not graduate. For example, it is clearly counterproductive to suspend students for being chronically absent.

Finally, given that being suspended in the 9th grade appears to greatly diminish a student's odds of graduating and enrolling in postsecondary schooling, and that clear evidence exists not only in Florida but across the nation that Black students and students with disabilities are suspended disproportionately, even after controlling for poverty, efforts to end this disproportionality must be undertaken with great urgency. The fact that high-poverty high schools with low suspension rates for Black students and students eligible for special education can be found in Florida and other states indicates that alternative disciplinary policies are feasible. Otherwise, given the central importance a high school diploma and postsecondary schooling have to adult success in the 21st century, we will knowingly be creating an unequal and ultimately less successful society.

NOTE

1. The percentages of students in the cohort who graduated from high school or dropped out do not total 100% because some students remained actively enrolled in school 2 years past their expected time of graduation.

REFERENCES

Balfanz, R., Herzog, L., & MacIver, D. (2007). Preventing student disengagement and keeping students on the graduation track in high-poverty middle-grades schools: Early identification and effective interventions. *Educational Psychologist, 42,* 223–235.

Center for Social Organization of Schools. (2007). *Falling off the path to graduation: Middle grade indicators in Indianapolis.* Baltimore, MD: Johns Hopkins University.

Everyone Graduates Center. (2010a). *Early indicator analysis: Arkansas.* Baltimore, MD: Johns Hopkins University.

Everyone Graduates Center. (2010b). *Early warning indicator analysis: Tennessee.* Baltimore, MD: Johns Hopkins University.

Everyone Graduates Center. (2010c). *Early indicator analysis for Metro Nashville Public Schools.* Baltimore, MD: Johns Hopkins University.

Everyone Graduates Center. (2010d). *Massachusetts segmentation study.* Baltimore, MD: Johns Hopkins University.

Everyone Graduates Center. (2010e). *Multiple pathways segmentation study: Austin Independent School District.* Baltimore, MD: Johns Hopkins University.

Everyone Graduates Center. (2011). *Early indicator analysis of high school and post-secondary outcomes: Florida.* Baltimore, MD: Johns Hopkins University.

Fabelo, T., Thompson, M. D., Plotkin, M., Carmichael, D., Marchbanks, M. P. III, & Booth E. A. (2011). *Breaking schools' rules: A statewide study of how school discipline relates to students' success and juvenile justice involvement.* New York, NY, and College Station, TX: Council of State Governments Justice Center and Texas A&M University Public Policy Research Institute. http://www2.mysanantonio.com/PDFs/Breaking_Schools_Rules_embargo_final_report.pdf

Freedberg, L., & Chavez, L. (2012). *Understanding school discipline in California: Perceptions and practice.* Oakland, CA: EdSource.

Georgia Appleseed Center for Law & Justice. (2011). *Effective student discipline: Keeping kids in class.* Atlanta, GA: Author. Retrieved from www.GaAppleseed.org/keepingkidsinclass

Harris, D., & Herrington, C. (2006). Accountability, standards, and the growing achievement gap: Lessons from the past half-century. *American Journal of Education, 112,* 209–238.

Losen, D. J., & Gillespie, J. (2012). *Opportunities suspended: The disparate impact of disciplinary exclusion from school.* Los Angeles, CA: The Civil Rights Project at UCLA.

Losen, D. J., & Martinez, T. E. (2013). *Out of school and off track: The overuse of suspension in American middle and high schools.* Los Angeles, CA: The Civil Rights Project at UCLA, the Center for Civil Rights Remedies.

MacIver, M., Balfanz, R., & Byrnes, V. (2009). *Advancing the "Colorado Graduates" agenda: Understanding the dropout problem and mobilizing to meet the graduation challenge.* Baltimore, MD: Johns Hopkins University, Center for Social Organization of Schools.

## CHAPTER 2

Racial Disparities in School Suspension and Subsequent Outcomes

Evidence From the National Longitudinal Survey of Youth

Tracey L. Shollenberger

Out-of-school suspension is common in U.S. schools and has become more common in recent years. Research from individual states and districts—including the Florida research presented by Balfanz, Byrnes, and Fox in the previous chapter—has consistently found that students who are suspended from school experience worse outcomes than their nonsuspended peers in the years following suspension. But do the associations between suspension and negative outcomes documented by research in individual states and districts exist at the national level? In this chapter, I use a national, longitudinal survey to follow a cohort of youth from their schooling years in the 1990s through roughly a decade after K–12 to present a national portrait of suspension and subsequent outcomes. I find that suspension is a common experience—affecting more than one in three U.S. youth—and is highly correlated with high school dropout, arrest, and incarceration. Although these associations are strong, I find that many suspended students were not participating in serious delinquency at the time they were first suspended from school. In addition, racial disparities in suspension cannot be explained by differences in serious misbehavior. This evidence reveals that the concerns that have arisen out of research in individual states and districts apply to the United States as a whole and offers support for addressing the use of suspension and persistent racial disparities at the national level.

SUSPENSIONS AMONG U.S. YOUTH: A NATIONAL PHENOMENON

Since the 1970s, several broad shifts have occurred in the way student behavior is managed in U.S. schools. Corporal punishment has declined, zero-tolerance policies have proliferated, and schools have adopted surveillance strategies once reserved for the criminal justice system (Hirschfield, 2010; Robers, Zhang, &

Truman, 2010; Simon, 2007). Against this backdrop, school administrators across the United States have come to rely increasingly on disciplinary strategies that exclude students from school in response to misbehavior. Out-of-school suspension—the barring of students from the school building for 132 or more school days—has become commonplace. During the 2009–2010 school year, 1 in 9 secondary students was suspended at least once, up from fewer than 1 in 12 in the early 1970s (Losen & Martinez, 2013). Among Black students, suspension rates are much higher than the national average: In high schools across the United States, an astonishing 30% of Black boys and 19% of Black girls are suspended each year (p. 9).

Critics have challenged the use of suspension based on lost instructional time, persistent racial disparities, and the association between suspension and long-term negative student outcomes. As a result, some states and districts have begun to take action to reduce both the use of suspension and racial disparities. However, many states and districts have not made changes, in part because they recognize that educators need tools to help keep schools safe and orderly and to promote academic achievement.

Research suggests, however, that continued reliance on suspension might be misguided. Although many school disciplinarians rely on suspension to maintain a safe learning environment and to deter future misbehavior, there is no systematic evidence that suspension accomplishes these goals (American Psychological Association Zero Tolerance Task Force, 2008). Instead, the research shows strong correlations between the use of suspension and a variety of negative school and student outcomes. Schools with high suspension rates tend to have low academic performance and poor school climate ratings (Christle, Nelson, & Jolivette, 2004; Skiba et al., 2015; Steinberg, Allensworth, & Johnson, 2015). Individual students who are suspended from school are more likely than their nonsuspended peers to experience a range of negative outcomes, including grade retention, high school dropout, arrest, and incarceration (Arum & Beattie, 1999; Balfanz, Byrnes, & Fox, Chapter 1; Bowditch, 1993; Fabelo et al., 2011; Marchbanks et al., Chapter 4). Increasingly, research from individual states and districts has controlled for important differences between suspended and nonsuspended students more carefully, yet the relationship between suspension and negative outcomes has persisted. This suggests that suspension might cause outcomes to worsen, rather than simply co-occurring with other problems.

This chapter contributes to the growing body of longitudinal research from states and districts across the country by showing that associations between suspension and subsequent negative outcomes found in state and local level studies represent a national phenomenon. The chapter uses data from the Bureau of Labor Statistics' National Longitudinal Survey of Youth 1997 to examine suspension experiences among nationally representative samples of White, Black, and Hispanic youth who attended secondary school during the late 1990s, following outcomes for roughly a decade after respondents turned 18. By tracking experiences with suspension across school years and correlating them with self-reported experiences of delinquency, arrest, and incarceration, this analysis answers three broad questions about suspension in the United States: *How prevalent is suspension during K–12? How strongly does being suspended correlate with subsequent negative outcomes? How well are racial disparities in suspension explained by differences in behavior?* After describing the methods and the results, the chapter concludes by making recommendations for policy based on these findings.

THE NATIONAL LONGITUDINAL SURVEY OF YOUTH 1997

I use data from the National Longitudinal Survey of Youth 1997 (NLSY97), which follows a cohort of nearly 9,000 youth born between January 1, 1980, and December 31, 1984.[1] Baseline interviews were conducted in 1997, when respondents were between 12 and 17 years old. Follow-up interviews are conducted annually. This analysis uses data from the baseline survey in 1997 through the 2010 survey, when respondents were between 26 and 31 years old.

The NLSY97 provides a unique opportunity to examine suspension and long-term outcomes among a nationally representative sample of youth. The data are exceptionally rich, containing detailed information about schooling experiences, delinquency, and arrest. Black and Hispanic youth were intentionally oversampled, which allows for reliable comparisons across racial and ethnic groups. Youth were recruited into the study based on the households in which they were living; therefore, relative to surveys administered to students at school, the NLSY97 is more likely to include responses from youth who were not attending school regularly. This is important because suspension and attendance problems often co-occur. Excluding the experiences of youth who do not attend school regularly (or have dropped out altogether) would underestimate the prevalence of suspension among all U.S. youth.

For some analyses, I present results separately by gender and by race and ethnicity. For comparisons by race and ethnicity, respondents are divided into three mutually exclusive groups: (1) White, non-Hispanic; (2) Black, non-Hispanic; and (3) Hispanic.[2] For simplicity, I refer to the first two groups as White and Black. Mixed-race youth and youth of other races (Asian, American Indian, etc.) are included in results for the full sample but are excluded from analyses disaggregated by race and ethnicity due to low sample size.

All of the statistics in this chapter are weighted so that the 8,984 youth who were surveyed represent the broader population of U.S. youth during the late 1990s. Accordingly, roughly half (49%) of the weighted sample is female. Two in three (67%) youth are White, 15% are Black, 13% are Hispanic, and the remainder identify as another race or multiple races. At the time of the baseline survey in 1997, the average age of respondents was 14.9. At the time of their most recent survey, which occurred in 2010 for most respondents, the average age was 27.4.

FINDINGS

1. How common is suspension during K–12, and what intensity is typical? In the NLSY97, respondents were asked whether they had been suspended during each school year and, if so, for how many total days.[3] Using these data, I examine both the cumulative risk of suspension during K–12 and the total number of days students missed due to suspension across school years. These analyses reveal that suspension was a common feature of the respondents' schooling experiences, with more than one in three youth (35%) suspended from school at least once during K–12. More than two in five boys (44%) were suspended, as was one in four girls (25%). Consistent with prior research, Black boys were at highest risk of suspension, with fully two in three (67%) suspended at some point during K–12. Nearly half of Hispanic boys (49%) and more than two in five Black girls (44%) were suspended, whereas rates for White boys, Hispanic girls, and White girls were lower (38%, 29%, and 19%, respectively).[4]

Figure 2.1 tracks these disparities as they emerge and expand over the course of the school career. (Here I refer to "on-time" grades K through 12, which are based on respondents' ages rather than the actual grades in which they were enrolled. For example, "on-time" grade 6 refers to the school year during which respondents turned 12 years old, whether or not they had been promoted to grade 6 by that time.) More than 1 in 10 Black boys (11%) had been suspended before or during "on-time" grade 4, more than 1 in 4 (27%) had been suspended by on-time grade 6, and fully half (50%) had been suspended by on-time grade 8. By contrast, only 3% of White boys had been suspended by grade 4, 9% by grade 6, and 23% by grade 8.

In addition to calculating the percentage of youth who had ever been suspended, I track individual students' experiences across school years. Among youth who were suspended at any point during K–12, roughly half were suspended during only 1 school year, and the other half were suspended during 2 or more school years. Many missed substantial instructional time due to suspension. Table 2.1 presents the total number of days all students were suspended from school across K–12. With this measure, as with prevalence, Black boys experienced the most suspension and White girls the least, with other groups of youth falling in between. Among all youth who were suspended, the typical total length of all suspensions during K–12 was between 1 and 2 school weeks (5–9 days). However, 1 in 10 boys (10%) was suspended from school for 20 days or more, meaning they missed at least 1 full month of school during K–12 due to suspension. Among Black boys, this figure was nearly one in five (19%).

2. How strongly is suspension associated with subsequent outcomes? Longitudinal research within individual states and districts has documented associations between suspension and a range of negative student outcomes, including low educational attainment, arrest, and incarceration. The findings presented here

Figure 2.1. Cumulative Risk of Suspension by "On-Time" School Grade

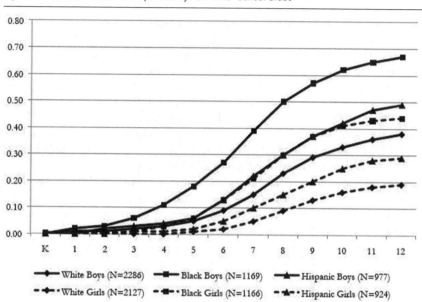

Table 2.1. Prevalence of Suspension and Cumulative Time Missed

	FULL SAMPLE	Boys				Girls			
		All	White	Black	Hispanic	All	White	Black	Hispanic
Ever suspended during K–12	.35	.44	.39	.67	.49	.25	.20	.45	.29
Total number of days suspended									
Zero	.65	.56	.61	.33	.51	.75	.80	.55	.71
1–4	.14	.17	.16	.21	.21	.12	.09	.19	.15
5–9	.08	.09	.07	.16	.10	.06	.05	.12	.07
10–19	.06	.08	.07	.11	.09	.04	.03	.07	.03
20 or more	.07	.10	.09	.19	.09	.03	.02	.07	.03
N	8984	4599	2286	1169	977	4385	2127	1166	924

confirm that these associations are national in scope and follow the story through the respondents' late 20s.

To understand how suspension relates to subsequent outcomes, I first compare students who were suspended at any point during their schooling careers to students who were never suspended. I then focus on students who had been suspended, examining whether the timing or length of suspension is further associated with negative outcomes. Specifically, I examine two factors: (1) early suspension (being suspended by age 12), and (2) substantial time missed (being suspended for 10 or more total days during one's school career).

Table 2.2 presents outcomes for White, Black, and Hispanic boys by the time of their most recent interview (mean age 27), broken down by suspension experience. The results are in the expected direction, but the magnitudes might be surprising. Nearly half of Black boys (46%), more than two in five Hispanic boys (42%), and more than one in three White boys (36%) who were suspended at any point during their school careers had not obtained a high school diploma by their late 20s.[5] While a substantial percentage of boys who were suspended had gone on to attend college, only a small share—9% of White boys, 7% of Black boys, and 5% of Hispanic boys—had obtained a bachelor's degree. Furthermore, the total length of suspension predicted educational attainment. For example, the graduation rate for Hispanic boys suspended 10 days or more was just 38%, compared to 81% for Hispanic boys who were never suspended.

The risk of arrest and incarceration was also highly stratified by suspension experience. Among White boys who were suspended 10 or more days, for example, 43% had been arrested three or more times, and 32% had been sentenced to confinement in a juvenile or adult correctional facility. The comparable statistics for White boys who had never been suspended were seven to eight times lower (6% and 4%, respectively). Similar patterns were found among Black and Hispanic boys.

Among boys who had never been suspended from school, a sizeable percentage (25% or more in each racial/ethnic group) had been arrested by their late 20s. However, only a small percentage was arrested three or more times or sentenced to confinement. Thus, although not all boys who were suspended from school were sanctioned by the juvenile or criminal justice systems, only a small percentage of boys who became chronic offenders by their late 20s had never been suspended from school.

Interestingly, controlling for suspension reduces racial gaps in educational attainment, suggesting that discipline and achievement gaps might indeed be "two sides of the same coin" (Gregory, Skiba, & Noguera, 2010, p. 59). For example, the Black–White gap in high school completion rates among youth who were never suspended is only 5 percentage points, compared to 15 percentage points for all White and Black boys. Similarly, controlling for suspension greatly reduces gaps in arrest and incarceration rates across racial and ethnic groups. The arrest and incarceration profiles for White, Black, and Hispanic boys who were suspended 10 days or more are remarkably similar.

Table 2.2. Boys' Long-Term Outcomes by Suspension Experience (Mean Age 27)

	White Boys					Black Boys					Hispanic Boys				
	All	Never Susp.	Any Susp.	Susp. by Age 12	Susp. 10+ Total Days	All	Never Susp.	Any Susp.	Susp. by Age 12	Susp. 10+ Total Days	All	Never Susp.	Any Susp.	Susp. by Age 12	Susp. 10+ Total Days
Obtained . . .															
High school diploma	.78	.87	.64	.56	.49	.63	.82	.54	.56	.42	.70	.81	.58	.58	.38
Any college	.54	.66	.35	.32	.23	.36	.53	.28	.31	.20	.43	.55	.31	.30	.24
Bachelor's degree or more	.26	.37	.09	.07	.03	.11	.19	.07	.08	.04	.12	.18	.05	.05	.03
Arrested . . .															
Ever	.39	.25	.63	.68	.76	.56	.34	.67	.68	.78	.47	.31	.63	.66	.80
Three or more times	.16	.06	.31	.36	.43	.28	.11	.37	.39	.52	.20	.08	.32	.30	.50
Sentenced to . . .															
Any confinement	.10	.04	.21	.28	.32	.22	.09	.28	.29	.38	.15	.07	.23	.20	.35
Jail	.08	.03	.15	.20	.23	.13	.07	.15	.14	.19	.10	.05	.15	.13	.22
Adult correctional facility	.03	.01	.07	.09	.11	.11	.02	.15	.17	.23	.05	.02	.08	.03	.14
Juvenile correctional facility	.02	.00	.04	.07	.08	.05	.01	.07	.08	.10	.04	.02	.07	.07	.13
Reform or training school	.00	.00	.01	.00	.01	.01	.00	.01	.01	.02	.01	.01	.01	.02	.01
N	2286	1405	881	213	355	1169	371	798	314	361	977	500	477	137	177

Table 2.3 presents outcomes for girls,[6] which in general parallel those of boys, with one exception: The association between suspension and criminal justice outcomes is weaker for Black girls than for any other group. Only half of Black girls who had been suspended 10 or more total days had been arrested by their late 20s, compared to roughly three in four White and Hispanic girls who had been suspended 10 or more days. Suspended Black girls were also less likely than suspended White and Hispanic girls to have been sentenced to a correctional facility. These findings could be due in part to a disconnect between the behaviors for which students are suspended from school and behaviors that can result in arrest. Prior research has documented that Black girls are especially likely to be suspended for defiance, dress code violations, and other subjective infractions (see Chapter 5), which might not be strongly associated with illegal activity.

3. To what extent is suspension explained by behavior? The strong correlation between suspension and negative outcomes for both girls and boys suggests two possibilities: (1) that schools are suspending students who are already at risk for dropout and arrest based on their behavior or other existing characteristics, and/or (2) that suspension influences subsequent trajectories of behavior, achievement, and punishment. Conventional wisdom suggests that suspended students are generally troubled youth who are punished first in school and then by the juvenile and criminal justice systems as their delinquency and noncompliance evolve into criminal activity. Critics of suspension, on the other hand, argue that suspension can *cause* later negative outcomes.

Unlike most administrative datasets, the NLSY97 contains extensive information on behavior, including annual self-reported data on delinquency and crime, which can inform this debate.[7] At the baseline survey, youth were asked whether they had ever participated in a range of behaviors, including destruction of property, theft (divided by items worth more and less than $50), other property crimes, drug sales, physical assault,[8] carrying a handgun, and gang involvement. (These questions did not distinguish between behaviors that happen inside and outside of school.) Using responses to these questions, I divide respondents into four mutually exclusive groups based on their delinquency experiences: (1) no delinquency; (2) property only (a composite measure of destruction of property, theft under $50, theft of $50 or more, and other property crimes); (3) violent only (a composite measure of physical assault, carrying a handgun, and gang involvement); and (4) both property and violent activities.

To shed light on the extent to which suspension reflects behavior problems, I compare these delinquency data to suspension experiences. I limit the analysis to the younger half of the sample (mean age 13 at baseline) in order to observe youth as early as possible in the schooling process. Table 2.4 presents the results.

Table 2.3. Girls' Long-Term Outcomes by Suspension Experience (Mean Age 27)

	White Girls					Black Girls					Hispanic Girls				
	All	Never susp.	Any susp.	Susp. by age 12	Susp. 10+ total days	All	Never susp.	Any susp.	Susp. by age 12	Susp. 10+ total days	All	Never susp.	Any susp.	Susp. by age 12	Susp. 10+ total days
Obtained . . .															
High school diploma	.82	.87	.61		.43	.77	.86	.65	.69	.56	.75	.80	.63		.47
Any college	.63	.70	.37		.26	.57	.69	.42	.45	.32	.50	.54	.40		.37
Bachelor's degree or more	.35	.42	.10		.04	.20	.29	.09	.10	.03	.18	.22	.09		.04
Arrested . . .															
Ever	.21	.14	.50		.76	.24	.14	.37	.43	.50	.19	.11	.41		.73
Three or more times	.06	.03	.21		.37	.06	.03	.11	.15	.18	.06	.01	.17		.37
Sentenced to . . .															
Any confinement	.04	.02	.13		.21	.04	.02	.07	.08	.12	.03	.01	.09		.19
Jail	.03	.01	.08		.12	.02	.01	.04	.07	.07	.02	.01	.04		.09
Adult correctional facility	.01	.00	.03		.04	.01	.01	.02	.03	.02	.01	.00	.02		.00
Juvenile correctional facility	.01	.00	.04		.09	.01	.01	.02	.01	.04	.01	.00	.04		.10
Reform or training school	.00	.00	.01		.02	.00	.00	.00	.00	.00	.00	.00	.01		.00
N	2127	1708	419	52	119	1166	619	547	162	169	924	660	264	45	60

Table 2.4. Boys' Early Participation in Delinquency by Suspension Experience (Subsample: Younger Half of Respondents, Mean Age 13)

	White Boys		Black Boys		Hispanic Boys	
Ever suspended?	No	Yes	No	Yes	No	Yes
No delinquency	.52	.21	.53	.35	.53	.42
Property only	.25	.29	.22	.24	.28	.21
Violent only	.07	.05	.07	.09	.05	.09
Both property and violent	.16	.45	.18	.32	.14	.28
N	856	227	230	295	295	153

Note: The property category includes destruction of property, theft, and other property crimes. The violent category includes physical assault, carrying a handgun, and belonging to a gang.

Two findings deserve special attention. First, White boys who had been suspended were more likely to report delinquency than were Black and Hispanic boys who had been suspended. Among White boys who had been suspended, nearly four in five (79%) reported some form of delinquency, and 45% reported both property and violent activities. Among suspended Black and Hispanic boys, the percentages reporting any delinquency (65% and 58%, respectively) and both property and violent behaviors (32% and 28%, respectively) were much smaller.[9] Second, large percentages of boys who had been suspended from school did not report ever having participated in any of the delinquent behaviors. This is true of more than two in five Hispanic boys (42%), more than one in three Black boys (35%), and just over one in five White boys (21%).

In short, the delinquency data reveal that many suspended youth were not participating in serious delinquency at the time they were first suspended from school. In addition, differences in serious misbehavior do not explain racial disparities in suspension, as suspended Black and Hispanic youth report lower levels of delinquency than do suspended White youth. These findings suggest that many youth are suspended from school for fairly minor misbehavior and do not pose a serious threat to school safety at the time they are first removed from school. For some suspended students, it is possible that schools' actions might increase their risk of involvement in more serious delinquency and illegal activity later on.

IMPLICATIONS FOR EDUCATION POLICY

Given that suspension rates have increased since the late 1990s, the findings presented in this chapter offer a conservative estimate of the prevalence and intensity of suspension in U.S. schools. Yet the prevalence of suspension within this cohort is alarmingly high: More than one in three youth (35%) and two in three Black boys (67%) were suspended at least once during their school careers. Following these youth through their late 20s paints a sobering picture of what we can expect to occur over the next decade among students who are being suspended today.

The findings in this chapter show that strong associations between suspension and negative outcomes are a national phenomenon. Students across the United States who are suspended from school are less likely than their nonsuspended peers to obtain a high school diploma and to obtain a bachelor's degree by their late 20s, and are more likely to be arrested, arrested multiple times, and sentenced to confinement in a correctional facility. Combined with evidence provided in Chapters 3 and 7 in this volume, these findings present a compelling case for reconsidering our national reliance on suspension.

Because suspension and negative outcomes are highly correlated, it is important from a policy perspective to understand the nature of these relationships: Does suspension simply identify youth who are already at risk for dropout and arrest, or does it increase students' likelihood of having negative outcomes? For policymakers concerned about human capital development and the provision of public safety, funding research that (1) rigorously examines the possibility of a causal relationship between suspension and subsequent outcomes, and (2) compares the costs and benefits of out-of-school suspension with those of alternative interventions should be a top priority.

The findings of this study have several additional implications for education policy at the federal, state, and district levels.[10] First, given that the basis for concern about the use of suspension—that is, substantial missed instructional time and racially disparate impact—has been documented nationally, policymakers should consider pursuing changes to federal policy to address the use of suspension. One option is to offer incentives that promote using promising alternatives to suspension, including restorative justice (see Chapter 10). Some national efforts to eliminate excessive and disparate disciplinary exclusion are already under way, including guidance on disparate impact jointly released by the U.S. Departments of Justice and Education in January 2014 and additional recommendations and resources developed as part of the Safe and Supportive School Discipline Initiative consensus project. Second, policymakers at the state and district levels should identify and support schools with high rates of exclusionary discipline, not to punish them but to provide additional support for revising their disciplinary practices and improving student outcomes. Third, policymakers at all levels should consider integrating measures of school discipline into accountability frameworks and facilitating data collection that will allow for the evaluation of progress over time. Bowditch (1993) noted 2 decades ago that suspension can be used to push struggling students out of school permanently; in the wake of the No Child Left Behind Act, accountability pressures on schools and individual teachers might be providing additional incentives for educators to use suspension to push out low achievers who misbehave. Finally, policymakers should fund evaluations of recent efforts in individual states and districts (e.g., Baltimore, Maryland, and Oakland, California) to reduce the use of suspension and related racial disparities in order to determine how the lessons learned in these pioneering districts can be scaled up to benefit students across the nation.

NOTES

1. Details on NLSY97 sampling procedures and survey questions were obtained from the Bureau of Labor Statistics website.

2. These terms reflect the wording of the survey. Unfortunately, I am unable to disaggregate the Hispanic category into subgroups.

3. Data on suspensions occurring prior to the baseline survey in 1997 were collected retrospectively.

4. Wallace, Goodkind, Wallace, & Bachman (2008) analyzed data from *Monitoring the Future*, a national survey of 10th-graders, between 2001 and 2005 (the same general cohort as NLSY97 youth). They found that 56% of Black boys, 43% of Black girls, 39% of Hispanic boys, 27% of White boys, 24% of Hispanic girls, and 12% of White girls had been suspended (p. 54). Rates presented in Figure 2.1 for "on-time" grade 10 (the school year in which respondents turn 16) are somewhat higher. This difference might be due in part to the fact that NLSY97 data include responses from youth who did not reach grade 10 or who were not attending school regularly by that time.

5. GEDs are excluded.

6. Statistics on early suspension among White and Hispanic girls are omitted, as very few had been suspended by age 12.

7. The portion of the survey that asks about delinquency and arrest is self-administered. Youth enter their responses directly into the computer rather than reporting them to interviewers.

8. I use the term "physical assault," whereas other publications refer to this as "engaging in assaultive behaviors" (Puzzanchera, 2000, p. 1). The survey asks: "Have you ever attacked someone with the idea of seriously hurting them or have *[sic]* a situation end up in a serious fight or assault of some kind?"

9. These White–Black and White–Hispanic differences are all statistically significant at a 95% confidence level (with t-statistics ranging from 3.16 to 4.68).

10. These results also have implications for criminal justice policy, as they suggest that schools might have the capacity to influence public safety.

REFERENCES

American Psychological Association Zero Tolerance Task Force. (2008). Are zero tolerance policies effective in the schools? An evidentiary review and recommendations. *American Psychologist, 63,* 852–862.

Arum, R., & Beattie I. (1999). High school experience and the risk of adult incarceration. *Criminology, 37,* 515–540.

Bowditch, C. (1993). Getting rid of troublemakers: High school disciplinary procedures and the prediction of dropouts. *Social Problems, 40,* 493–509.

Bureau of Labor Statistics, U.S. Department of Labor. (2010). *National Longitudinal Survey of* Youth 1997 Cohort, 1997–2010 (rounds 1–14). Columbus, OH: Center for Human Resource Research, The Ohio State University.

Christle, C., Nelson, M., & Jolivette, K. (2004). School characteristics related to the use of suspension. *Education and Treatment of Children, 27,* 509–526.

Fabelo, T., Thompson, M. D., Plotkin, M., Carmichael, D., Marchbanks, M. P. III, & Booth E. A. (2011). *Breaking schools' rules: A statewide study of how school discipline relates to students' success and juvenile justice involvement.* New York, NY, and College Station, TX: Council of State Governments Justice Center and Texas A&M University Public Policy Research Institute. Retrieved from http://www2.mysanantonio.com/PDFs/Breaking_Schools_Rules_embargo_final_report.pdf

Gregory, A., Skiba, R. J., & Noguera, P. A. (2010). The achievement gap and the discipline gap: Two sides of the same coin? *Educational Researcher, 39*(1), 59–68.

Hirschfield, P. J. (2010). School surveillance in America: Disparate and unequal. In T. Monahan & R. Torres (Eds.), *Schools under surveillance: Cultures of control in public education* (pp. 38–54). New Brunswick, NJ: Rutgers University Press.

Losen, D. J., & Martinez, T. E. (2013). *Out of school and off track: The overuse of suspension in American middle and high schools.* Los Angeles, CA: The Civil Rights Project at UCLA, the Center for Civil Rights Remedies.

Puzzanchera, C. M. (2000). *Self-reported delinquency by 12-year-olds, 1997.* Washington, DC: U.S. Department of Justice.

Robers, S., Zhang, J., & Truman, J. (2010). *Indicators of school crime and safety: 2010* (NCES 2011-002/ NCJ 230812). Washington, DC: U.S. Department of Justice, Bureau of Justice Statistics, Office of Justice Programs, and U.S. Department of Education, National Center for Education Statistics.

Simon, J. (2007). *Governing through crime: How the war on crime transformed American democracy and created a culture of fear.* New York, NY: Oxford University Press.

Wallace, J. M. Jr., Goodkind, S., Wallace, C. M., & Bachman, J. G. (2008). Racial, ethnic, and gender differences in school discipline among U.S. high school students: 1991–2005. *The Negro Educational Review, 59*(1–2), 47–62.

## CHAPTER 3

Security Measures and Discipline in American High Schools

Jeremy D. Finn and Timothy J. Servoss

Proponents of high security and strict disciplinary codes at American high schools argue that these measures make schools safer and create an orderly learning environment. However, the same practices can also create prison-like conditions that make some students feel ill at ease and others anxious that serious misconduct might occur at any time (Brooks, Schiraldi, & Ziedenberg, 2000). These same factors can make students feel defensive and contribute to their emotional and physical disengagement from school. And some students are likely to be affected more than others, in particular males, minorities, students who perceive teachers as unwelcoming or unfriendly, or and those who have been disciplined for infractions of school rules (see McNeely, Nonnemaker, & Blum, 2002; Skiba, Michael, Nardo, & Peterson, 2002).

With the shooting of schoolchildren in Newtown, Connecticut, and the subsequent calls for more police in schools, the policy relevance of this study has increased precipitously. As a response to that tragedy, the federal government has made funds available to districts across the country to hire additional school resource officers (law-enforcement officers assigned to schools) or counselors. Although some child advocates have expressed increasing concern about excessive security at schools, many states and districts have shown strong interest in adding SROs and other high-security measures.

This study examined the relationships among misbehavior, suspensions, and security measures in a nationwide sample of 10th-grade students in public high schools. The purpose was twofold; first, we wanted to ask if invasive security measures are being implemented for reasons unrelated to misbehavior or to school safety. We viewed security measures as discretionary actions taken by administrators that are based in part on student behavior, in part on administrators' capacity to deal effectively with misbehavior, and in part on other less relevant school characteristics. We asked whether decisions to implement security measures reflect such characteristics as school enrollment, the racial/ethnic and socioeconomic composition of the student body, the school's location, the level of crime in the school neighborhood, or the school's suspension rate.

The second purpose was to examine conditions related to high suspension rates and to high racial/ethnic and gender inequities in suspensions. We found such inequities in suspensions by race and gender, even when controlling for differences in student misbehavior. We went beyond that to ask whether disparities in suspensions are increased by high levels of school security or in particular types of schools, such as those with large enrollments, large proportions of minority students, or high percentages of students from low-income families.

Using data from the Education Longitudinal Study of 2002 (ELS: 2002), a survey of 10th-grade students across the United States and their schools, we examined relationships with out-of-school suspensions and total suspensions from the classroom (in school plus out of school).

The following were the main findings regarding school security measures:

- A high degree of school security is associated with increased suspension rates generally.
- A high degree of school security is associated with increased Black–White disparities in the total number of suspensions. Moreover, most Black students are enrolled in schools with a high degree of security.

Regarding suspensions, we found the following:

- African American students and Hispanic/Latino students are suspended at higher rates than non-Hispanic Whites, even beyond what would be predicted from different levels of misbehavior.
- Out-of-school suspensions are more frequent at schools in higher crime neighborhoods, where students might experience an environment not conducive to positive educational or social outcomes.

THE EFFECTS OF EXCLUSIONARY DISCIPLINE

Suspending or expelling a student from school might be necessary to protect the welfare of others, yet little if any research has documented any positive effects of suspension. In fact, the research suggests that out-of-school suspensions, intended as a remedy for misbehavior, fail to deter further misconduct and might even encourage it (Brooks, Schiraldi, & Ziedenberg, 2000; Hyman & Perone, 1998; Noguera, 1995). Furthermore, absence from school for any reason interferes with learning, an effect that is heightened among students having academic or behavior difficulty (Balfanz & Byrnes, 2012; Fabelo et al., 2011). A suspended student is disengaged from the sequence of instruction and is likely to experience alienation from school altogether (Resnick, Harris, & Shew, 1997; Stewart, 2003). Suspended students' need for educational and personal support when they return to school is likely to be greater than what they receive. This combination of factors can accelerate a downward spiral of failure and disengagement; thus it is little wonder that suspensions, together with low academic achievement and grade retention, are the strongest student-level predictors of dropping out (Rumberger, 2011). This study examined the role of school security as a factor that might contribute to increased student suspensions and/or increased racial/ethnic or gender disparities in suspensions.

OVERVIEW OF THE RESEARCH

This study addressed questions about schools' security levels and their connections with schools' overall suspension rates and the suspension of individual students. Data to answer the questions were drawn from national surveys of students and their schools. The main database consisted of students in public schools who participated in the Education Longitudinal Study of 2002 conducted by the National Center for Education Statistics (NCES). This was augmented by information from the Common Core of Data (CCD), also compiled by NCES, and by schoolwide suspension rates from the Civil Rights Data Collection (CRDC). The ELS:2002 data (base year) and CCD data are from the 2001–2002 school year; the CRDC data are from the 2000 survey, which provided enrollments in 1999–2000 and suspensions in 1998–1999. All U.S. public schools were included.

The ELS: 2002 survey data were collected from a nationally representative sample of 10th-grade students. Surveys were administered to school administrators, students, parents, and teachers. The sample for the present study consisted of 8,775 10th-grade students (66% White, 16.1% Black, 17.9% Hispanic) in 500 public schools.[1] The schools spanned all four major geographic regions of the United States (Northeast, Midwest, South, and West) and were located in urban, suburban, and rural areas (25.6%, 51%, and 23.4%, respectively).[2]

Schools in the survey covered the full range of public high school characteristics, such as enrollments, percentages of minority students, and percentages of socioeconomically disadvantaged students. Most of the schools (87.4%) included only grades 9–12; the remainder also had some earlier grades, such as middle school and high school or K–12. We controlled for enrollment and grade-span differences in the analysis.

The student response rate for the ELS survey was 87%, quite good by conventional standards. However, nonresponders would have included students currently skipping school, suspended, incarcerated, or in the process of dropping out, as well as those out of school for health reasons and others who refused to participate. Nonresponse due to these reasons could create a downward bias in reports of suspensions and misbehavior.

The data collected in these surveys were analyzed using multilevel forms of regression analysis, which allowed us to examine school features and characteristics of individual students. Multiple regression was important in order to find out if the main independent variables (school characteristics) were related to suspension rates above and beyond the impact of other background characteristics. All analyses used school and student sampling weights so that the weighted sample approximated the national population of 10th-graders and their schools. (See Finn and Servoss, 2013, online draft for full details., http://tinyurl.com/JanCRPconference.)

Statistical results are reported as nonsignificant or significant. Statistical significance indicates that the result is reliable, or replicable from one study to another. We also report whether the relationship between variables is weak, moderate, or strong (or small, moderate, or large). This indicates the relative importance of one variable to another. A relationship between two variables can be statistically significant but not very important from a practical perspective, so both kinds of information are needed.

Four sets of variables were created from the survey responses in order to address study's concerns: school security measures, suspensions, student misbehavior, and other background information.

School Security Measures

The ELS:2002 administrator questionnaire asked each principal whether, during the current school year, the school had each of 20 security measures in place, from those that were relatively innocuous (e.g., dress code, closed campus during lunch hours) to others that were more invasive (e.g., metal detectors, drug testing).

For this study, seven measures were selected that were the most salient to all members of the school community: (1) metal detectors at the school entrance, (2) random metal detector checks on students, (3) drug testing, (4) random sweeps for contraband, (5) security cameras, (6) police or security guards on site during school hours, and (7) random "dog sniffs" to check for drugs.

The seven measures were used to obtain a score that represented a school's total security environment. The score was obtained by scaling (Rasch, 1960), which weighs individual security measures according to the frequency with which they are used. Measures that are used less often and are generally more invasive contributed more to the total score than frequently used security measures.[3]

Approximately 9% of schools reported having none of the seven security measures; the greatest number of measures in a single school was five. The median number of security measures in the schools in our sample was one. For some of our analyses, high- and low-security schools were defined as the upper one third and lower one third of schools on the Rasch scale, respectively. The median numbers of security measures in the two groups were three and one, respectively.

Suspensions

This study is unusual in that we were able to analyze the data on both the total number of students suspended from a school alongside data on a sample of individual students in the same school. The proportion of students in a school who were given out-of-school suspensions in 1998–1999, not including students with disabilities, was drawn from the Civil Rights Data Collection school-level files.

In ELS: 2002, each student reported the number of times she or he received in-school and out-of-school suspensions during the previous school year. Responses were ordered from "never" to "10 or more times." Both questions had a high proportion of "nevers" (86.2% for in school, and 91.9% for out of school). We suspected that students might underreport their own suspensions, although these percentages were not inconsistent with other published suspension rates.

We analyzed student suspensions from ELS: 2002 in two ways. The first was out-of-school suspensions alone, consistent with the data tabulated by OCR. The second was the total number of suspensions from the classroom for each student, whether the suspension was served in school or out of school. We viewed this as reflecting the schools' general dispositions toward discipline. Due to the high proportion of "nevers" and small proportion of multiple suspensions, both suspension variables were rescored as "never" or "one or more suspensions."[4]

Student Misbehavior

In this study, we assessed multiple misbehaviors and the frequency of each. On ELS: 2002, each student self-reported his or her misbehavior and was rated by their English and math teachers. The responses were combined into two scales, self-reported and teacher-reported, using the Rasch method. The resulting scales represented assessments of the overall severity of a student's misbehavior.

The student questionnaire asked, "How many times did the following things happen to you in the first term of this school year?" The list included getting into a fight, arriving late at school, skipping classes, being absent from school, and not following rules. The teacher questionnaire asked each student's two teachers to report whether they had communicated with the student's parents about disruptive behavior or absenteeism, had communicated with the guidance counselor about the student's disruptive behavior, whether the student had fallen behind due to a disciplinary action, and how often the student was absent, tardy, inattentive, or disruptive in class. ELS: 2002 did not ask about other behaviors (e.g., drug or alcohol use in school, bringing a weapon to school, theft, gang activities).

Other Background Information

School characteristics used in the study were enrollment, the proportion of students eligible for free or reduced-price lunch (as a proxy for poverty), and the extent of crime in the school neighborhood as reported by the school principal; the ELS: 2002 response categories were high, moderate, low, and mixed, from which we created three categories, high (2% of schools), moderate/mixed (21%), and low (77%).

SCHOOL SECURITY AND SUSPENSION RATES

The data analysis addressed four specific questions: What types of schools have the highest security levels? What types of schools have higher or lower suspensions rates? Are particular racial or gender groups suspended more often than others? Are high levels of security associated with increased racial disparities in suspensions?

What Types of High Schools Have the Highest Levels of Security?

This question was answered in two ways: by computing correlations between security and other school characteristics, and by comparing the highest one third of schools on the security scale (high security) to the lowest one third (low security). The extent of school security was correlated significantly with all school characteristics studied—that is, enrollment, percentage Black and Hispanic students, percentage eligible for free or reduced-price lunch, and school suspension rates.

The strongest correlation was with the percentage of Black students in the school. That is, the percentage of Black students enrolled was more highly related to security levels than was any other characteristic. The correlation was weaker, but still positive and significant, for the percentage of students eligible for free or reduced-price lunch. The correlation of security levels with the percentage of Hispanic/Latino students was weak and statistically significant but in the opposite direction: There was a slight tendency for schools with higher percentages of Latino students to have lower security levels.

When compared to low-security schools, higher security schools were

- Larger (average enrollment in high-security schools was 921; 521 in low-security schools)
- Had a higher proportion of Black students (average percentage of Blacks in high-security schools was 21.5%; 5.4% in low-security schools)
- Had a higher percentage of students on free lunch (high security, 28.3%; low security, 25.6%)
- Had higher percentages of students suspended (high security, 14.0%; low security, 7.5%)

School security was also related significantly to neighborhood crime and urbanicity. About 90% of schools in high-crime neighborhoods had high levels of security, compared to 27% of schools in low-crime neighborhoods; only 24% percent of rural schools had high levels of security. We did not find that urban communities necessarily had a high concentration of high-security schools, or that suburban communities had far more low-security schools.

Individual security measures. The use of security measures in U.S. schools is pervasive (see Table 3.1). Approximately half of all public schools with 10th-grade

Table 3.1. Comparing Individual Security Measures Between High- and Low-Security Schools

During this school year, is it a practice of your school to do the following . . .	Overall %	High Security %	Low Security %
Use one or more random dog sniffs to check for drugs	52.5	80.5	27.1
Use police or paid security at any time during school hours or during arrival or departure	52.0	83.8	24.0
Use one or more security cameras to monitor the school	35.0	67.1	7.5
Perform one or more random sweeps for contraband	27.8	56.1	3.0
Require drug testing for any students	14.3	33.6	3.5
Perform one or more random metal detector checks on students	7.9	25.5	0.0
Require students to pass through metal detectors each day	1.4	4.7	0.0

students used random "dog sniffs" to check for drugs and/or had police or paid security officers on duty during the school day. About one third of schools had security cameras to monitor school areas, and over one fourth of schools performed random checks for contraband. A smaller percentage—but many schools, nevertheless—required drug testing and/or performed personal metal detector checks on students. Approximately 1.4% of schools required students to pass through metal detectors each day.

Schools classified as high security presented a picture in which invasive security measures were even more common. Over three fourths of high-security schools had a police presence and used dogs to check for drugs; two thirds had security cameras inside or outside the school; over half performed random sweeps for contraband; and one third required drug testing. Half of the schools in this group had three or more of the seven security measures considered.

What Types of Schools Have Higher or Lower Suspension Rates?

The schoolwide out-of-school suspension rates in our sample ranged from no students suspended to almost 80%. The median suspension rate was 6.6%, and the mean was 10.0%; that is, half of the schools suspended fewer than 6.6% of their students and half suspended more. Ten percent of schools suspended 20% or more of their students in 1 school year—that is, 5 students in a typical class of 25. The most extreme example we found is a small number of schools (1.5%) that suspended over half of their students, up to a maximum of 79.8%.

The same characteristics related to security levels were also correlated with suspensions. Schools with higher suspension rates tended to be larger and had higher percentages of Black students and students from low-income homes. Further, like the correlation with security, the strongest statistically significant predictor of suspension rates was the percentage of Black students in the school. The correlation of suspension rates with the percentage of Hispanic/Latino students was small and not statistically significant.

The relationship between suspensions and school location also paralleled those of security levels, especially the association with neighborhood crime. Over half (58.3%) of schools in high-crime neighborhoods had suspension rates in the top one third, and only 16.7% were in the lowest one third. In general, rural schools with lower security levels had fewer suspensions than did urban or suburban schools.

Are Particular Gender or Racial/Ethnic Groups Suspended More Often Than Others?

ELS: 2002 data allowed us to distinguish out-of-school suspensions for individual 10th-grade students from any exclusion from the classroom (whether the student was kept in school or sent out of school)—that is, "total suspensions."[5] The data revealed that males were suspended at a substantially higher rate than females (see Table 3.2) in terms of one or more out-of-school suspensions (10.6% versus 6.5%), and one or more total suspensions (out of school plus in school; 21.2% versus 12.8%). African American students were suspended at a higher rate than Hispanic/Latino students, who in turn were suspended at higher rates than non-Hispanic White students. This same rank order was found for out-of-school suspensions (16.0%, 10.8%, and 8.5%, respectively) and total suspensions from the classroom (31.6%, 21.5%, and 13.0%, respectively).

The largest out-of-school suspension percentage (16.0% of Black 10th-grade students) means that approximately one of every six Black 10th-grade students was excluded from school at least once during the 2000–2001 year, a number that has increased appreciably in recent years.

We examined whether race and gender differences in suspensions were statistically significant above and beyond other school characteristics (school urbanicity, neighborhood crime, racial/ethnic and socioeconomic composition of the student body, school size, and the level of security). In terms of gender, the odds of a male being suspended out of school was still twice as great as the odds of a female being suspended—a large and statistically significant difference.

Table 3.2. Suspensions by Race and Gender

	Male	Female	Total
Percentage suspended (out of school)			
White	8.5	4.4	6.4
African American	17.5	14.6	16.0
Hispanic/Latino	13.3	8.4	10.8
Total	10.6	6.5	8.5
Percentage suspended (total suspensions)			
White	17.0	8.9	13.0
African American	35.7	27.3	31.6
Hispanic/Latino	26.4	16.7	21.5
Total	21.2	12.8	17.1

Note: Total suspensions are based on both in- and out-of-school suspensions.

In terms of race/ethnicity, all comparisons were statistically significant. The odds of a Black student being suspended out of school were 1.8 times greater than the odds of a White student receiving an out-of-school suspension; the odds of a Black student being excluded from the classroom (total suspensions) were 2.2 times greater than that of Whites. These effects are all large. Similar patterns were found for Hispanic/Latino students.

Disproportionate Suspensions Relative to Misbehavior. Our analysis of racial and gender differences also considered the misbehavior of individual students as reported by the students and their teachers. Students who were suspended were generally reported to have worse behavior than those who were not. The correlations between suspensions and misbehavior ratings ranged from weak to moderate, but all were statistically significant.

When misbehavior was entered into the regressions as student-level control variables, males were still suspended at substantially higher rates than females (the odds of being suspended were 1.6 to 1.9 times greater for males than for females). Black students were still suspended more times in total than White students by a factor of 1.8. In other words, if one Black and one White student had the same behavior rating, the odds of the Black students being excluded from the classroom or school were 1.8 times greater than those of the White student. Likewise, Latino students had 1.6 greater odds of being given an out-of-school suspension than White students with the same behavior ratings.

Are High Levels of School Security and Other School Characteristics Associated With Increased Disparities in Suspensions?

We considered six school characteristics, of which one was the use of security measures. Others included school enrollment, the composition of the student body (percentage Black, percentage Hispanic, percentage qualified for free or reduced-price lunch), and features of the school setting (urbanicity, neighborhood crime).

The effect of security on the Black–White disparity in total suspensions from the classroom (among students with similar behavior ratings) was statistically significant. Greater Black–White disparities occurred in schools that had higher degrees of security. To illustrate the relationship, we computed predicted probabilities of total suspensions of Black and White students in the low- and high-security schools. The probability of suspension was similar for White students in high- and low-security environments (12.8% and 11.8%, respectively). However, the probability of suspension for Black students was greater in high-security environments (20.2%) than in low-security environments (16.3%).

Viewed from a different perspective, there was no significant difference in total suspensions between Black students and White students in low-security schools. However, significantly more Black students than White students were suspended from the classroom in high-security schools; the odds of a Black student being suspended was 2.7 times greater than for a White student.

Most important, the Black-White difference in total suspensions remained statistically significant and was almost as large (2.2 times greater for Black students than White students) even when teacher and student ratings of misbehavior were included in the regressions. The relationship of security with out-of-school suspensions was not statistically significant, but it was in the same direction as for total suspensions (i.e., bigger disparities in high-security schools).

In sum, Black students who had the highest suspension rates generally were all more likely to be suspended than Whites—even Whites with similar behavior ratings—when security in a school was high. This was not the case for Hispanic students.

LIMITATIONS OF THE STUDY

Several features of ELS:2002 limited the conclusions we could draw from this study. For one, the frequency of suspensions was reported but not the length, which might have been related to student or school characteristics. The students' and teachers' reports of behavior and principals' reports of neighborhood crime also might have been subject to bias. For example, if students tend to underreport their misbehavior or punishments, the impact of a selected factor on these outcomes might be harder to detect. Finally, the survey did not ask about more severe misbehavior or violent behavior, which might have stronger relationships with suspensions. Thus we were unable to examine relationships in as much depth as we desired.

SUMMARY AND RECOMMENDATIONS
FOR POLICY AND PRACTICE

Security measures, like exclusionary discipline, are intended to make schools safer and more orderly, but they do not always accomplish these aims. Instead they can usurp scarce resources and help to create a setting that alienates students, particularly those already at risk of academic failure and dropping out.

The use of security measures was widespread in 2002, when our data were first collected. High-security schools were prevalent in all geographic regions of the United States and in both suburban and urban districts—about 35% of suburban schools in this study were classified as high security. Since that time, partially in response to school violence such as that in Columbine and Newtown, there has been a dramatic increase in the use of security measures (Addington, 2009). As a result, in 2010 almost 70% of schools had security guards or police officers and over 61% had cameras in public areas (Robers, Kemp, & Truman, 2013).

Positive effects of these measures are largely undocumented, but the costs are clear to school administrators. One of the few comprehensive studies of the cost of security measures found that spending in one state (Texas) was positively related to the percentage of minority students in the district and negatively related to a district's wealth; in other words, spending was highest in districts that could afford it the least (DeAngelis, Brent, & Ianni, 2011). These spending issues are particularly important considering this study's findings that both the security and suspension rates were strongly correlated with the percentage of Black students in a school.

Our study also found the following: Neighborhood crime is related to school suspension rates; high levels of security are correlated with other school characteristics but do not necessarily have positive impacts; and the degree of security, related to suspension rates, generally, is also related to racial disparities in total suspensions.

Neighborhood crime is related to school suspension rates. Over half of the schools in high-crime neighborhoods were in the top one third in terms of suspension rates. It is not clear whether students excluded from school contribute to creating a high-crime neighborhood or whether the school is sending them into neighborhoods that already have high crime levels. These findings are similar to those in Chapter 8. It is clear, however, that out-of-school suspensions in these communities can be harmful above and beyond the loss of instructional time resulting from excluding students from school.

High levels of security are correlated with other school characteristics but do not necessarily have positive impacts. High-security schools tended to be larger than low-security schools, with enrollments averaging 921 students or more. They had substantially higher percentages of African American students (averaging about 20%), and tended to be located in neighborhoods with moderate to high crime rates.

Few if any studies have documented benefits of school security measures, but several studies suggest adverse consequences. Recently, Judge Steven Teske of Georgia testified to the U.S. Senate that placing police in schools in Clayton County, Georgia, led to a dramatic increase in arrests, many for minor offenses.[6] Other adverse consequences have been suggested, including the cost: DeAngelis, Brent, and Ianni (2011) report that an average of $28 per student was spent on security measures in Texas in 2008–2009, a number that undoubtedly increases each year.

And in terms of student attitudes and behavior, a review by these authors concluded, "one relatively consistent finding from this work: security measures are *negatively* but weakly associated with perceptions of safety [and] security and enforcement practices were related weakly but positively to school disruption and school crime" (Servoss & Finn, 2013, pp. 7–8). Research has also shown that when students view school rules as being too harsh or inequitably applied misbehavior can increase and attitudes toward school and a sense of school belonging can suffer (Bryk & Thum, 1989; Hyman & Perone, 1998). High levels of security might have the same impact.

The present study found that security measures do not reduce school suspensions but, rather, might work in tandem with suspensions to create an environment that can be alienating for some or all students.

The degree of security, related to suspension rates generally, is also related to racial disparities in total suspensions. The percentage of Black students suspended in high-security schools (20.2%) was significantly greater than the percentage of White students suspended (11.8%), but the percentage of total suspensions of Black students in low-security schools was similar to that of Whites.

Both disproportionate suspensions and security measures might be reactions to the large number of Black students in a school (the "racial threat" hypothesis) or other race-related phenomena. It is also possible that both are linked to school size, contributing to administrators' perceptions that behavior management requires additional resources.

The study leads to five recommendations for education policy and practice:

Recommendation 1. Because out-of-school suspensions can have harmful educational consequences for students and because suspensions might be ineffective in controlling student behavior, it is recommended that, to the extent feasible, out-of-school suspensions should be used only as a measure of last resort for students who misbehave continually or who are a threat to property or to others.

Although student misbehavior of the types examined in this study (absenteeism, disruptiveness, and even fights among students) is inevitable, alternative approaches to discipline that do not exclude students from the school community should be encouraged.

Recommendation 2. School administrators and education boards should carefully consider the costs and the anticipated benefits of implementing security measures and examine the limited research on the subject. Alternatives to exclusionary discipline might also serve as alternatives to the need for security. High-security environments should be implemented only as a last resort, given the potential for harm that exceeds the real benefits.

Recommendation 3. Further research is needed to understand the full impact of security measures in schools. Policymakers and researchers should be encouraged to undertake this line of research with urgency.

Recommendation 4. Schools should be required to explain clearly to students, parents, and teachers the reasons for their security measures and for disciplinary actions to be taken if infractions occur. State or federal policies requiring that the information be provided should be considered.

Recommendation 5. Schools and districts should ensure that disciplinary actions are administered fairly and are proportional to student misbehavior, and that exclusionary discipline is used only as a measure of last resort. Data on the application of disciplinary policies, and on the extent to which they are understood clearly by students and teachers, should be reviewed regularly by schools and districts.

Implementing these recommendations will also help ensure that schools and districts are in compliance with federal civil rights law. Specifically, if high-security measures are not fulfilling their intended purpose of improved safety, or if there are equally effective approaches for meeting security needs, their disparate impact might be unlawful (see the guidance document issued by the U.S. Departments of Justice and Education in January, 2014).

NOTES

Work on this chapter was supported in part by a grant from the Spencer Foundation entitled High School Regulatory Environment, Student Perceptions, and Dropping Out.

1. Of these, 7,138 students in 448 schools had all variables and were used in the multivariate analyses.

2. These are the actual (unweighted) percentages in the sample.

3. The overall score accounted for 80.4% of the variability among schools, indicating that the single score was a good summary of schools' overall security environments. The score ranged from 5.6 (low-security school) to 12.8 (high-security school), with an average of 8.7.

4. We checked the reasonableness of this by performing an analysis to see if relationships were different for infrequent suspenders and frequent suspenders as compared to nonsuspenders and found no difference in results between the two suspended groups.

5. The suspension data for this and the following questions were taken from individual student responses in ELS: 2002.

6. The Honorable Steven C. Teske testified before the Senate Subcommittee on the Constitution, Civil Rights, and Human Rights Subcommittee Hearing on "Ending the School to Prison Pipeline" on December 12, 2012.

REFERENCES

Addington, L. A. (2009). Cops and cameras: Public school security as a policy response to Columbine. *American Behavioral Scientist, 52,* 1426–1445.

Balfanz, R., & Byrnes, V. (2012). *The importance of being in school: A report on absenteeism in the nation's public schools.* Baltimore, MD: Johns Hopkins University Center for Social Organization of Schools.

Brooks, K., Shiraldi, V., & Ziedenberg, J. (2000). *School house hype: Two years later.* Washington, DC: Justice Policy Institute.

Bryk, A. S., & Thum, Y. M. (1989). The effects of high school organization on dropping out: An exploratory investigation. *American Education Research Journal, 26,* 353–383.

Bureau of Justice Statistics. (2012). Number of violent victimizations, personal thefts/larcenies, rape/sexual assaults, robberies, aggravated assaults, and simple assaults by region, 1993–2011. Generated using the NCVS Victimization Analysis Tool at www.bjs.gov.

DeAngelis, K. J., Brent, B. O., & Ianni, D. (2011). The hidden cost of school security. *Journal of Education Finance, 36,* 312–337.

Fabelo, T., Thompson, M. D., Plotkin, M., Carmichael, D., Marchbanks, M. P. III, & Booth E. A. (2011). *Breaking schools' rules: A statewide study of how school discipline relates to students' success and juvenile justice involvement.* New York, NY, and College Station, TX: Council of State Governments Justice Center and Texas A&M University Public Policy Research Institute. Retrieved http://www2.mysanantonio.com/PDFs/Breaking_Schools_Rules_embargo_final_report.pdf

Hyman, I. A., & Perone, D. C. (1998). The other side of school violence: Educator policies and practices that may contribute to student misbehavior. *Journal of School Psychology, 36*(1), 7–27.

McNeely, C. A., Nonnemaker, J. M., & Blum, R. W. (2002). Promoting school connectedness: Evidence from the National Longitudinal Study of Adolescent Health. *Journal of School Health, 72,* 138–146.

Noguera, P. A. (1995). Preventing and producing violence: A critical analysis of responses to school violence. *Harvard Educational Review, 65,* 189–212.

Rasch, G. (1960). *Probabilistic models for some intelligence and attainment tests.* Copenhagen, Denmark: Danmarks Paedagogiske Institut.

Resnick, M. D., Harris, K. M., & Shew, M. (1997). Protecting adolescents from harm: Findings from the National Longitudinal Study on Adolescent Health. *Journal of the American Medical Association, 278,* 823–832.

Robers, S., Kemp, J., & Truman, J. (2013). *Indicators of school crime and safety: 2012* (NCES 2013-036/NCJ 241446). Washington, DC: U.S. Department of Education, National Center for Education Statistics, and U.S. Department of Justice, Bureau of Justice Statistics.

Rumberger, R. W. (2011). *Dropping out: Why students drop out of high school and what can be done about it.* Cambridge, MA: Harvard University Press.

Servoss, T. J., & Finn, J. D. (2013, November). *School security: For whom and with what results?* Paper presented at the annual conference of the UCEA, Indianapolis, Indiana.

Skiba, R. J., Michael, R. S., Nardo, A. C., & Peterson, R. L. (2002). The color of discipline: Sources of racial and gender disproportionality in school punishment. *Urban Review, 34,* 317–342.

Stewart, E. A. (2003). School social bonds, school climate, and school misbehavior: A multilevel analysis. *Justice Quarterly, 20,* 575–604.

U.S. Department of Justice and U.S. Department of Education (2014, January 8). *Dear colleague letter: Nondiscriminatory administration of school discipline.* Washington, DC: Author. Retrieved from http://www.justice.gov/crt/about/edu/documents/dcl.pdf

The Economic Effects of Exclusionary Discipline on Grade Retention and High School Dropout

Miner P. Marchbanks III, Jamilia J. Blake, Eric A. Booth,
Dottie Carmichael, Allison L. Seibert, and Tony Fabelo

Disciplinary sanctions are used to manage student behavior in schools at an alarming rate. Whereas some scholars have alluded to the detrimental effects exclusionary discipline has on student achievement, few longitudinal investigations document the association of discipline practices with students' long-term academic outcomes (see Chapters 1 and 2). Particularly lacking are studies that explore the economic relationship between discipline and grade retention and/or dropping out.

This study highlights the added risk for grade retention and dropping out that is associated with suspensions, and in light of these significant associations it breaks new ground by also estimating the economic costs related to exclusionary discipline. To the extent that school discipline is related to negative academic effects that present economic hardship for communities and states, educational agencies should reexamine the need for exclusionary discipline.

In 2011, the average high school dropout rate was 7.1% in the United States, with dropout rates of 5.0% for Whites, 7.3% for African Americans, and 13.6% for Hispanics. More troubling is the fact that only 79.6% of White students graduate high school nationally; minorities fare worse, with 61.7% of African Americans and 68.1% of Hispanics graduating (Swanson & Lloyd, 2013). These statistics continue a 40-year trend wherein dropout rates for Black and Hispanic students have exceeded that of Whites (National Center for Education Statistics, 2012b). Given the societal and economic impact of high school dropout rates on future employment and involvement in the criminal justice system (Belfield, Levin, & Rosen, 2012), scholars have called for explanations, and remedies, for the racial disproportion in high school noncompletion (Orfield, Losen, Wald, & Swanson, 2004; Swanson, 2006). Federal accountability measures attached to federal funds already call for improvements in graduation rates. With policymakers giving increased attention to reducing dropout, many researchers have moved beyond describing who drops out of school to the more fundamental questions of why.

In general, there are apparently two types of students that fail to complete high school: students who are pulled out of school and those who are pushed out (Bradley & Renzulli, 2011; Jimerson, Anderson, & Whipple, 2002). Students who are pulled out of school are forced to leave due to personal circumstances such as pregnancy, or by the need to support their family financially. Most of these students would complete school if they did not have demands that conflict with their desire to graduate (McNeal, 1997).

Conversely, students who are pushed out appear to exhibit undesirable traits that officials perceive as troublesome. They share many characteristics of students who are frequently subject to inequitable disciplinary practices (Bradley & Renzulli, 2011): They are academically disengaged, have tumultuous relationships with other students and school staff, and have a history of academic and disciplinary problems (see Chapters 1, 2, and 7). These students are believed to drop out because of feelings of alienation that arise, at least in part, from their frequent involvement in the school discipline system.

Students who are retained in grade represent a subset of students at risk of being pushed to drop out. The dominant perception is that retained students fail to complete high school because they are not academically capable of doing so. However, Jimerson and colleagues (2002) found retention itself to be a greater predictor of dropout than low academic performance. Across 17 studies, which controlled for many background variables, students' history of retention, not academic performance, proved to be most predictive of dropping out.

Few empirical investigations have explored the impact of persistent exposure to exclusionary discipline, which involves removing students from the classroom, on grade retention and dropout. Because children of color are disproportionately subject to sanctions involving removal from the classroom (see Chapters 1, 2, 3, and 7), research that establishes how exclusionary discipline contributes to racial/ethnic disparities in educational outcomes is important for educators and policymakers who are interested in creating a more efficient system of public education—and one that produces more successful and productive citizens regardless of race or ethnicity.

This study begins by examining the degree to which exposure to exclusionary discipline contributes to students' risk for dropping out, and to the increased risk that a disciplined student will be retained in grade. If exclusionary discipline also has economic significance, then more should be known about the costs of such a practice. A second goal of this study, then, is to determine the economic impact of exclusionary discipline by identifying its relationship to high school dropout and grade retention.

The authors of the report *Breaking Schools' Rules* (Fabelo et al., 2011) described the strong relationship between discipline and failing to graduate. This study is an extension of that analysis, and it also controls for individual- and school-level characteristics that can mitigate the effect of exclusionary discipline on student achievement. We tracked nearly one million Texas students over several years, and our findings provide an unprecedented exploration of the degree to which school discipline is related to increased levels of dropout and grade retention. This study takes an additional step by offering an assessment of the economic costs of school discipline that result from increased rates of grade retention and dropout.

OVERVIEW OF THE RESEARCH

Within this section, we set the stage for the research by discussing our sample and data sources. We continue with an examination of our measures and conclude with an overview of our data analytic strategy.

Sample and Data Sources

Our sample was drawn from the Texas Education Agency's (TEA) Public Education Information Management System (PEIMS), which is a statewide repository that contains student records collected by all Texas school districts. Educational records from 1999 to 2007 were extracted for all Texas students enrolled in 7th grade at a public school during the 2000–2001, 2001–2002, or 2002–2003 academic years. The three cohorts were scheduled to graduate in 2006, 2007, and 2008, respectively. Students' progress was tracked from 7th grade through at least their cohort's 12th-grade year and up to 2 years beyond to allow for evidence of completion for students who were retained. In addition to education records, data on the characteristics of the schools and districts students attended were included to provide contextual information about their educational environment.[1]

Measures

Individual-Level Student Characteristics. The PEIMS database provides a method to track Texas students throughout their public school career. For the purpose of this study, we included the following individual-level student characteristics as predictor variables in the analyses: student demographic characteristics, attendance history, grade promotion, special status (e.g., disability status, English proficiency, gifted and talented), and standardized test performance consistent with the extant school dropout literature (Hammond, Linton, Smink, & Drew, 2007). A full list of control variables is available in Appendix Table 4.1 at the end of the chapter. The sample was nearly evenly divided between White and Hispanic students, at 43% and 40%, respectively; African American students made up 14% of the sample.

Discipline Contact. For the purpose of this study, we used each of the reported disciplinary events included only in the PEIMS database: in-school suspension (ISS)—removed from the classroom but kept at the home campus; out-of-school suspension (OSS)—removed from the school for up to 3 days; expulsion—permanent or long-term removal from the school system; Disciplinary Alternative Education Placement (DAEP)—long-term housing on a campus designed to educate students who have exhibited serious or persistent behavior problems; or Juvenile Justice Alternative Education Placement (JJAEP)—long-term housing on a campus run by the juvenile justice department and designed to educate students who have exhibited serious or persistent behavior problems.

Within our study cohorts, the majority of the students (60%) were subject to discipline during the period studied. The racial breakdown reveals deep disparities: 75% of African American students and 65% of Hispanics were disciplined, compared to 49% of White children. Furthermore, when we applied multivariate analyses that controlled for 83 variables to isolate the effects of race on disciplinary actions, we found that African American students had a 31% higher chance of experiencing a discretionary school disciplinary action, compared to otherwise identical White students (Fabelo et al., 2011).

School Dropout. School dropout served as a dependent variable. When a student leaves a school, either by withdrawal or by not returning at the start of a new school year, the district is required to report a "leaver code" indicating why the student no longer attends the school. Some leaver codes simply indicate that a student transferred to another district, whereas others indicate that a student graduated. Before 2005–2006, Texas classification of dropouts was not strict. For instance, students who completed all required coursework but failed the state standardized test required to graduate were not counted as dropouts (Texas Education Agency, 2008). Beginning in the 2005–2006 school year, however, Texas adopted the more stringent National Center for Education Statistics definition for dropouts. Students who left school and were unaccounted for were not counted as dropouts (Losen, Orfield, & Balfanz, 2006). For the purposes of this study, we used the definition of dropping out used by the TEA during each year for which data were extracted.

Grade Retention. Grade retention, a dependent variable in the analyses, was determined by the student's grade in the current year relative to the prior year. Students who were in the same grade in the fall as in the spring of the previous school year were classified as being retained.

School-Level Characteristics. A complementary dataset to the PEIMS, the Academic Excellence Indicator System (AEIS), includes a variety of school-level measures, such as school-level indicators of wealth and expenditures, teacher demographics and professional experience, student–teacher ratios, campus-wide attendance rates, and much more. For the purpose of this study, the following variables were extracted from the AEIS: cohort measures and staff measures. As mentioned earlier, a full list of control variables is available in Appendix Table 4.1 at the end of this chapter.

Data Analytic Strategy

The study analyzed the effect of discipline on the probability that students would drop out or be retained at least once during their secondary school career. Both of these are terminal outcomes, meaning that once a student has been retained or has dropped out he or she is not included in subsequent years' models. The analyses used multivariate techniques that statistically controlled for over 40 factors to produce a more accurate estimate of the true relationship between discipline and grade retention/dropout. The most straightforward approach, then, was to calculate the change in the probability of the outcome of interest when a student was disciplined.

To ensure that changes in dropout/grade retention rates were not the result of other factors, we also controlled for over 40 variables associated with academic failure and exclusionary discipline in prior research (Hammond et al., 2007). These variables included measures of students' academic performance, socioeconomic status, race/ethnicity, and disabilities. We also included measures of students' school environment that were believed to be important predictors of students' academic outcomes, such as student–teacher ratios, and district wealth. We used the results of these logistic regression analyses to identify the difference in dropout/retention rates for students who were disciplined and those for students who had no school disciplinary experience. To quantify the economic effects of exclusionary discipline, we assigned an economic value to the resulting difference in rates, based on available measures and previous economic studies.

WHAT ARE THE ECONOMIC EFFECTS
OF EXCLUSIONARY DISCIPLINE ON DROPOUTS?

Overall, 31% of our study cohort did not graduate high school; 6.7% dropped out. Although 10% of those who were disciplined dropped out and roughly 40% of them failed to graduate, only 2% of those who were not disciplined dropped out, with 18% not graduating during the period of study. These numbers represent the official dropouts; they ignore many others who did not receive a diploma, such as those enrolled in a GED prep course.

As Table 4.1 indicates, a "typical" student who received one in-school suspension (ISS) placement during the year was 23.7% more likely to drop out during that year than a student who received no discipline after controlling for other factors. This finding is statistically significant. The effects of school discipline occur each year that a student is present at school. This makes the overall likelihood

Table 4.1. School Discipline and Likelihood of Dropout

Characteristic	Label	Raw Probability	Percentage Increase
Base	No discipline	0.0005	—
	One in-school suspension	0.0006	23.7

of dropping out dependent on tracking this outcome over multiple academic years, rather than for just a single year. We calculated the effects of exclusionary discipline (including ISS, OSS, expulsion, disciplinary alternative education placement, and juvenile justice alternative education placement) on the probability that a student will drop out of school. The students in our cohort who were disciplined at least once (ISS or worse) between 7th and 12th grade averaged 1.4 disciplinary removals per year. These students were 23.5% more likely to drop out at some point during their secondary school career—a conservative value.[2]

We note again that Texas increased the strictness of its dropout measure during the time the study cohorts were in school. For instance, students who could not pass the standardized tests required to graduate were previously not counted as dropouts; thus, if the more inclusive measure of dropout were used in all years, dropout rates would be higher. In fact, the official dropout rate for the class of 2007 was twice as high as for the class of 2005, the last class completely counted under the old rules (Texas Education Agency 2008, pp. 56, 94).

The 24% increase in dropout rates associated with those who are disciplined provides a platform from which to investigate the costs associated with school discipline, through its relationship with dropping out. If the 59.6% of students who were disciplined dropped out at rates comparable to their peers who avoided punishment (e.g., the 23.5% increase in dropping out vanished), the overall dropout rate in Texas would be approximately 14% lower (23.5% x 59.6%). Though this measure applies the multivariate rate to all disciplined individuals, the relationship would still be substantive if the real value were only a fraction of this amount. For instance, Table 4.2 shows the predicted effects if the relationship between school discipline and dropout were reduced by much smaller values.

A recent study examined the economic costs associated with dropouts from a single Texas cohort (Alvarez et al., 2009). This impressive analysis used a vast array of data to calculate these values. First, adjusting for the demographics of the state, the study found that a single cohort's dropouts had between $5.0 billion and $9.0 billion in present-value lost wages over the course of their careers. Using Texas

Table 4.2. Reduction in Dropout with Hypothetical Lower Relationships Between School Discipline and Dropout

Hypothetical Relationship	Overall Dropout Reduction	Low Estimate	High Estimate
1%	0.60%	$31,890,324	$57,435,946
5%	2.98%	$159,451,622	$287,179,728
10%	5.96%	$318,903,243	$574,359,456
15%	8.94%	$478,354,865	$861,539,184
20%	11.91%	$637,806,487	$1,148,718,913

state comptroller data, the study also found that the state forgoes between $279 million and $507 million in lost sales tax revenue over the course of the cohort students' lifetimes. The study next examined increased welfare costs associated with dropout, finding the value to be between $404 million and $736 million. These welfare figures are conservative because they ignore the difference in the number of children dropouts have relative to graduates—a key predictor of welfare expenses. The study subsequently explored the increased criminal justice costs associated with dropouts, which it found to be between $595 million and $1.0 billion. Finally, the study acknowledged that dropouts do provide savings to the state in one area—the cost of education. The authors estimated this amount to be between $625 million and $1.1 billion.

The total social cost of dropping out for the lifetime of each cohort of students in the Alvarez et al. (2009) study was between $5.4 billion and $9.6 billion. We don't know with certainty the direct causal effects of discipline on dropping out. However, the statistical model demonstrates that discipline is associated with a 14% higher risk for dropping out in Texas. If policymakers could remove the 14% elevation in dropout associated with school discipline, the total lifetime savings for each cohort would be between $750 million and $1.35 billion.

In other words, these estimates demonstrate that exclusionary discipline is likely attached to tremendous hidden costs. Even if reducing suspensions lowered dropouts by 1% for each cohort, Texas would save millions per cohort. Table 4.2 indicates the cost savings associated with lower discipline if the relationship between exclusionary practices and dropout were attenuated. If the relationship between discipline and dropping out were reduced from 23.5% to 20%, the cost savings to the state would be between $112 million and $202 million per year (roughly $443 per student in the cohort).

WHAT ARE THE ECONOMIC EFFECTS OF
EXCLUSIONARY DISCIPLINE ON RETENTION?

As mentioned, one area in which dropouts save the state money is by removing its need to spend money on their education. However, this relatively small savings pales in comparison to the dramatic lifetime costs associated with dropping out of school. This section demonstrates what happens to the "best case" marginalized students— those who are retained rather than dropping out. These students do continue their education but, as we demonstrate, this does not occur without costs.

Table 4.3 details the relationship between school discipline and first-time grade retention within 1 school year. Although all types of discipline were included in the model, we report on ISS as the exemplar sanction because it is the most common and least serious; thus, when we refer to "disciplinary sanctions" moving forward, we are referring to the less severe ISS. A typical student with no disciplinary record has a small probability of grade retention (0.013). A single ISS encounter nearly doubles the probability to 0.025 and is statistically significant.

In order to conduct the economic analysis, the probability that a student will be retained during her or his secondary school career is needed. A student who matriculates from 7th grade to 12th grade has six chances to be retained. Our results illustrate the serious effect school discipline can have on long-term prospects for grade retention. A typical student who is never disciplined has a probability of being retained during his or her secondary school career of only 0.034. Recall that the students in our cohort who were disciplined in the 7th through 12th grades averaged 1.4 discipline encounters per year. A typical student with this level of discipline has a 0.067 probability of being retained, which is nearly double the rate for students with no prior discipline history. Furthermore, students who are given ISS once in the 9th grade are 46.2% more likely to be retained during junior/senior high than their peers who were never disciplined. A single disciplinary event at any time during a student's secondary academic career has a profound relationship on the likelihood that she or he will repeat a grade. To the extent that minority students are involved in school discipline more often than their White counterparts, as documented earlier, they are also at higher risk for grade retention and dropping out.

When a student is retained, there are serious economic consequences for both the state and the student. The state and its school districts combined spend

Table 4.3. School Discipline and Likelihood of Grade Retention

Characteristic	Label	Raw Probability	Percentage Increase
Base	No discipline	0.013	—
	One in-school suspension	0.025	91.9%

an average of $11,543 a year per student (Texas Education Agency, 2012). When a student is retained, the state is forced to spend this amount for an additional year, which absorbs funds that would otherwise be available for other purposes. Of course, we cannot establish the direct causal effects of discipline on retention. However, the statistical model demonstrates that discipline is associated with a higher risk for being retained.

The analyses here examine the likelihood a student will be retained at least once. If a student is retained multiple times, the additional costs are felt multiple times as well. If anything, then, the cost estimates we present are conservative. To the extent that a student is retained multiple times, the costs to the state would be greater than reported here.

These additional costs are magnified by the size of the Texas public school system. Texas has over 4.9 million students, approximately 10% of all public school students nationally (National Center for Education Statistics, 2012a; Texas Education Agency, 2012). Each year, Texas receives more than 350,000 new students. For instance, the 2010–2011 8th-grade cohort had 354,139 students (Texas Education Agency, 2012). Therefore, when calculating annual costs, it is necessary to extrapolate from the students modeled in the study to all students enrolled in the same grade and school year.

Using the 2010–2011 8th-grade cohort for size and the racial breakdown from our study (14% African American, 39% Hispanic, 43% White), Table 4.4 displays the discipline rate by gender and race/ethnicity, and after controlling for over 40 variables, and indicates the predicted increase in grade retention associated with school discipline for these groups. Discipline among the three largest races/ethnicities in Texas leaves a per-year increase in retention of 6,603 students. Though discipline-based retention of less than 2% of the cohort might seem trivial, the economic effects are profound. Spending an additional $11,543 on each of these students results in a total annual cost of over $76 million.

The student does not fare much better. An additional year in school likely signals delayed entry into the workforce. Students who begin their career late miss out on the earning potential that more time would give them. Individuals with a minimum wage full-time position will miss out on $14,500 in earnings during the school year.[3] When the entire cohort is considered, more than $96 million in purchasing power is lost.

There are also lost sales tax revenues. The state comptroller reports that households earning less than $29,233 spend 6% of their income on sales tax (Combs, 2011). This translates to $870 per person, or $5.7 million in lost sales tax revenue.

Students obtaining a higher paying job would only magnify the costs of delayed entry. For instance, a beginning career in the Army would provide $18,194, plus substantial benefits and allowances (United States Army, 2012). Furthermore, because many wages/salaries are determined by time on the job, the lower earning power resulting from delayed entry can affect students for the duration of their careers.

Table 4.4. School Discipline Related to Predicted Grade Retention and Cost Increases

Race	Gender	Discipline Rate	Increased Retention	Education Costs	Lost Wages	Lost Sales Tax	Total	Per Capita
Black	Male	83%	623	$7,191,125	$9,033,294	$541,998	$16,766,417	$773
Black	Female	70%	405	$4,677,509	$5,875,759	$352,546	$10,905,813	$503
Latino	Male	74%	2,094	$24,170,351	$30,362,133	$1,821,728	$56,354,212	$806
Latina	Female	58%	1,270	$14,656,332	$18,410,882	$1,104,653	$34,171,866	$489
White	Male	59%	1,491	$17,209,625	$21,618,259	$1,297,096	$40,124,980	$526
White	Female	37%	721	$8,317,218	$10,447,861	$626,872	$19,391,951	$254
Total		60%	6,603	$76,222,160	$95,748,187	$5,744,891	$177,715,239	$529

Table 4.5. School Discipline Related to Predicted Grade Retention and Cost Increases Assuming Lower Association

Percent of Model	Increased Retention	Education Costs	Lost Wages	Lost Sales Tax	Total	Per Capita
5%	332	$3,811,108	$4,787,409	$287,245	$8,885,762	$26
25%	1,659	$19,055,540	$23,937,047	$1,436,223	$44,428,810	$132
50%	3,319	$38,111,080	$47,874,094	$2,872,446	$88,857,619	$265
75%	4,978	$57,166,620	$71,811,140	$4,308,668	$133,286,429	$397

Table 4.5 indicates that even if the relationship between discipline and retention is dramatically lower than the statistical model predicts, substantial costs are
still present. The total relationship between school discipline and grade retention
costs the state over $44 million even if the association is only one fourth as strong
as the multivariate model posits.

SUMMARY

The results indicate that the negative effects of school discipline do not end with
exclusionary suspension or expulsion. Involvement in school discipline is associated with at least two further deleterious outcomes—grade retention and dropping
out of the school system. The effects of these negative outcomes are felt not only
by the individual but by society as a whole.

Previous research has largely neglected the economic costs associated with
school discipline. This research shows that students who are disciplined are more
likely to be retained and to drop out, and that there are serious economic costs associated with these negative outcomes. We estimate that those who are disciplined
are significantly more likely to drop out. This increase in dropout is associated
with $750 million in increased costs and lost wages over the lifetime of each co-
hort. Furthermore, grade retention associated with discipline costs the state of
Texas $178 million per year.

This study ignores other economic costs associated with school discipline.
For instance, Fabelo et al. (2011) established that individuals who are disciplined
are much more likely to move into the juvenile justice system, whereas our analysis looks only at involvement in the adult justice system. As such, our results are
conservative.

Our results are likely generalizable to other jurisdictions. In another statewide study, Balfanz (see Chapter 1) finds a similar relationship in Florida between
school discipline and dropout. If similar economic analyses were applied there,
results would likely be similar.

RECOMMENDATIONS FOR POLICY/PRACTICE

The results of this study should be interpreted with several limitations in mind.
One such limitation is the method in which school dropout was conceptualized.
There is controversy surrounding how states measure school dropout rates. The
ambiguity in the way Texas codes students who exit school prior to graduating
forced us to adopt an overly conservative and restrictive definition of dropout
that might not extend to other studies that measure this construct more liberally.
As mentioned, Texas relies on student exit codes to determine number of dropouts. However, many students likely exit school while claiming to pursue home

schooling or to move out of the state. Furthermore, in calculating dropout rates, the state discards student data when the outcome records are missing (Losen et al., 2006). This restrictive definition likely led to a dramatic undercount of dropouts within our cohort. For instance, only 7% of students within our cohort were categorized as dropouts, compared to 31% of students who did not graduate high school for all reasons combined. Despite these limitations, education agencies and taxpayers would be well served to explore the economic burden exclusionary discipline places on schools and society as a whole. Because administrators can affect the level of discipline that occurs in their schools, they can act to reduce discipline and, in turn, any deleterious economic effects it brings (Booth, Marchbanks, Carmichael, & Fabelo, 2012; Fabelo et al. 2011).

It is important to understand, as Table 4.5 shows, that the economic costs associated with discipline are distributed as unequally as discipline itself. As mentioned earlier, Black students were 31% more likely to be disciplined after controlling for all other variables (Fabelo et al., 2011; see also Chapters 2, 3, 7, and 9 in this book). We recommend that educational agencies adopt evidenced-based programs that reduce school officials' use of punitive and exclusionary measures to manage student behavior, and that extra attention be given to programs that reduce these outcomes for children of color. Although alternatives likely will not be free, cost-conscious policymakers must take into account the cost associated with suspensions described here.

One approach that might prove cost-effective is investing in dropout-prevention programs that are linked to tracking discipline. To do this, educational administrators would need to identify students who are at risk for receiving frequent disciplinary sanctions by monitoring the number of classroom and office discipline referrals these students receive. Students who receive a number of discipline referrals (e.g., more than the mean for their grade) should be included in two distinct types of dropout-prevention programs adopted by the school: a dropout-prevention program that focuses on gaining the academic skills needed for school success and a dropout-prevention program that fosters school engagement by building positive relationships with meaningful adults in the student's school (Sugai, Sprague, Horner, & Walker, 2000). In addition to addressing at-risk students' academic skill deficits, school officials should adopt prevention programs that attempt to reduce feelings of being disconnected from school and encourage school completion. Programs that use adult mentors to monitor at-risk students' attendance, motivation, and engagement in school might foster levels of belonging that will be helpful in disrupting the cycle of exclusionary discipline and high school dropout.

These are just some possible approaches to alternative disciplinary measures. The U.S. Department of Justice and the U.S. Department of Education have formed the Safe and Supportive School Discipline Initiative (U.S. Department of Education, 2014), and the Council of State Governments Justice Center has created a national consensus-building project around school discipline (Morgan, Salomon, Plotkin, & Cohen, 2014). Each of these efforts produces detailed policy recommendations.

In closing, this research adds to the policy discussion by identifying the economic costs associated with school discipline. Using a robust sample of 900,000 students, our analyses show that receiving exclusionary discipline is associated with students' negative academic outcomes and that serious economic costs for both the student and state are associated with these negative outcomes. In that minority students are overrepresented in the area of school discipline (see Chapters 1, 2, and 7), they likely are experiencing higher levels of grade retention and dropout as well. Policymakers should explore programs that can disrupt or eliminate this relationship and/or prevent disciplinary actions in the first place, as doing so may lead to substantial cost savings.

NOTES

Portions of this research were supported by Grant #(2012-JF-FX-4064) awarded by the Office of Juvenile Justice and Delinquency Prevention, Office of Justice Programs, U.S. Department of Justice. The opinions, findings, and conclusions or recommendations expressed in this publication are those of the authors and do not necessarily reflect those of the Department of Justice and are not endorsed by the Texas Education Agency, the Texas Higher Education Coordinating Board, CSG, or the state of Texas.

1. The sample follows the same design as the *Breaking Schools' Rules* design. For a more in-depth discussion, please visit http://csgjusticecenter.org/wp-content/uploads/2012/08/Breaking_Schools_Rules_Report_Final.pdf for a copy of the report.

2. The multivariate dropout rate reported is substantially smaller than the overall dropout rate. This is due to the base individual reported being the "typical" student. Such a student has never failed a standardized test and is not poor or classified as at risk of dropping out of school by TEA.

3. Calculation: $7.25/hour X 40 hours X 50 weeks.

REFERENCES

Alvarez, R., Brennan, S., Carter, N., Dong, H. K., Eldridge, A., Fratto, J., . . . Thorburn, P. (2009). *The ABCD's of Texas education: Assessing the benefits and costs of reducing the dropout rate.* College Station, TX: Texas A&M University, The Bush School of Government and Public Service.

Belfield, C. R., Levin, H. M., & Rosen, R. (2012). *The economic value of opportunity youth.* Retrieved from http://files.eric.ed.gov/fulltext/ED528650.pdf

Booth, E. A., Marchbanks, M. P., Carmichael, D., & Fabelo, T. (2012). Comparing campus discipline rates: A multivariate approach for identifying schools with significantly different than expected exclusionary discipline rates. *Journal of Applied Research on Children: Informing Policy for Children at Risk, 3*(2), 1–22.

Bradley, C. L., & Renzulli, L. A. (2011). The complexity of non-completion: Being pushed or pulled to drop out of high school. *Social Forces, 90,* 521–545.

Combs, S. (2011). *Tax exemptions & incidence: A report to the governor and the 82nd Texas legislature.* Retrieved from http://www.window.state.tx.us/taxinfo/incidence/96-463TaxIncidence02-11.pdf

Fabelo, T., Thompson, M. D., Plotkin, M., Carmichael, D., Marchbanks, M. P. III, & Booth E. A. (2011). *Breaking schools' rules: A statewide study of how school discipline relates to students' success and juvenile justice involvement.* New York, NY, and College Station, TX: Council of State Governments Justice Center and Texas A&M University Public Policy Research Institute. Retrieved from http://www2.mysanantonio.com/PDFs/Breaking_Schools_Rules_embargo_final_report.pdf

Hammond, C., Linton, D., Smink, J., & Drew, S. (2007). *Dropout risk factors and exemplary programs.* Clemson, SC: National Dropout Prevention Center, Communities in Schools.

Jimerson, S. R., Anderson, G., & Whipple, A. (2002). Winning the battle and losing the war: Examining the relation between grade retention and dropping out of high school. *Psychology in the Schools, 39,* 441–457.

Losen, D., Orfield, G., & Balfanz, R. (2006). *Confronting the graduation rate crisis in Texas.* Cambridge, MA: The Civil Rights Project at Harvard University.

McNeal, R. (1997). Are students being pulled out of high school? The effect of adolescent employment on dropping out. *Sociology of Education, 70,* 206–220.

Morgan, E., Salomon, N., Plotkin, M., & Cohen, R. (2014). *The school discipline consensus report: Strategies from the field to keep students engaged in school and out of the juvenile justice system.* New York, NY: Council of State Governments Justice Center.

National Center for Education Statistics. (2012a). *Enrollment in educational institutions, by level and control of institution: Selected years, 1869–70 through fall 2019.* Retrieved from http://nces.ed.gov/programs/digest/d10/tables/dt10_003.asp

National Center for Education Statistics. (2012b). *Percentage of high school dropouts among persons 16 through 24 years old (status dropout rate), by sex and race/ethnicity: Selected years, 1960 through 2011.* Retrieved from https://nces.ed.gov/programs/digest/d12/tables/dt12_128.asp

Orfield, G., Losen, D., Wald, J., & Swanson, C. (2004). *Losing our future: How minority youth are being left behind by the graduation rate crisis, 2004.* Cambridge, MA: The Civil Rights Project at Harvard University.

Sugai, G. P., Sprague J. R., Horner, R. H., & Walker, H. M. (2000). Preventing school violence: The use of office discipline referrals to assess and monitor school-wide discipline interventions. *Journal of Emotional and Behavioral Disorders, 8*(2), 94–101.

Swanson, C. B. (2006). *High school graduation in Texas: Independent research to understand and combat the graduation crisis.* Bethesda, MD: Editorial Projects in Education Research Center.

Swanson, C. B., & Lloyd, S. C. (2013). *Graduation in the United States.* Retrieved from http://www.edweek.org/media/education-week-diplomas-count-graduation-rates-2013.pdf

Texas Education Agency. (2008). *Secondary school completion and dropouts in Texas public schools 2006–07.* Retrieved from http://ritter.tea.state.tx.us/research/pdfs/dropcomp_2006-07.pdf

Texas Education Agency. (2012). *2011 state AEIS report.* Retrieved from http://ritter.tea.state.tx.us/perfreport/aeis/2011/state.html

United States Army. (2012). *Army base pay and basic pay chart.* Retrieved from http://www.goarmy.com/benefits/money/basic-pay-active-duty-soldiers.html

United States Department of Education. *School climate and discipline.* Retrieved from http://www2.ed.gov/policy/gen/guid/school-discipline/index.html

Appendix Table 4.1. Variables Used in the Multivariate Models

Label	Definition
Charter school	Attends a charter school
Title I school	Attends a Title I school
Campus attendance rate	Attendance rate based on all students
Student/teacher ratio	The # of students per teacher on campus
% economically disadvantaged	% of campus eligible for free or reduced-price lunch
Avg. actual salaries of teachers	Avg. salary paid to each FTE teacher at the campus
Avg. years experience of teachers	Avg. years experience for teachers at the campus
District wealth per capita	Total taxable property value per student
Suburban county	Student lives in a suburban county
Non-metro adjacent county	Student lives in a non-metro county adjacent to a metro county
Rural county	Student lives in a rural county
At risk of dropping out	Student is at risk of dropping out (TEA designation)
Gifted	Student is classified as gifted
Has failed a TAKS test	Student h as failed a TAAS/TAKS test (state test) before
Failed last TAKS test	Student failed at least one section of the last TAAS/TAKS test (state test)
Retained	Student was retained in the previous year
Years behind	# of years student is behind expected grade level
Attendance rate	Student's attendance rate
7th grade	Student is in the 7th grade
8th grade	Student is in the 8th grade
9th grade	Student is in the 9th grade
10th grade	Student is in the 10th grade
11th grade	Student is in the 11th grade
Cohort year	The # of years the student's cohort has been in the study

(continued)

Appendix Table 4.1. *(continued)*

Label	Definition
African American	Student is African American
Latino	Student is Hispanic
Other race	Student is not a White, Hispanic, or Black student
Male	Student is male
Autism	Student is diagnosed with autism
Emotional disturbance	Student is diagnosed with an emotional disturbance
Learning disability	Student is diagnosed with a learning disability
Mental retardation	Student is diagnosed with mental retardation
Physical disability	Student has orthopedic, auditory, visual impairment, speech impairment, noncategorical early childhood or other health impairment
Traumatic brain injury	Student is diagnosed with a traumatic brain injury
Disciplined	Student was disciplined
Encountered TJPC in the past	Student was referred to TJPC in the past
# of ISS disciplinary actions	# of in-school suspensions
# of OSS disciplinary actions	# of out-of-school suspensions
# of DAEP disciplinary actions	# of referrals to a DAEP
# of JJAEP disciplinary actions	# of referrals to a JJAEP
# of expulsion disciplinary actions	# of expulsions
# of fine disciplinary actions	# of truancy-related fines
# of no action disciplinary actions	# of discipline events where no action was taken
# of unknown disciplinary actions	# of discipline events were the action was not reported
Title I Ind.	Student receives Title I services
Economical disadvantage	Student is eligible for free or reduced price lunch
Limited English Proficiency	Student classified as having limited English proficiency
Migrant	Student is classified as a migrant
# of schools attended	# of schools the student attended in the year

## CHAPTER 5

Challenging Middle-Class Notions of Femininity

The Cause of Black Females' Disproportionate Suspension Rates

Jamilia J. Blake, Bettie Ray Butler, and Danielle Smith

Black males have historically been at the center of the national and empirical debate on school suspension. The suspension rates for Black females generally are described in the context of reports emphasizing the discriminatory experiences of Black males. The common tendency to overlook the high rates of suspension experienced by Black females is troubling, as the average suspension rate for Black females across grade levels nationwide was 13% in 2009. This is 5 percentage points higher than the national average for all students and 8 percentage points higher than all female students (Losen & Martinez, 2013). The pendulum shifted in 2010, when the public face of youth who are subjected to disproportionate exclusionary discipline practices broadened to include Black females (Dillon, 2010; Lewin, 2012). This public attention marked a small yet important victory for Black females in that it signaled the end of the silent struggle with school discipline that Black females have grappled with for decades (Mendez & Knoff, 2003; Taylor & Foster, 1986). Although it appears that Black females are now etched into the national portrait of youth who are vulnerable to punitive disciplinary practices, limited public and scholarly attention has been devoted to explaining why these girls are at elevated risk for school suspension. Understanding Black females' disciplinary experiences is essential for those shaping education policy and formulating preventive and alternative discipline strategies to manage student behavior.

This chapter explores the nature of Black females' disciplinary infractions in an effort to inform school discipline policies that address the specific needs of Black male and Black female students in K–12 public institutions. The major goal of this study was to determine if the disciplinary experiences of Black female students were significantly different from those of their White female peers by investigating the type of infractions female students are referred for and the discipline sanction assigned to these students for that violation. For reasons that are consistent with the literature, we expected to find racial variation in the rates of suspension, with Black female students having higher rates of both out-of-school suspensions (OSS) and in-school suspensions (ISS) for offenses similar to those of their White counterparts.

Although a number of factors are believed to contribute to disproportionate disciplinary practices, racial/ethnic bias has been implicated most frequently (Fenning & Rose, 2007; Monroe & Obidah, 2004). It is well documented that teachers have lower academic and behavioral expectations of Black students than of White students, and that these expectations shape teachers' instructional and behavioral management practices. Rarely mentioned, however, is the gendered nature of teachers' racialized expectations and how this influences schools' use of draconian measures to manage Black students' behavior, male and female alike (Downey & Pribesh, 2004; Tenenbaum & Ruck, 2007).

Teachers tend to perceive Black females as having greater academic promise than Black males and thus are much more optimistic about Black females' academic trajectory (Tenenbaum & Ruck, 2007). Some argue that teachers' glowing perception of Black females' achievement potential means these girls are under less surveillance in the classroom than Black males, shielding them from harsh and inequitable discipline (Rollock, 2007). This position naively uses Black males' behavior as the standard by which to evaluate Black females, conveniently ignoring how gender and race shape teachers' views of acceptable behavior.

We believe that Black females' race, gender, and socioeconomic status gives them a unique and paradoxical social position in the education system (Collins, 2000). Instead of Black females having less supervision in the classroom and being subjected to laxer behavioral standards because of their academic potential, we propose that they are in fact held to higher behavioral standards than all of their peers, male and female. We suspect that K–12 educators show less tolerance for Black girls' behavior violations of decorum and enforce discipline more stringently for these girls' transgressions in an effort to regulate their behavior (e.g., loud talking, provocative dress, overly expressive gestures, etc.), which teachers perceive as undermining their educational potential. Unlike Black males, who are purported to be inequitably disciplined due to the stereotype of Black males as violent and dangerous, we assert that Black females discipline sanctions are fueled by a different set of stereotypes—those stemming from sexual scripts enacted when Black females deviate from White middle-class gender norms or "ladylike" behavior (Monroe, 2005; Stephens & Phillips, 2003). Societal and media stereotyping paint Black females as hypersexual, boisterous, aggressive, and unscrupulous (Collins, 2000; West, 1995). Unfortunately, these stereotypes underlie the implicit bias that shapes many educators' view of Black female students as sexually promiscuous, hedonistic, and in need of socialization (Rahimi & Liston, 2009).

Within the K–12 education system, school discipline policies are used to maintain order and to socialize future citizens (Raby, 2005). Disciplinary sanctions that result from violations of these policies serve as a means to normalize unruly youth and deter troublesome behavior. This partially explains why Black girls who are loud, outspoken, indignant, and perceived as dressing provocatively are consistently identified as needing greater social control by educators (Evans, 1988; Grant, 1984; Morris, 2005). If these females were of another race/ethnicity, they might be considered assertive, independent, inquisitive, and creative leaders; however, their social position in the public schools and within the larger society subjects them to teachers' reprimands and chastisement for being "unladylike" (Morris, 2007).

Essentially, Black females who inadvertently defy White middle-class gender norms—which values female invisibility, marked by silence, diffidence, and modesty in appearance—in their speech and deportment challenge educators' notion of femininity (Brown & Gilligan, 1993). To many school officials, these young women represent unsociable jezebels whose behavior is in desperate need of remediation. The disproportionate issuing of school discipline sanctions to Black females for gender nonconformity reflects a subconscious attempt to police and correct the moral deficiency that is perceived to plague Black females and subvert their educational attainment. In our prior study of urban elementary and secondary Black female students from one school district, we found some support for this notion (Blake, Butler, Lewis, & Darensbourg, 2011). When comparing reasons for female suspension by race, our findings indicated that Black females were more likely to be suspended for defiance, improper dress, and threatening other students than were White females. Countering administrators' rhetoric that suspension is used to remove dangerous students, the infractions for which Black females in our study were most frequently suspended reflect behaviors that were more likely to threaten White middle-class standards of femininity and gender expression than to threaten the safety of other students (i.e., physical fighting [Noguera, 2003]. These findings provide tentative evidence for the role gendered racial/ethnic bias plays in Black females' risk for school suspension; however, they are limited in that they are noncausal and isolated to a single school district. Thus it is plausible that our findings reflect only the culture of the school district we sampled and not educators as a group. The purpose of this study is to conduct a state-level investigation into the disciplinary infractions Black females are accused of and the sanctions they receive in K–12 education settings relative to White females to understand whether Black females' risk for suspension is driven by their violation of White middle-class gender norms.

OVERVIEW OF RESEARCH

Using cross-sectional descriptive analysis, we examined secondary discipline data from the Ohio Department of Education (ODE) for the 2012–2013 academic year (Ohio Department of Education, 2013b). ODE is unique in that it is one of the few state education agencies to disaggregate school discipline data by race and sex, and by the type of infraction for which students are disciplined. For the 2012–2013 academic school year, ODE reported the total K–12 enrollment for the state at approximately 1.8 million students (Ohio Department of Education, 2013a). Female students represented 48.5% (829,117) of all students enrolled in Ohio public schools. Table 5.1 shows the racial composition of the state's female student population and percentage of the total sanctions each group received for misbehavior.

Do Racial Disparities in School Discipline Disproportionately Affect Black Females?

In our cohort, White females constituted an overwhelming majority of the female student body; Black female students made up only 16% of the total female student population. One would thus expect Black females to receive about 16% of all disciplinary exclusions. In fact, 53.4% of all the exclusions meted out to females were meted out to Black females.

Of course, this disproportionality suggests only that the Black females' share of discipline was higher than one would expect—it does not tell us whether Black females were suspended at high rates in absolute terms. Unfortunately, if we compare the rate of disciplinary exclusions per 100 students (Table 5.2) we see that Black females also had the highest rate[1] of disciplinary sanctions: 48.4 per 100 enrolled. This rate was nearly seven times the rate for White females (7.2 per 100) and by far the highest of all racial/ethnic minority females in the state. Table 5.2 makes it clear that Black females had the highest rate of both OSS (27.52) and ISS (12.70). These disturbing disparities call for closer examination into the reasons for the different suspension rates of Black and White female students.

Are There Racial Differences in School Suspension Rates?

By using cross-tabulations, we were able to show how often administrators used suspension in response to certain infractions committed by Black females. Black female students had the highest suspension rate for each infraction category (Table 5.3). For disobedience/disruptive behavior—which was defined as "an unwillingness to submit to authority, refusal to respond to a reasonable request, or any act that disrupts the orderly conduct of a school function; behavior that substantially disrupts the orderly learning environment (i.e., dress code violations, inappropriate language, cursing, inappropriate gestures)"—Black females' OSS rate was 16.3 and ISS was 10.0, the highest female student rates listed (Ohio Department of Education, 2012). Essentially, this means that 16 out-of-school suspensions and 10 in-school suspensions in this category were meted out to Black females for every 100 Black females enrolled. In comparison, White females received 1.5 OSS and 1.9 ISS per 100 White females enrolled.

Table 5.1. Demographics and Disciplinary Sanctions of Female Students

	White	Black	Hispanic	Multiracial	Asian	American Indian/ Alaskan Native	Total
							Race
Student enrollment							
Percentage enrolled	73.4%	16.0%	4.2%	4.4%	1.9%	0.1%	
Number enrolled	607,955	132,827	34,685	36,214	15,877	1,107	828,665
Disciplinary actions: number of incidents							
All school exclusions[a]	43,779	64,251	4,752	7,222	251	142	120,397
Out-of-school suspension	18,710	36,549	2,428	3,491	98	71	61,347
In-school suspension	16,534	16,872	1,475	2,532	94	58	37,565

Note: Data are based on enrollment and discipline sanctions from the 2012–2013 academic year.
Pacific Islander female students were omitted due to a lack of data per ODE policy, reducing enrollment size from 829,117 to 828,665. All disciplinary actions represent duplicated sanctions.
Only the most severe type of disciplinary sanction issued for a single infraction was reported.
[a] The "all school exclusions" category includes the following disciplinary actions: expulsion, out-of-school suspension, in-school suspension, in-school alternative discipline, and emergency removal by district personnel.

79

Table 5.2. Rate of Exclusions Per 100 Students Enrolled

					Race	
	White	Black	Hispanic	Multiracial	Asian	American Indian/Alaskan Native
			Disciplinary actions			
All school exclusions[a]	7.20	48.37	13.70	19.94	1.58	12.83
Out-of-school suspension	3.08	27.52	7.00	9.64	0.62	6.41
In-school suspension	2.72	12.70	4.25	6.99	0.59	5.24

Note: Rates are calculated per 100 students. All disciplinary actions represent duplicated sanctions. Only the most severe type of disciplinary sanction issued for a single infraction was reported.
[a] The "all school exclusions" category includes the following disciplinary actions: expulsion, out-of-school suspension, in-school suspension, in-school alternative discipline, and emergency removal by district personnel.

Black females also received the lion's share of OSS for fighting/violence. There were seven out-of-school suspensions for fighting per 100 Black female students. Conversely, White female students had a rate of only 0.8 OSS for the same infraction. Black female students had the second highest rate of out-of-school suspensions for truancy, with one OSS issued to a Black female for every 100 Black females enrolled. Although this number is relatively small, the comparison to the rates of White females—just 0.2 OSS for truancy infractions per 100—was pronounced.

How Often Are School Suspensions Used as a Disciplinary Response?

The cross-tabulation analysis in Table 5.3 indicates that the frequency of suspension was highest for both Black and White female students for disobedience infractions. However, it should be noted that when we compared the use of OSS to ISS within the respective racial groups by category (Table 5.3), we found that Black females most frequently received an OSS for disobedience, whereas White females more often received an ISS for the same infraction. It is noteworthy that the higher frequency category of disobedience, which also is the most subjective and vague, had the largest percentage point difference in OSS between Black and White females—more than 14 percentage points—which dwarfed the differences in all other categories.

Table 5.3. Infraction Type and Discipline Sanction by Race

	Race	
Infraction Type by Disciplinary Sanction	Black	White
Rate of out-of-school suspension		
Disobedience/disruptive behavior	16.3	1.5
Fighting/violence	7.0	0.8
Harassment/intimidation	1.5	0.2
Truancy	1.0	0.2
Rate of in-school suspension		
Disobedience/disruptive behavior	10.0	1.9
Fighting/violence	1.6	0.5
Harassment/intimidation	0.5	0.1
Truancy	0.3	0.1

Note: Rates are calculated as suspensions per 100 students.

To establish which differences were statistically significant, we applied a difference of means test to the observed Black–White differences in sanctions per enrollment (ISS and OSS). In conducting these analyses, we sought to determine whether Black females were significantly more likely than White females to receive suspensions for a given infraction, or if the difference observed might reasonably be expected to occur by chance. Our analysis indicated that the differences found between Black and White female students were statistically significant for disobedience for both OSS and ISS and for OSS for fighting. All the other differences by category were not statistically significant.

SUMMARY AND IMPLICATIONS OF KEY FINDINGS

In a broad sense, our findings partially support our claims that Black females' violation of gender norms influences their risk for suspension.

Our findings revealed that Black females received more severe discipline sanctions in the form of out-of-school suspensions than White females for disobedience. The Ohio Department of Education's inclusion of dress code violations and defiance (i.e., unwillingness to submit to authority) as disobedient and disruptive behaviors, as well as Black females' elevated suspension risk for this infraction, supports our theory that Black girls are suspended frequently for infractions that counter White middle-class norms of femininity and female respectability. Although the data from Ohio did not indicate the specific number of dress code violations and defiance citations for which Black females were suspended most often, the fact that Black females were more likely than White girls to be removed from school for this type of infraction broadly parallels the findings from our prior work (Blake et al., 2011). Failure to submit to authority and wearing clothing that calls attention to oneself defy the female "invisibility" that is at the core of White middle-class norms of gender expression. It appears that the assertiveness that has earned many Black females academic and occupational success has created a double-edged sword for them within modern-day K–12 educational settings, as it puts them at greater risk for inequitable discipline due to cultural misinterpretations of the intent behind their behavioral "transgressions" (Ladner, 1972).

Additional findings from the current study also reveal that when compared to White females, Black females receive more out-of-school suspensions for fighting. Few would argue that physical violence and fighting that pose a danger or lead to serious physical injury do not warrant removal from the mainstream classroom. However, it is worth noting that physical fighting, like defiance, is viewed as unfeminine. The literature has frequently indicated that "girls don't fight," or at least that respectable middle-class White females do not fight (Crick, 1997), as fighting is the antithesis of what it means to be ladylike. Ladies do not lose control and do not visibly express anger or handle conflict with their fists. They instead use silence, manipulation, and cruel words to psychologically control and strategically destroy the social status, interpersonal relationships, and self-esteem of their "enemies." These covert behaviors can be as disruptive to school order as fighting and are equally detrimental to girls' social and psychological development (Brown & Gilligan, 1993; Underwood, 2003). In many schools, these covert forms of aggression can go unnoticed by school officials or even be ignored, getting administrators' attention only when they escalate into physical violence, which counters gender norms. Such responses from administrators uphold the presumption that females do not and should not fight, and when they do they must be punished in order to correct this unfeminine trait.

Physical fighting might not be the first response to disagreements for all Black females, however. For Black females from poverty-stricken inner-city communities, physical fighting approaches a necessary evil. Jones (2009) found that for many Black females from these communities fighting was often a last resort for conflict resolution but critical for posturing and warding off future physical attacks. Black females' failed attempt to initially resolve conflict nonviolently necessitates the implementation of more culturally salient antiviolence prevention programs in schools. It also suggests that there are critical periods when school officials should intervene to prevent the escalation of youth violence, rather than using suspension to address such altercations.

The findings from this study shed important light on why Black females are disproportionately suspended, but they should be interpreted in light of the study's limitations. Data from this study were drawn from a secondary dataset, which limited our ability to examine causality in Black females' risk of suspension (e.g., the number of infractions that resulted in a suspension) or to test directly for implicit bias in levying disciplinary actions. Due to our inability to disaggregate the data by socioeconomic status, race, and gender, our findings provide an incomplete depiction of Black females' disciplinary experiences.

Despite these limitations, however, our findings represent an important advancement in the school discipline literature. Based on these findings, we encourage policymakers and practitioners to consider whether there are factors specific to the experiences of Black females that need to be understood and addressed more competently in the course of remedying disproportionate suspension rates. This study also calls for further investigation of Black females' risk of suspension through a gendered lens. Given studies suggesting that Black females are held to the behavioral standards of White females rather than those of their Black male counterparts, analyses of school discipline by gender should be conducted to assess the root causes of Black females' elevated risk for school suspension (Blake et al., 2011).

RECOMMENDATIONS FOR POLICY AND PRACTICE

The alarm bell has sounded for many advocates, who are now calling for a moratorium on school suspensions. The federal government also is working on a major policy initiative to reduce disparities in discipline, especially where there is excessive use of suspension as a response to minor offenses (U.S. Department of Justice Civil Rights Division and U.S. Department of Education Office of Civil Rights, 2011). Along with guiding principles to help schools implement disciplinary practices that foster a safe environment while keeping students in school, the departments of education and justice jointly issued legal guidance stating that even an unintended racially disparate impact of discipline might violate students' federal protection against discrimination (U.S. Department of Education, 2014; U.S. Department of Justice Civil Rights Division and U.S. Department of Education Office of Civil Rights, 2014). This has resonated with an increasing number of schools and districts across the country, which have chosen to replace most suspensions with less punitive alternatives (Ahmed, 2013; NPR Staff, 2013). Though these changes in school policy are promising, they are not sweeping, which indicates that national education policies are still needed to address inequitable school discipline practices.

To fully unearth and understand the inequitable disciplinary experiences of Black females, we recommend that two policies be implemented: (1) Reports of school discipline data should include both the nature of the sanction and the reason it was issued, and (2) the number of school-based mental health professionals available to provide behavioral consultation services to teachers and to support the implementation of social–emotional prevention programs should be increased.

Reports of school discipline data should include both the nature of the sanction and the reason it was issued. We recommend that states be mandated to release to the public their data on student discipline by race, gender, type of infraction, and disciplinary sanction issued. These data should provide information on the cross-section of these groups rather than reporting on race separately from gender. In our search of state-level discipline datasets, we found that few state education departments provided all four aspects of this information. When these agencies did include the reason for suspension or expulsion, the data limited comparisons within race or gender, which prevented the analyses necessary to understand the disciplinary experiences of ethnic minority females. School disciplinary data that include the reason for referral, as well as information on the offending student's race and gender, is vital to examining school discipline from a gendered framework. Education agencies that can state not only who is inequitably disciplined but also why the inequity occurs are better equipped to conduct root cause analyses (U.S. Department of Education, 2014).

Root cause analyses of inequitable disciplinary experiences can help education institutions understand more fully whether teachers' implicit bias is contributing to socially marginalized students' elevated receipt of exclusionary discipline sanctions (Darensbourg, Perez, & Blake, 2010). These analyses also can inform and evaluate the development and selection of nonpunitive alternatives for managing student misbehavior.

Increase the number of school-based mental health professionals available to provide behavioral consultation services to teachers and to support the implementation of social–emotional prevention programs. We recommend that school funds be earmarked to increase the hiring of school-based mental health professionals (e.g., school psychologists and counselors) who can provide behavioral consultation services to teachers and help to implement social–emotional learning to prevent misbehavior for students. School disciplinarians might be insensitive to the unique educational experiences of Black females, for example, and school psychologists who have significant cultural competency training can help bridge that gap. Because school psychologists serve multiple school campuses, they often bring a more objective perspective to understanding student misconduct than campus-based practitioners tend to do.

School psychologists can be instrumental in disrupting the disparate impact of school suspension on Black youth by consulting with teachers on behavior management and working with them to build positive student–teacher relationships (Darensbourg et al., 2010). School psychologists can assist teachers who over-refer students to the office for misconduct by observing their classroom management practices and providing consultation on how to handle challenging students. Research suggests that teachers benefit from explicit instruction on classroom behavior management and are more likely to exude confidence in their classroom discipline strategies when such supports are provided (Nelson, Colvin, & Smith, 1996). Behavioral consultations with teachers can focus on altering their social cognitions about Black females and the reasons for these students' transgressions. These consultations can also help teachers identify and develop proactive classroom behavior management and nonpunitive disciplinary strategies to manage student behaviors. School psychologists and counselors also can assist in implementing social and emotional learning programs for students to help them develop skills for negotiating conflicts. The shortage of school-based mental health professionals in public schools has prevented school psychologists and counselors from playing a vital role in reducing racial/ethnic disparities in school suspension (American School Counselor Association, 2013; Charvat, 2008).

CONCLUSION

The gravity of school suspension for Black females is evident when one considers the potential inequitable use of suspension has to derail the educational attainment and academic future of Black female students (Aud, Fox, & Kewal-Ramani, 2010). Black females who have been suspended are at elevated risk for teenage pregnancy, involvement with the juvenile justice system, and high school dropout (Acoca, Le, Poe-Yamagata, & Muckelroy, 2000; Clark, Petras, Kellam, Ialongo, & Poduska, 2003; also see Chapter 2 of this book). Such events significantly limit the educational and occupational attainment and financial stability of Black females as they transition into womanhood. The association between school suspension and broad economic and physical health outcomes indicates that disproportionate school discipline is not only a pressing educational issue for Black females but a significant public health and societal concern.

In order to address the disparate impact of school suspension on Black females, we recommend that educational stakeholders use similar state-level discipline data to conduct analyses of the root causes of inequitable disciplinary practices. The Ohio Department of Educations' discipline data provide a model of reporting procedures for state discipline data that could aid in developing this policy. In addition to providing more comprehensive reporting procedures, we recommend that additional education funding be focused on (1) increasing the number of school-based mental health professionals available in public schools to provide indirect services to teachers that ensure that behavioral consultations on classroom behavior management are available to struggling teachers, and (2) implementing direct services that make social–emotional learning programs accessible to students in schools.

NOTES

Completion of this chapter was made possible by a grant awarded by the Office of Juvenile Justice and Delinquency Prevention (OJJDP) to the first author (Award Number 2012-JF-FX-4064). The conclusions of the researchers are not necessarily endorsed by OJJDP or the Ohio Department of Education.

1. This rate was calculated by taking the total number of sanctions for Black female students (64,251) and dividing it by their total enrollment (132,827). This number was then multiplied by 100 to yield the number of disciplinary incidents that occurred per 100 Black female students.

REFERENCES

Acoca, L., Le, T., Poe-Yamagata, E., & Muckelroy, A. (2000). *Educate or incarcerate? Girls in the Florida and Duval County juvenile justice systems.* Washington, DC: National Council on Crime and Delinquency.

Ahmed, D. (2013, December 9). Bronx schools reduce policing and suspensions with support from parents. *Huffington Post.* Retrieved from http://www.huffingtonpost.com/tag/school-suspensions

American School Counselor Association. (2013). *Public elementary and secondary school student enrollment and staff counts from the common core of data: School year 2010–2011, first look.* Retrieved from http://www.schoolcounselor.org/asca/media/asca/home/Ratios10-11.pdf

Aud, S., Fox, M., & Kewal-Ramani, A. (2010). *Status and trends in the education of racial and ethnic groups* (NCES 2010–015). Washington, DC: Department of Education.

Blake, J., Butler, B., Lewis, C., & Darensbourg, A. (2011). Unmasking the inequitable discipline experiences of urban black girls: Implications for urban educational stakeholders. *The Urban Review, 43,* 90–106. doi:10.1007/s11256–009–0148–8

Brown, L. M., & Gilligan, C. (1993). Meeting at the crossroads: Women's psychology and girl development. *Feminism & Psychology, 3,* 11–35.

Charvat, J. L. (2008). *Estimates of the school psychology workforce.* Bethesda, MA: National Association of School Psychologists.

Clark, M. D., Petras, H., Kellam, S. G., Ialongo, N., & Poduska, J. M. (2003). Who's most at risk for school removal and later juvenile delinquency? *Women & Criminal Justice, 14*(2–3), 89–116. doi:10.1300/J012v14n02_05

Collins, P. H. (2000). *Black feminist thought: Knowledge, consciousness, and the politics of empowerment*: New York, NY, Psychology Press.

Crick, N. R. (1997). Engagment in gender normative versus gender nonnormative forms of aggression: Links to social-psychological adjustment. *Developmental Psychology, 33*, 610–617.

Darensbourg, A., Perez, E., & Blake, J. J. (2010). Overrepresentation of African American males in exclusionary discipline: The role of school-based mental health professionals in dismantling the school to prison pipeline. *Journal of African American Males in Education, 1*(3), 196–211.

Dillon, S. (2010, September 3). Racial disparity in school suspensions. *The New York Times*. Retrieved from http://www.nytimes.com/2010/09/14/education/14suspend.html?_r=0

Downey, D. B., & Pribesh, S. (2004). When reace matters: Teachers evaluations of students' classroom behavior. *Sociology of Education, 77*, 267–282.

Evans, G. (1988). Those loud black girls. In D. Spender & E. Sarah (Eds.), *Learning to lsoe: Sexism and Education* (pp. 183–190). London, England: Women's Press.

Fenning, P., & Rose, J. (2007). Overrepresentation of African American students in exclusionary discipline the role of school policy. *Urban Education, 42*, 536–559.

Grant, L. (1984). Black girls' "place" in desgreated classrooms. *Sociology of Education, 57*, 98–111.

Jones, N. (2009). *Between good and ghetto: African American girls and inner-city violence*. New Brunswick, NJ: Rutgers University Press.

Ladner, J. (1972). *Tomorrow's tomorrow: The Black woman*: Lincoln, NE: University of Nebraska Press.

Lewin, T. (2012, March 6). Black students face more discipline, data suggests. *New York Times*. Retrieved from http://mobile.nytimes.com/2012/03/06/education/black-students-face-more-harsh-discipline-data-shows.html

Losen, D. J., & Martinez, T. E. (2013). *Out of school and off track: The overuse of suspension in American middle and high schools*. Los Angeles, CA: The Civil Rights Project at UCLA, the Center for Civil Rights Remedies.

Mendez, L. M. R., & Knoff, H. M. (2003). Who gets suspended from school and why: A demographic analysis of schools and disciplinary infractions in a large school district. *Education & Treatment of Children, 26*, 30.

Monroe, C. R. (2005). Why are "bad boys" always black?: Causes of disproportionality in school discipline and recommendations for ghange. *The Clearing House: A Journal of Educational Strategies, Issues and Ideas, 79*, 45–50.

Monroe, C. R., & Obidah, J. E. (2004). The influence of cultural synchronization on a teacher's perceptions of disruption: A case study of an African American middle-school classroom. *Journal of Teacher Education, 55*, 256–268.

Morris, E. W. (2005). "Tuck in that shirt!" Race, class, gender, and discipline in an urban middle school. *Sociological Perspectives, 48*, 25–48.

Morris, E. W. (2007). "Ladies" or "Loudies"? Perceptions and experiences of Black girls in classrooms. *Youth & Society, 38*, 490–515.

Nelson, J. R., Colvin, G., & Smith, D. J. (1996). The effects of setting clear standards on students' social behaviors in common areas of the school. *The Journal of At-Risk Issue, 3*, 10–19.

Noguera, P. A. (2003). Schools, prisons, and social implications of punishment: Rethinking disciplinary practices. *Theory into Practice, 4*, 341–350.

NPR Staff. (2013, June 2). Why some schools want to expel suspensions. *National Public Radio*. Retrieved from http://www.npr.org/2013/06/02/188125079/why-some-schools-want-to-expel-suspensions?ft=1&f=1001

Ohio Department of Education. (2012). *Reporting student data*. In ODE EMIS manual (2nd ed. vol. 1, pp. 1–193): Columbus, OH: Ohio Department of Education.

Ohio Department of Education. (2013a). *Enrollment data*. Retrieved from http://education.ohio.gov/Topics/Data/Frequently-Requested-Data/Enrollment-data

Ohio Department of Education. (2013b). *Interactive local report card (iLRC): Discipline reports on school discipline data.* Retrieved from http://bireports.education.ohio.gov

Raby, R. (2005). Polite, well dressed and on time: Secondary school conduct codes and the production of docile citizens. *Canadian Review of Sociology, 42*(1), 71–91.

Rahimi, R., & Liston, D. D. (2009). What does she expect when she dresses like that? Teacher interpretation of emerging adolescent female sexuality. *Educational Studies, 45,* 512–533.

Rollock, N. (2007). Why Black girls don't matter: Exploring how race and gender shape academic success in an inner city school. *Support for Learning, 4,* 197–202.

Stephens, D. P., & Phillips, L. D. (2003). Freaks, gold diggers, divas, and dykes: The sociohistorical development of adolescent African American women's sexual scripts. *Sexuality and Culture, 7,* 3–49.

Taylor, M. C., & Foster, G. A. (1986). Bad boys and school suspensions: Public policy implications for Black boys. *Sociological Inquiry, 56,* 498–506.

Tenenbaum, H. R., & Ruck, M. D. (2007). Are teachers' expectations different for racial minorities than for European American students? A meta-analysis. *Journal of Educational Psychology, 99*(2), 253–273.

U.S. Department of Education. (2014). *Guiding principles: A resource guide for improving school climate and discipline* (pp. 1–27). Washington, DC: U.S. Department of Education.

U.S. Department of Justice Civil Rights Division and U.S. Department of Education Office of Civil Rights. (2011). *Supportive school discipline initiative.* Retrieved from http://www.ed.gov/news/pres-releases/secretary-duncan-attorney-general-holder-announce-effort-respond-school-prison-p

U.S. Department of Justice Civil Rights Division and U.S. Department of Education Office of Civil Rights. (2014). *Dear colleague letter on the nondiscriminatory administration of school discipline.* Retrieved from http://www2.ed.gov/about/offices/list/ocr/letters/colleague-201401-title-vi.html

Underwood, M. (2003). *Social aggression among girls*: New York, NY: Guilford Press.

West, C. M. (1995). Mammy, sapphire, and jezebel: Historical images of Black women and their implications for psychotherapy. *Psychotherapy: Theory, Research, Practice, Training, 32,* 458–466.

## CHAPTER 6

Disturbing Inequities

Exploring the Relationship Between Racial Disparities in Special Education Identification and Discipline

Daniel J. Losen, Jongyeon Ee,
Cheri Hodson, and Tia E. Martinez

Students with disabilities are entitled by law to receive special education, which includes individualized supports and services, including behavioral supports if needed, to help them succeed in school. So it is especially disturbing that nationally, in 2011–2012, their out-of-school suspension rate for grades K–12 was more than twice as high as their nondisabled peers (Office for Civil Rights, 2014). They are also more likely than their nondisabled peers to be suspended repeatedly (Losen & Gillespie, 2012). In 2011–2012, across K–12, as described in the table below, the rates were much higher for students with disabilities who were Black or American Indian and male, with more than one out of every four having been suspended at least once (27%) (see Table 6.1; OCR, 2014).

The data from different school levels (elementary, middle, and high) reveal even deeper disparities. For students with disabilities, the risk for suspension at the elementary school level is 4.1%. This rises to 19.3% at the secondary level (Losen & Martinez, 2013). Whereas students with disabilities are about twice

Table 6.1. National (K–12) Suspension Risk by Race, Disability, and Gender 2011–2012

United States	American Indian/Alaska Native	Asian	Native Hawaiian/ Other Pacific Islander	Black/African American	Latino	White
Male	29%	10%	25%	27%	17%	12%
Female	20%	6%	18%	19%	10%	6%

Source:. U.S. Department of Education Office for Civil Rights Data Collection: Data Snapshot (School Discipline) at page 3, March 2014.

as likely as their nondisabled peers to be suspended at each level, the 2 percent point gap at the elementary level increases fivefold at the secondary level to a 10 percent point gap.

When we look at the intersection of race, disability, and gender at the secondary level, we find that 24% of Black secondary students, 31% of Black secondary school students with disabilities, and 36% of Black secondary school males with disabilities were suspended from school in 2009–2010 (Losen & Martinez, 2013).

It is worth noting that this national average masks even more extreme situations. For example, using U.S. Department of Education data for the 2009–2010 academic year, of the 1,136 U.S. school districts that have at least 50 Black males with disabilities, 211 had suspension rates for Black males with disabilities at the secondary level of over 50% (Losen & Martinez, 2013). These are averages for large districts, which means there are individual schools in each of these high-suspending districts with even higher suspension rates.

Researchers have consistently found that getting suspended from school correlates with a dramatic increase in a student's risk for dropping out and involvement in the juvenile justice system (see Chapters 1, 2, and 4). Unfortunately, our national data-collection efforts do not rigorously track the number of students incarcerated by race and disability status. Despite this weakness in the data collection, the Office of Special Education Programs' (OSEP) national data consistently show dramatic disparities. When we examined OSEP's 2011–2012 data, we found that Black students with disabilities constituted 19% of all students with disabilities, yet they represented 50% of students with disabilities in correctional institutions.

This chapter asserts that this status quo must be rejected because federal, state, district, and school-level policies and practices are likely contributing to the high rates of disciplinary exclusion experienced by all students with disabilities, particularly Black students with disabilities. This chapter seeks to promote a better understanding of the relationship between the risk for being identified as having a disability, and disparate patterns of school discipline. We have centered our analysis on Blacks with disabilities because they have the highest risk for suspension, and because the federal Individuals with Disabilities Education Act (IDEA) requires that every state reviews each district's data and address significant levels of disproportionality by race with regard to identification, placement, and discipline. It is worth noting that as this chapter was being written, on June 19, 2014, the U.S. Department of Education submitted a request for public comment on the actions that the Department should take to address the fact that "Data collected by the Department's Office of Special Education Programs (OSEP) and Office for Civil Rights (OCR) shows significant racial and ethnic disparity . . . including identification by disability category, educational placement, and disciplinary action. Based on these data, the Department has been concerned about the very small number of LEAs [Local Educational Agencies] that have been identified by their States as having significant disproportionality, and the resulting limited funds that LEAS are required to use for CEIS [coordinated early intervening services] to address that significant disproportionality" (Federal Register, 2014, p. 35155). Not only are few states identifying any districts pursuant to the IDEA (Skiba & Losen, 2012), but those districts that are identified often do not understand what factors contribute to the disparate patterns within their district.

SETTING THE STAGE

Closer Examination of Possible Contributing Factors to High Rates and Significant Disparities That Schools Can Influence. The racial disparities we observed are significant, in part because the data indicate that extraordinary numbers of Black students with disabilities are subjected to out-of-school suspension (OSS). We focused our deeper analysis of the data on the exploration of two possible contributing factors to these higher rates of suspensions for Black students with disabilities. We chose differential exposure to novice teachers (1–2 years of experience) and risk for identification as having special education needs because they can possibly be affected by education policy, so that if our findings had statistical significance they would more likely have policy relevance as well. In addition to the aforementioned IDEA requirements, the Elementary and Secondary Education Act (ESEA) requires that each state ensure that poor and minority students are not taught at higher rates by inexperienced teachers. By its own admission, the U.S. Department of Education has stated that this federal requirement has not been effectively implemented (McNeil, 2014).

Further, we chose these two factors because prior research suggests they are connected, although our analysis looks at the degree to which each independently predicts higher suspension rates.

Differential Exposure to Inexperienced Teachers. First- and second-year teachers tend to have comparatively lower classroom management and instructional skills due to their inexperience, and researchers have suggested that this low level of experience contributes to the higher likelihood that students in general are suspended from school (Morrison et al., 2000). Research has also established that poor and minority students are more likely than their counterparts to be taught by novice teachers. This differential exposure to novice teachers would be expected to contribute to the increased risk for suspension documented for Black students and Black students with disabilities (Losen & Martinez, 2013). For a variety of reasons, researchers have suggested that novice teachers might also be more likely than their experienced colleagues to refer minority students for special education evaluation. Specifically, a review of the research by the National Academy of Sciences (NAS) in the 2002 publication *Minorities in Gifted and Special Education* (National Research Council, 2002c) concluded that "the school experience itself contributes to racial disproportion in academic outcomes and behavioral problems that lead to placement in special and gifted education . . ." at least in part because "Schools with higher concentrations of low-income, minority children are less likely to have experienced, well-trained teachers" (National Research Council, 2002c, p. 358).

Although the impact novice teachers (1 or 2 years of experience) have on the suspension rates of Black students with disabilities was not studied directly by the NAS researchers, we would expect that being taught by novice teachers would predict a statistically significant increase in this group's risk for suspension from school. The NAS report also suggests that the impact of teacher inexperience might be greatest in urban districts (National Research Council, 2002c). Rothstein (2000, p. 175) stated similarly that one of the greatest inequities in education is the uneven distribution of teachers within urban districts.[1]

Of course, other factors besides differential exposure to novice teachers, including the possibility of unconscious bias (Harry, Klingner, Sturges, & Moore, 2002; Oswald, Coutinho, Best, & Nguyen, 2001) might contribute to higher risk that Black students are identified as having special education needs. Under the IDEA, it states, pursuant to review of district-level data for large racial/ethnic disparities identification, placement, and discipline, if "significant disproportionality" is found, the district must take action to address the issues and must spend 15% of their federal special education funding on coordinated early intervening services (20 U.S.C. Section 1418[d]) (IDEA, 2004).] Toward the goal of understanding the extraordinarily high suspension rates of Black students with disabilities, and helping districts explore possible contributing factors they could control, this chapter further explores whether schools that tend to identify a high number of Black students as having emotional disturbance (ED), intellectual disability (ID, formerly mental retardation), or specific learning disabilities (SLD) also tend to suspend Black students with disabilities at higher rates. The combination of factors that contribute to a greater likelihood that Black students will be identified for special education in these disability categories might also contribute to the disparate discipline of Black students with disabilities. If identification in these categories predicts higher suspension rates for Black students with disabilities, but not for their White peers, questions are raised about systemic racial bias in the treatment of Black students with disabilities. In fact, prior studies have suggested that Black students with emotional disturbance do receive less and lower quality care than their White counterparts (Osher, Woodruff, & Sims, 2002). We would thus expect to see lower rates of suspension in disability categories in which Blacks are not likely to be identified at higher rates than Whites, such as autism.

As we will discuss in our recommendations and conclusion, current federal policy requirements that address the overrepresentation of minorities in the special education categories of ED, ID, and SLD, as well as disparities in discipline, have been criticized (GAO, 2013). Beyond the possible steps the Department of Education initiates after reviewing the responses to its RFI, when reauthorization of the IDEA is taken up by Congress, our findings could also have implications for amendments to the statutory requirements.

The Breakdown of the Data From Over 70,000 Schools Across the Nation. To conduct our analysis, we worked with the school-level data for 2009–2010 collected by the U.S. Department of Education Office for Civil Rights. Specifically, the data come from 72,168 schools from nearly 7,000 school districts from nearly every state.

Choice of Disability Categories. In 2002, the NAS noted that "racial disproportionality in special education was historically markedly higher in the high-incidence categories of mild mental retardation, emotional disturbance, and to a lesser extent learning disabilities, categories in which the problem is often identified first in the school context and the disability diagnosis is typically given without confirmation of an organic cause . . ." and nonexistent in categories typically diagnosed by medical professionals (National Research Council, 2002b, p. 1).

Our own analysis of the most recent national data available also shows that these three disability categories are three of the four in which students with disabilities are most likely to be suspended or expelled from school (Table 6.2).

Table 6.2. Suspension Risk by Disability Category[a]

Disability Category	Suspension Rate
Emotional disturbance	32.88
Other health impairment	14.68
Specific learning disability	13.06
Intellectual disability (mental retardation)	10.17
Traumatic brain injury	8.00
Deafness/Blindness	7.06
Hearing impairment	5.94
Orthopedic impairment	5.74
Multiple disabilities	4.65
Developmental delay	4.52
Autism	4.32
Visual impairment	4.32
Speech or language impairment	3.68

Forty-two states had complete data.
Sources: Civil Rights Data Collection National Estimations (2009–2010); IDEA Data Center: Part B-Child Count (2009–2010)

We added a school-level analysis of autism to these three historically problematic and subjective categories for two reasons. First, over the last 10 years the
risk for autism has increased dramatically, such that it is no longer a "low-inci-
dence" category. Like the high-incidence categories, autism involves a degree of
subjectivity in diagnosis. Second, autism is one of the few categories in which
Black students are at a substantially lower risk for identification compared to
White students.

To put the more detailed analysis in perspective, we first provide the values
for the risk for special identification by disability category for the entire sample
(Table 6.3). It should be noted that these values apply only to the sample used in
our analysis and are not identical to those for the nation.[2]

Table 6.3. Disability Risk for Identification by Category

2009–2010 Disability Category	American Indian	Asian/Pacific Islander	Black	Hispanic	White	All Races
Autism	.04	.31	.30	.23	.62	.45
ED	.30	.02	.81	.20	.56	.48
ID	.34	.10	1.25	.44	.56	.62
SLD	4.11	.71	5.32	4.67	4.03	4.19

Next, in Table 6.4 we provide the risk for suspension for the school-level sample (combining elementary, middle, and high). These are not per-school averages;
they provide the average risk for suspension by subgroup for students attending all
the schools in the entire sample.

Table 6.4. Average Suspension Rates for All Schools in Sample

Subgroup	Percentage of Enrolled Students Suspended at Least Once (2009–2010)
All students	7.28
Black	16.60
Black with disabilities	23.77
Black males with disabilities	26.84
White	4.75
Whites with disabilities	9.16
White males with disabilities	11.19

To complete our review of the descriptive findings, we have grouped the schools in our study by increases in Black enrollment. Table 6.5 provides a general sense of how suspension rates for the subgroups we studied varied when the percentage of Black school-level enrollment rose. This is noteworthy because our additional analyses controlled for both Black and White enrollment. The pattern in the chart shows that the risk for suspensions for all Black students, Black students with disabilities, and Black males with disabilities rises steadily until Blacks make up about 30% to 40% of the total enrollment. This is the point at which suspension rates of Black students with disabilities appeared highest, at 27.63% (K–12), although they are consistently above 20% risk for suspension in schools where they constitute more than 10% of total enrollment. Suspension risk levels for White students with disabilities similarly rises with increases in Black enrollment. Although beyond the scope of this analysis, the fact that schools with enrollment of 95% to 100% Black students had markedly lower suspension rates for Blacks with disabilities is worth exploring further.

What Did We Find When We Controlled for Different Enrollment Levels and Other Factors? The dual explorations of this chapter are the impact of the risk of novice teachers and disability identification on the risk for suspension of Black students with disabilities. We also performed the same analysis for Black male students with disabilities and Black students in the aggregate to understand how our findings compare to suspension trends we observed in the descriptive analysis. To understand whether the predictive power of the tested variables was unique to Black students with disabilities, or more universal, we conducted the same analysis for White students, White students with disabilities, and White male students with disabilities. Finally, because suspension rates are much higher at the middle and high school level than in elementary schools, we ran the analysis at each of these three school levels.

To explore the possible impact of our two factors—novice teachers and identification in certain special education categories—on the risk for suspension, we controlled for the possible impact of enrollment and many other variables using a method called a multivariate regression analysis. For example, one of our analyses answers the question, "What is the predictive impact of having a higher percentage of Blacks identified as having emotional disturbance on the suspension rate of all Black students with disabilities after the potential impact of the percentage of enrolled Black students, percentage of enrolled White students, percentage of novice teachers, percentage of Blacks identified as having intellectual disabilities, percentage of Blacks identified as having autism, and percentage of Blacks identified as having specific learning disabilities have been accounted for?" Our full set of findings and more detailed description of the methods and justification are available in the longer online version of this chapter (Losen, Hodson, Ee, & Martinez, http://tinyurl.com/JanCRPconference). For the purpose of informing policymakers, this chapter provides the summary of our statistically significant findings.

Table 6.5. Average School-Level Suspension Rates for Sample, Disaggregated by Percentage of Black Students in Total Enrollment

Percentage of Black Enrollment	Number of Schools	Percentage of Black Students Suspended			Percentage of White Students Suspended		
		All	Students With Disabilities	Males with Disabilities	All	Students With Disabilities	Males With Disabilities
0–5%	30,411	9.64	15.92	18.84	3.76	7.63	9.44
5–10%	8,589	11.48	18.50	21.45	4.50	8.82	10.79
10–15%	5,146	13.57	21.23	24.28	5.37	10.34	12.51
15–20%	3,482	14.15	22.14	25.21	5.72	10.64	12.90
20–25%	2,573	15.49	23.69	26.84	6.13	11.52	14.16
25–30%	2,139	17.07	26.02	29.32	7.15	12.62	15.15
30–40%	3,019	18.27	27.63	30.90	7.88	13.71	16.32
40–50%	2,241	18.25	27.22	30.93	8.31	14.14	16.76
50–60%	1,564	18.18	26.35	29.62	9.74	15.65	18.32
60–70%	1,210	19.09	26.05	29.04	10.73	15.63	18.11
70–80%	1,064	19.26	25.97	29.04	10.71	14.06	16.92
80–90%	1,127	19.65	25.39	28.30	13.29	17.53	20.44
90–95%	795	19.67	26.05	29.29	12.68	15.64	17.57
95–100%	8,808	16.27	20.76	23.04	12.74	13.02	15.12

Exposure to Novice Teachers Predicted a Slight Increase in Suspension Risk. Our regression analysis showed that across each school level, after controlling for the other factors, a 1% point increase in the level of novice teachers predicted a weak, yet statistically significant, increase in suspension rates for all students, all Black students, all White students, Black male students, White male students, and all Black students with disabilities. A similarly weak yet statistically significant predictive value for novice teachers was found for suspension of White students with disabilities at the elementary level, but not at the middle or high school levels.

Identification in Some Disability Categories Studied Predicted Increases in Suspension Risk for Black and White Students with Disabilities. The results revealed that among the tens of thousands of schools, those schools that identified more Black students as having emotional disturbance or specific learning disabilities were also found to suspend Black students with disabilities at higher rates. Our most consistent finding across these analyses was that, for both Black and White students, a 1-point increase in the percentage of students identified as having emotional disturbance predicted a statistically significant increase in the risk for out-of-school suspension at each level (elementary, middle, and high). We found that schools with higher identification rates in these two categories predictably had higher suspension rates. This predictive power of identification for suspension was consistently found for the suspension risk for all Black students, Black students with disabilities, and Black males with disabilities. The strongest finding for Blacks was that at the elementary school level, a 1 point increase in Black students' identification as having emotional disturbance predicted a 2.3% increase in the suspension rate for all Black students in elementary school. The findings for the predictive power of Whites having emotional disturbance on White suspensions were consistent with those for Blacks, and sometimes slightly stronger. A similar pattern and consistency was found with regard to the predictive power of specific learning disabilities on higher risk for suspension for both Black and White students. Conversely, being identified as having autism consistently predicted a decrease in the risk for out-of-school suspension, and the autism results were among the strongest. For Black and White students, a 1 point increase in the rate of identification for autism predicted between a 1% and 5% decrease, respectively, in rate of suspension.

Our findings for intellectual disability (ID) were highly inconsistent and did not suggest a clear pattern or policy relevant finding. For example, for both Blacks and Whites, a higher identification rate for ID predicted a statistically significant *increase* in the risk for suspension for *all* Black students and for *all* White students but predicted a *decrease* in the risk for suspension among both Black and White students *with disabilities*. Further inconsistencies were found from one school level to the next.

LIMITATIONS AND RATIONALE

This regression analysis could be criticized as insufficient if we hoped to prove un-equivocally that the factors we analyzed *caused* higher suspension rates for Black students with disabilities. Regression analyses examine relationships—they do not determine causality—and ours is no exception. An ideal school-level study would control for more variables, including school-level poverty, and the attitude of the school principal among likely contributing factors. In Chapter 9, for example, Skiba et al. do control for poverty in a multivariate regression analysis of the use of out-of-school suspension, and they find that race is predictive even after con-trolling for poverty. In addition, the national CRDC database we had access to did not contain school-level data on the discipline rates by race by disability category; nor did it contain data on the percentage of poor students for each school.

On the other hand, controlling for some variables in an attempt to find what contributes to observed racial inequality raises the dilemma that some of the con-trolled variables might be products of racial discrimination or too entangled with each other to show a distinct contribution when analyzed separately (Losen & Orfield, 2002). Our purpose, however, was not to rule out possible contributors or define the relative strengths of all contributing factors, but merely to explore the possibility of connections among factors schools can control and the high rates of discipline for Black students with disabilities—specifically, the connections among disability categories in which Black students are typically overrepresented: exposure to inexperienced teachers and discipline. Whereas the descriptive statis-tics from this chapter's introduction give rise to logical inferences that discipline disparities are related to these factors, the results of our regression analyses reveal whether there is a statistically significant relationship and, if so, its strength.

IMPLICATIONS OF OUR FINDINGS FOR POLICYMAKERS

As mentioned in our introduction, exposure to inexperienced teachers has long been thought to contribute to the overidentification of Black students in special education (National Research Council, 2002a). The results of our regression anal-ysis show that greater exposure to novice teachers predicts a relatively weak but statistically significant higher risk for every subgroup's suspension risk, including Blacks with disabilities. The regression analysis for predicting Black students' risk for suspension, however, controlled for Black students identified as having emo-tional disturbance, specific learning disability, intellectual disability, or autism. It also controlled for the level of Black enrollment. The analysis was done in paral-lel fashion for White students. In other words, the degree to which having nov-ice teachers predicts an increase in discipline rates was detected after controlling for any effect that higher identification for any disability category or enrollment demographics might have on these discipline rates. Thus, our findings suggest that education policy aimed at ensuring a more equitable distribution of novice teachers might help reduce both the overidentification of Black students in high-incidence categories as well as help reduce the high rates of suspension, including those experienced by Black students with disabilities.

The fact that we found a consistent pattern of suspension prediction for novice teachers on suspension rates of both Black students with disabilities at all levels, and White students with disabilities in elementary school, points to an issue regarding the distribution of novice teachers, which is one that schools and districts can control.

In regard to identification in certain special education categories, again our study suggested a similar impact on both Black and White students with respect to suspension rates, but the category seemed to matter a great deal. Specifically, there might be a common problem with the behavioral supports and services provided to ED and SLD students that predicted an increase in suspensions. For these two categories, our predictive findings are consistent with the descriptive statistics presented earlier (Table 6.2) that showed that students with disabilities in these two categories (without regard to race) were the first and third most likely to be suspended.

One plausible explanation might be that students with emotional disturbance and specific learning disabilities simply misbehave more *because of their disability*. However, suspending students for behavior that is a manifestation of their disability is unlawful. Moreover, schools are obligated to determine if the disability is causing the misbehavior; thus this possible explanation is connected to a factor schools can control—namely, their legal responsibility not to suspend children because of their disabilities.

Specifically, the IDEA contains both substantive requirements and procedural protections to help prevent schools from unlawfully excluding any students whose disabilities cause problematic behavior. If a student's disability manifests itself as inappropriate behavior of a kind or to a degree that interrupts the student's learning or that of others, the school is obligated to provide the student with a behavioral improvement plan, or to consider placing the student in a more restrictive educational setting, if the special education team determines that it is appropriate based on an individualized evaluation. When not used as a punishment, placement in a more restrictive setting to ensure appropriate behavioral supports and services are provided is not regarded as a suspension from school (U.S. Department of Education, 2009). As an additional safeguard, Congress requires schools to conduct a manifestation determination hearing for a single (or cumulative suspensions) suspension in excess of 10 days in a given school year. If the behavior is found to be a manifestation of a student's disability, the school may not remove the student from the current placement. Exceptions exist only when the student poses a serious physical threat to self or others. There are also many additional requirements in the IDEA, including requirements to conduct behavioral assessments and provide behavioral improvement plans intended to ensure that any student with a disability (regardless of disability category) who exhibits behavioral problems receives the individualized special education supports and services that she or he needs to succeed. No student with a disability may be denied access to education because they have a disability.

If most schools were meeting their legal and moral obligations to identify students with disabilities, and then meeting their individualized needs, including providing the needed behavioral supports and placements when warranted, one would expect students with disabilities to be excluded from school at a rate similar to that of their nondisabled peers. The findings from our regression analyses, when combined with the descriptive data showing students with disabilities at twice the risk for suspension as those without, raise many serious questions. Are some schools discounting the behavioral attributes of some disabilities? Are they failing to provide the needed supports, services, and procedural safeguards? This is known as a denial of their right to a free appropriate public education (FAPE). If some students are being denied FAPE, this raises a related question of whether this failure is more common for some disability categories than others?

Students with disabilities are not supposed to be treated any differently if their misconduct is not directly caused by their disability. For example, having dyslexia should not except a student from having to obey school rules, assuming that the student has been given the necessary support to read and understand them. On the other hand, it is likely inappropriate to suspend a student with ADHD for leaving his seat, or a student with Tourette's syndrome for blurting out an inappropriate word. The large disparities observed together with the fact that being identified as having ED or SLD predicts higher suspension rates suggest that schools are overlooking the disability-connected behaviors, at least for these two high-incidence categories.

It is also worth noting that, compared to White students, Blacks are overidentified in the two categories that consistently predict increased suspensions and underidentified for autism, the category that consistently predicts lower suspension rates for both Black and White students. This pattern of categorical over- and underidentification might have a net disparate impact on Black students and might partially explain why Black students with disabilities are suspended out of school at much higher rates than White students with disabilities. Although they fall far short of proof, the empirical trends combined with the predictive values by category also raise the question of whether there is an unlawful racially disparate impact connected to the disparities in identification by disability category. (The legal analysis under disparate impact theory is described in the conclusion of this book.)

The legal analysis for whether a school policy or practice violates federal civil rights protections on the basis of race is also a good tool for shaping sound educational policy. The first question civil rights investigators ask is whether the policy or practice in question has a disparate harmful impact on a protected subgroup. If so, the question becomes whether the policy or practice can be justified because it is educationally necessary. If not, the policy or practice would likely violate the law. But even if found to be necessary, the question becomes whether there is a policy or practice that would effectively serve the same necessary purpose, but would have a less discriminatory impact. If so, persisting with the more harmful policy or practice would also violate civil rights law. As discussed further in our recommendations that follow, there are both law-enforcement policies and extant statutory requirements intended to address many of the questions and concerns raised by these findings.

RECOMMENDATIONS
FOR POLICYMAKERS

The following section provides practical recommendations for policymakers.

Increase Federal Education Resources for the Monitoring and Enforcement of Civil Rights Laws. The disparate disciplinary exclusion of students with disabilities in general and the confluence of race and disability with regard to the same raise a host of law and policy issues. There are clear legal concerns regarding the rights of students with disabilities to a free, appropriate public education (Kim, Losen, & Hewitt, 2010). It is also worth mentioning that formal guidance regarding discipline policies and practices that might violate Title VI on the basis of race, issued by the U.S. education and justice departments to states and districts in 2014, does make clear (in footnote 4) that the same "disparate impact" approach (described above) applies to students with disabilities (Departments of Education & Justice, 2014). One obvious recommendation is that the federal guidance on discrimination in discipline be expanded to add specific examples of how antidiscrimination law applies to discipline disparities regarding students with disabilities. Another straightforward recommendation is that the federal government direct more resources to the agencies responsible for monitoring and enforcing the legal protections against discrimination afforded to students with disabilities.

Improve the Enforcement of the IDEA's Provisions on School Discipline Disparities. Equally important to education policymakers is the fact that federal statutory obligations pursuant to the IDEA require states to review discipline disparities, by race, among students with disabilities. Among the several IDEA provisions is the requirement that each state annually and publicly report data on the incidence and duration of school discipline among students with disabilities, broken down by race, gender, English learner status, and disability category, including suspensions of 1 day or more (20 U.S.C. Sec. 1418 [a]) (IDEA, 2004).] A review of all 50 states' public reporting reveals that only 8 are even approaching compliance with this requirement (Center for Civil Rights Remedies, 2014).

Beyond improvement to the public reporting of data, the IDEA's federal policy requirements regarding discipline disparities are one of three areas falling under the broader rubric of racial disproportionality in special education. At the outset, we mentioned that the federal government has itself noted concerns about the implementation of these requirements. Thus it is worth reviewing the following details of the policy. Following federal guidance to the states from the Department of Education's Office of Special Education Programs, issued in 2007, the statutory requirements are clear:

> States have a separate obligation, under 20 U.S.C. 1418(d) and 34 CFR §300.646, to collect and examine data to determine whether significant disproportionality based on race or ethnicity is occurring in the State and LEAs of the State with respect to the identification of children as children with disabilities, including identification as children with particular impairments; the placement of children in particular educational settings; and the incidence, duration, and type of disciplinary actions, including suspensions and expulsions. States must make this determination on an annual basis. . . .
>
> [I]n the case of a determination of significant disproportionality with respect to the identification of children as children with disabilities, the placement in particular educational settings of such children, or disciplinary actions, the SEA must require the LEA to reserve the maximum amount (15%) of the flow-through funds it receives under Part B of IDEA to provide comprehensive coordinated early intervening services. (OSEP, 2007)

Among the many activities that might be considered coordinated early intervening services are "(1) professional development for teachers and other school staff to enable such personnel to deliver scientifically based academic and behavioral interventions . . . and (2) providing educational and behavioral evaluations, services, and supports" (20 U.S.C. Sec 1412 [f]) (IDEA, 2004).

Unfortunately, the U.S. Government Accounting Office issued a report criticizing the U.S. Department of Education for its poor implementation of the provisions regarding special education disproportionality. The report, which was issued in February 2013 for Senator Harkin, chair of the Senate Health Education Labor and Pensions Committee, pointed out that federal oversight had allowed states to define "significant disproportionality" to such a high bar that the states never identified any districts as having a problem (GAO, 2013). The results of this analysis clearly suggest that the disparate discipline rates for Blacks with disabilities are exacerbated by the disparate identification rates in at least two categories, ED and SLD, in which Blacks are overidentified in comparison to Whites. However, our findings suggest that part of the problem might lie in the quality of behavioral supports and services provided to students in those categories, regardless of race. Thus where states identify districts as having significant disproportionality in discipline, or in identification, they should consider the possible connections between overidentification and higher rates of discipline.

Improve Procedural Protections to Eliminate Unjust Disciplinary Exclusion. In addition, because our analysis raises serious doubts about the quantity and quality of the manifestation determination hearings, further research regarding these procedures is warranted. However, our study examined suspensions of 1 day or more. The procedural protections of a "manifestation determination" are triggered only when students with disabilities are suspended for more than 10 days. One overarching concern is that these procedural protections are not working at all. Another might be that they are ineffective because they do not apply to the vast majority of students with disabilities who are usually suspended for 10 days or less (or because their cumulative suspensions do not exceed 10 days in a given year). One solution might be to lower the threshold from 10 days to 3 days. Another would be to drop the annual resetting of the count of days of suspension and have the manifestation determination triggered when the cumulative suspension record of a student with disabilities exceeds the 10-day point at any time in his or her academic career.

Improve the Enforcement of State Obligations to Ensure That Poor and Minority Students Have Equitable Access to Experienced Teachers. Our analysis of the impact of novice teachers shows a consistent, albeit not robust, influence on suspension rates for every subgroup we analyzed, and consistently statistically significant for Black students with disabilities. There is already a federal requirement in Title I of the Elementary and Secondary Education Act of 2001 that every state receiving federal funding implement a plan to eliminate the greater frequency with which poor and minority students are taught by uncertified, inexperienced, and "out-of-field teachers." However, like the provisions for racial disproportionality, this requirement has been criticized as being poorly implemented. In 2014, the federal government acknowledged this failure. According to *Education Week,* Education Secretary Arne Duncan stated, "We don't have one district that systemically identifies their most successful teachers and principals and places them with the kids and communities that need them most" (McNeil, 2014). Our analysis suggesting that novice teachers appear to be a factor in the likelihood of suspension, including for Black students with disabilities, further supports the need for additional policy work and better enforcement of current federal policy in this area.

Additionally, we know from other research that schools with high concentrations of poor and minority students tend to have higher concentrations of novice teachers. The descriptive analysis tracking suspension risks in schools by percentage of Black enrollment and Skiba et al.'s findings in Chapter 9 suggest that efforts to reduce racial and socioeconomic isolation might also help reduce Black students' overall risk for suspension.

Knowing what we do about the negative impact of out-of-school suspension, the data on all students with disabilities should be enough to call for a change to education policies and practices. The fact that particular subgroups of students with disabilities are suspended out of school at much higher rates than other groups suggests an urgent need for additional policy and practice remedies that address the needs of the most vulnerable subgroups. Along these lines, and consistent with the concerns raised by Blake, Butler, and Smith in Chapter 5, more should be done to monitor and intervene where the disparities are found at the confluence of race, disability, and gender.

Step up Federal Oversight and Enforcement of Current Law. Finally, the federal policy issues highlighted here all involve requirements that belong to state and local educational agencies. In other words, state and local educators are ultimately responsible for looking closely at the issues raised and taking action. Most recently, the Office of the Attorney General for the state of New York raised concerns about the Syracuse City School District's discipline policies and practices and possible violations of both state and federal civil rights laws and the disparate the impact on students by race and disability. Following an investigation, in July 2014 the OAG entered into an agreement that included many changes to district policy and practice (Schneiderman, 2014). Though the findings we present do not point to any clear or simple solution, they do suggest that there are factors education policymakers can influence that could help reduce the grossly disproportionate impact of high suspension rates experienced by Black students with disabilities.

NOTES

1. In Chapter 9, Skiba et al. share the finding that higher Black enrollment predicts higher out-of-school suspension rates for Black students in Indiana, after controlling for poverty and type of suspension rates. Although their study of statewide suspension rates did not find "teacher's average years of experience" to predict higher Black suspension rates in the state of Indiana, our analysis focused exclusively on "novice" teachers.
2. A comparison with national rates shows that our sample's rates tend to be slightly lower than rates reported by OSEP for the 2009–2010 school year.

REFERENCES

Center for Civil Rights Remedies & CSG Justice Center. (2014). *Nationwide survey of state education agencies' online school disciplinary data.* Retrieved from http://civilrightsproject.ucla.edu/resourc es/projects/center-for-civil-rights-remedies/school-to-prison-folder/online-data-resources/ nation-wide-survey-of-state-education-agencies2019-online-school-disciplinary-data
Federal Register. (2014). *Notices, 2014.* Retrieved from http://www.gpo.gov/fdsys/pkg/FR-2014-06-19/ pdf/2014-14388.pdf

GAO. (2013). *Individuals with Disabilities Educational Act: Standards needed to improve identification of racial and ethnic overrepresentation in special education.* (GAO-13-137). Washington, DC: Author.

Harry, B., Klingner, J., Sturges, K. M., & Moore, R. F. (2002). Of rocks and soft places: Using qualitative methods to investigate disproportionality. In D. Losen & G. Orfield (Eds.), *Racial inequity in special education* (pp. 71–92). Cambridge, MA: Harvard Education Press.

Kim, C., Losen, D., & Hewitt, D. (2010). *The school-to-prison pipeline: Structuring legal reform*: New York, NY: NYU Press.

Losen, D., & Orfield, G. (Eds.). (2002). *Racial inequity in special education*: Cambridge, MA: Harvard Education Press.

Losen, D. J., & Gillespie, J. (2012). *Opportunities suspended: The disparate impact of disciplinary exclusion from school.* Los Angeles, CA: University of California, Los Angeles.

Losen, D. J., Hodson, C., Ee, J., & Martinez, T. E. (2014). *Disturbing inequities: Exploring the relationship of discipline disparities for students with disabilities by race with gender with school outcomes.* Los Angeles: University of California, Los Angeles. Retrieved from http://tinyurl.com/JanCRPconference

Losen, D. J., & Martinez, T. E. (2013). *Out of school and off track: The overuse of suspension in American middle and high schools.* Los Angeles, CA: The Civil Rights Project at UCLA, the Center for Civil Rights Remedies.

McNeil, M. (2014, February 18). Scrutiny rises on placement of best teachers. *Education Week.* Retrieved from http://www.edweek.org/ew/articles/2014/02/19/21equity_ep.h33.html?tkn=WQXFoTW0GoN8cftfOExHLZEprt75vPQ2ssJ/

Morrison, G. M., Anthony, S., Storino, M. H., Cheng, J. J., Furlong, M. J., & Morrison, R. L. (2000). School expulsion as a process and an event: Before and after effects on children at risk for school discipline. *New Directions for Youth Development, 92*, 45–71.

National Research Council. (2002a). Asessment practices, definitions, and classification criteria. In S. Donovan & C. T. Cross (Eds.), *Minority students in special and gifted education* (pp. 243–276). Washington, DC: National Academies Press.

National Research Council. (2002b). Executive Summary. In S. Donovan & C. T. Cross (Eds.), *Minority students in special and gifted education* (pp. 1–14). Washington, DC: National Academies Press.

National Research Council. (2002c). Recommendations. In S. Donovan & C. T. Cross (Eds.), *Minority students in special and gifted education* (pp. 357–385). Washington, DC: National Academies Press.

OSEP. (2007). *Disproportionality of racial and ethnic groups in special education* (OSEP 07-09). Washington, DC: United States Department of Education. Retrieved from https://www2.ed.gov/policy/speced/guid/idea/memosdcltrs/osep07-09disproportionalityofracialandethnicgroupsinspecialeducation.pdf

Osher, D., Woodruff, D., & Sims, A. E. (2002). Schools make a difference: The overrepresentation of African American youth in special education and the juvenile justice system. In D. Losen & G. Orfield (Eds.), *Racial inequity in special education* (pp. 93–116). Cambridge, MA: Harvard Education Press.

Oswald, D. P., Coutinho, M. J., Best, A. M., & Nguyen, N. (2001). Impact of sociodemographic characteristics on the identification rates of minority students as having mental retardation. *Mental Retardation, 39*(5), 351–367.

Rothstein, R. (2000). Equalizing education resources on behalf of disadvantaged children. In R. D. Kahlenberg (Ed.), *A Nation at risk: Preserving public education as an engine for social mobility* (pp. 31–92). New York, NY: Century Foundation Press.

Schneiderman, A. G. (2014). A. G. Schneiderman announces agreement addressing school discipline issues in Syracuse. Retrieved from http://www.ag.ny.gov/press-release/ag-schneiderman-announces-agreement-addressing-school-discipline-issues-syracuse

Skiba, R., & Losen, D. (2012). *Suspended education.* Montgomery, AL: Southern Poverty Law Center. Retrieved from http://www.splcenter.org/get-informed/publications/suspended-education

Individuals with Disabilities Education Improvement Act [IDEA]. 20 U.S.C. Section 1400 et seq. 2004

U.S. Department of Education. (2009, June). *Q and A: Questions and answers on discipline procedures.* Retrieved from http://idea.ed.gov/explore/view/p/,root,dynamic,TopicalBrief,7, http://idea. ed.gov/explore/view/p/%2Croot%2Cdynamic%2CQaCorner%2C7%2C

U.S. Departments of Education and Justice. (2014). *Nondiscriminatory administration of school discipline guidance.* Washington, DC: U.S. Departments of Justice and Education. Retrieved from http://www.justice.gov/crt/about/edu/documents/dcl.pdf

U.S. Department of Education Office for Civil Rights. (2014). *Civil rights data collection data snapshot: School discipline.* Retrieved from http://www2.ed.gov/about/offices/list/ocr/docs/crdc-dis cipline-snapshot.pdf

Reducing Suspensions by Improving Academic Engagement Among School-Age Black Males

Ivory A. Toldson, Tyne McGee, and Brianna P. Lemmons

Understanding punitive school discipline from the lens of academic engagement has shown that there is not only a discipline problem but an underlying education problem that leads to later behavioral issues with students. This research in particular shows how closely related discipline, academic engagement, and truancy are in terms of students' low academic achievement, especially in the case of Black males and Black males with disabilities. Ultimately, the cycle of disengagement and receipt of disciplinary actions leads to lower academic achievement and the disparate involvement of Black males in the juvenile and, eventually, adult justice systems.

Black students are currently about 2.3 times more likely to be suspended than White students (Hinojosa, 2008). The longstanding and persistently disproportional rates of suspension between races have persisted despite mounting evidence that suspensions are ineffective at correcting behavior and commonly precede dropping out (Dupper, Theriot, & Craun, 2009; also see Chapter 1 of this book). Out-of-school suspensions (OSS) continue to be a widely used form of school discipline in the United States.

This study addresses the excessive use of suspensions and other disciplinary actions against Black males who are disengaged from school due to dissatisfaction with school, lack of academic socialization, and/or disability. Disciplinary referrals have been found to be related to aggressive behaviors and disengagement from school. Findings reveal that academic disengagement and receiving disciplinary referrals have a cyclical relationship among Black males, which can ultimately lead to dropping out. Strategies to engage these students are discussed.

CURRENT STANCE OF SUSPENSION
AS A DISCIPLINARY PRACTICE IN SCHOOLS

Use of Suspension

Elevated public awareness and perceptions of violence have increased schools' reliance on suspensions, zero-tolerance, and other exclusionary disciplinary policies (Christle, Nelson, & Jolivette, 2004; Skiba & Peterson, 1999). General concerns surrounding the subjectivity in disciplinary referrals has led to a repudiation of punitive disciplinary practices. Through ethnographic research, Vavrus and Cole (2002) found that many suspensions resulted from a buildup of nonviolent events, in which one student often carries the brunt of many students' misbehaviors.

Antecedents to Suspensions

McConville and Cornell (2003), for example, found that students' self-reports of aggressive behavior significantly correlated with suspensions. However, Morrison, Anthony, Storino, and Dillon (2001) found that students with repeated suspensions, whether in school or out of school, were suspended for more attitudinal offenses than aggressive delinquent behaviors. Academic challenges have also been noted as a significant yet often overlooked antecedent to disciplinary referrals (Tyler-Wood, Cereijo, & Pemberton, 2004).

Black students with disabilities and, especially, with behavioral disorders were also more likely to be suspended (Krezmien, Leone, & Achilles, 2006), especially Black males (Osher, Woodruff, & Sims, 2002). Unfortunately, among students of all races, being suspended just once (Chapter 1), as well as being retained in a grade (Jimerson, Anderson, & Whipple, 2002; Stearns, Moller, Potochnick, & Blau, 2007), often precedes dropping out (Balfanz, Herzog, & Mac Iver, 2007).

Although some people attribute disproportionate disciplinary rates to higher levels of misbehavior, it has been shown that cultural expressions such as movement and speech might be misinterpreted as threatening to teachers who lack cultural awareness (Day-Vines & Day-Hairston, 2005). One study found that Black students with a history of disciplinary referrals were more likely to be viewed negatively by their teachers and tended to receive less deference (Gregory & Thompson, 2010). Natural adaptations to life in some impoverished areas have also been found to indirectly influence students' chances of being suspended from school (Kirk, 2009). Antisocial behaviors typically are more acceptable and, often, necessary for survival in impoverished areas (Gottfredson & Hirschi, 1990).

Engagement Versus Disengagement

Student engagement, as defined by Furrer and Skinner (2003), is the effort, enjoyment, and interest expressed while participating in academic activities. Because they are involved in classroom interactions, show genuine interest in learning, and are motivated, engaged students are less likely to be bored, inattentive, or disrespectful (Skinner & Belmont, 1993). Conversely, disengaged students have lower grades, are less likely to aspire to higher educational goals, and are more likely to drop out of school (Kaplan, Peck, & Kaplan, 1997).

Disengaged Teachers

With the understanding that Black students use teachers as tools to navigate an unfamiliar school system (Kesner, 2000), teachers must be able to engage in emotion and perception management in such a way that does not discourage student learning and engagement (Reyes, Brackett, Rivers, White, & Salovey, 2012). Teachers' perceptions, expectations, and behaviors are often shaped by stereotypes and thus impede learning for minority students. Findings from Crosnoe, Johnson, and Elder (2004) suggest that strong teacher–student relationships are positively related to higher levels of student academic achievement.

OVERVIEW OF THE RESEARCH

This study is a secondary analysis of 4,164 Black, White, and Hispanic 8th- and 10th-grade males who completed *Monitoring the Future: A Continuing Study of American Youth* (Johnston, Bachman, O'Malley, & Schulenberg, 2008); please see Appendix 1 of this chapter's online version for a detailed description of the methodology. Two items were used to measure students' experiences with suspensions and disciplinary referrals. The first question asked, "Have you ever been suspended or expelled from school?" and offered response options of "yes" and "no." The second question read, "Now thinking back over the past year in school, how often did you get sent to the office, or have to stay after school, because you misbehaved?"

Select interval items from the *Monitoring the Future* questionnaire were used to measure school and non-school-related factors, as a relationship is deemed to exist with disciplinary referrals by the authors. Through statistical testing, contributing factors that were most relevant were ascertained, including grades; academic disengagement; drugs, alcohol, and weapons use at school; attitudes/feelings toward school; classroom interruptions; hopelessness; positive self-worth; thrill-seeking behaviors; aggressive behaviors; general delinquency; and parental involvement.

FINDINGS

This section includes a description of the sample population, the methods applied to address research agenda, and the statistical findings.

Composition of Sample Population

Participants of this study included 703 Black males (6.7%), 709 Black females (6.7%), 2,757 White males (26.1%), 2,886 White females (27.3%), 704 Hispanic males (6.7%), and 736 Hispanic females (7 percent) for a total of 8,495 participants. Ninety-six percent were public school students. Fifty-one percent of participants were in the 8th grade, and 49% were in the 10th grade.

The majority (67.8 percent) of participants attended school in large metropolitan areas. Twenty-six percent of the total sample reported being suspended at least once.

Findings revealed statistically significant differences in the percent of Black, White, and Hispanic male students who reported having been suspended or expelled from school, with 59% of Black male students reporting they had been either suspended or expelled from school, compared to 42% percent of Hispanic males and 26% of White males. As a whole, a smaller percentage of female students reported a previous suspension or expulsion. However, 43% of Black females reported having been suspended or expelled from school, as compared to 26% and 11% of Hispanic and White females, respectively.

School-Related Factors and Disciplinary Referrals

Our study applied a statistical method called MANOVA to test the hypothesis that students who report having received fewer disciplinary referrals will have experienced fewer classroom interruptions and will have fewer incidents of truancy and be less likely to show involvement with drugs, alcohol, or weapons while at school. In addition, the same statistical analysis was used to test the hypothesis that students who reported receiving fewer disciplinary referrals will report higher grades, have a more positive attitude about school, and a higher level of academic engagement than students with more disciplinary referrals.

The analysis revealed that when examined through the lens of race, Black and Hispanic students reported having lower grades, more positive attitudes about school, and lower levels of academic engagement than their White counterparts. Hispanic students reported a higher frequency of truancy than did Black and White students.

The analysis revealed that grades and attitudes about school each has an inverse relationship with disciplinary referrals, meaning positive attitudes and higher grade-point averages are related to lower receipts of referrals. This linear relationship was found to be more robust for White students than for Black and Hispanic students. Significant main effects were shown for race, as well as significant interaction effects between race and disciplinary referrals, which points to the disproportionate appropriation of referrals to minorities.

The relationship between delinquency at school and academic disengagement each had a positive relationship with disciplinary referrals. Delinquency at school had an interaction effect revealing that the strongest association between delinquency and disciplinary referrals was for White students. Of all factors measured, academic disengagement had the strongest relationship with disciplinary referrals.

Non-School-Related Factors and Disciplinary Referrals

A second analysis was conducted to test the assertion that non-school-related factors including hopelessness, positive self-worth, thrill-seeking behaviors, aggression, delinquency, and parental involvement have a statistical relationship with disciplinary referrals among Black, White, and Hispanic male students. The analysis revealed that all six measures had a statistically significant relationship with the reported frequency of disciplinary referrals. Aggressive behavior and delinquent behavior had the most substantial relationship with reported disciplinary referrals. Significant differences surfaced among Black, Hispanic, and White students for three of the six measures: thrill-seeking behavior, aggressive behavior, and parental involvement.

Factors Related to Disciplinary Referrals

Of the school and non-school-related factors that were examined, six had very strong correlations with disciplinary referrals. These factors were used to create a path model to determine their direct and indirect effects on the reported frequency of disciplinary referrals received by male students (see online draft; Toldson, McGee, & Lemmons, 2013, http://tinyurl.com/JanCRPconference). In other words, by tracking the differences each variable made for each subgroup by race with gender, our analysis revealed that Black males often followed a somewhat different path to lower school performance than did other subgroups.

Racial Differences in Disciplinary Referrals. Given the large number of variables that had significant main effects for race, race differences were further examined. On analyzing the data, by calculating the goodness of fit for each group, no strong racial differences were revealed. For school-related behaviors, disciplinary referrals exhibited the strongest direct and total negative effects on grades for all races. That is, classroom interruptions and truancy were most strongly related to disciplinary referrals and lower grades. For non-school-related behaviors, aggressive behaviors had the strongest total effects on disciplinary referrals for all races. Academic disengagement had the strongest direct effect on disciplinary referrals for both Black and White males. However, for Black males, academic disengagement had a significant direct impact on truancy. Similarities and differences in the path toward more school participation and higher levels of academic success for Black, White, and Hispanic male students were noted.

DISCUSSION

Consistent with the literature on racial disparities in suspension and disciplinary referrals (Day-Vines & Day-Hairston, 2005; Eitle & Eitle, 2004; Kirk, 2009), this study found stark racial differences in the reported number of suspensions among Black, Hispanic, and White males. At 59%, twice as many Black males reported being suspended or expelled as compared to White males. When examining differences by both genders and race, more males reported having been suspended or expelled than their female counterparts. However, far more Black females reported being suspended than did White males.

The associated school-related and non-school-related factors examined were unsuccessful in fully accounting for the variance in reported suspensions or expulsions and disciplinary referrals across racial groups. The current literature suggests that racial disparities in suspensions and disciplinary referrals might be explained by the influence of associated school-related and non-school-related factors such as cultural mismatches, lack of cultural awareness among teachers (Day-Vines & Day-Hairston, 2005), and racial composition of schools (Eitle & Eitle, 2004).

The existing literature suggests that several school-related factors and student characteristics are antecedents to school suspension and disciplinary referrals. In this study, Black and Hispanic males generally reported more positive attitudes toward school and were less likely to report seeking satisfaction from "thrill-seeking" behaviors, both of which had statistically significant relationships with fewer reported disciplinary referrals. However, Black and Hispanic males reportedly engaged in more aggressive behaviors, had lower grades, and exhibited higher levels of academic disengagement than did White males.

For Black and White males, academic disengagement was the strongest predictor of disciplinary referrals. However, the two other predictors—aggressive behavior and school crime—were far stronger predictors of disciplinary referrals for White males than for Black males. Further, for Black males, but not White males, academic disengagement was a strong predictor of truancy. Finally, for both groups, truancy and disciplinary referrals predicted lower grades. Compared to White males, this indicates that Black males are more likely to abandon school in response to feeling academically disengaged. Much too often this cycle leads disengaged students into the school-to-prison pipeline (American Civil Liberties Union, n.d.).

In this study, highly disengaged students reported frequently failing to complete or turn in their assignments, not working up to their full potential, arriving to class late without an approved excuse, and finding schoolwork difficult to understand. Overall, the purpose of this study was to determine whether strategies are possible to reduce the frequency of disciplinary referrals and subsequent suspension, particularly among students who are disproportionally subjected to these disciplinary measures. This study found evidence that disciplinary referrals are more associated with negative attitudes and academic disengagement than the use of drugs, alcohol, and weapons at school. This implies that disciplinary referrals can be mitigated by

improving the structure and culture of the school to promote more positive attitudes about learning, more resources to help students learn appropriate school and
class etiquette, and providing extra assistance with schoolwork. Like previous studies, this study found an "attitude-achievement paradox" (Mickelson, 1990) among
Black male students, whereby their positive attitudes about school did not translate
to successful academic outcomes. These findings suggest that academic engagement
is a possible mediator between attitudes and grades.

Although this study revealed racial differences in disciplinary referrals and
suspensions, the racial differences revealed in examining the factors associated
with more reported disciplinary referrals do not reasonably account for the significant differences in suspension rates among Black students. As previously stated,
Black males tend to not report negative attitudes about school and do not report
using drugs, alcohol, and weapons while at school, yet they are subject to more
suspensions than any other group examined. The high suspension rates of Black
males paired with that of Black females suggest that school culture and climate
might account for much of the racial differences in suspensions. This study found
no direct effect of drug, alcohol, and weapon use at school on disciplinary referrals
for Black males, but a significant link for White males. Thus, one inference, supported by these statistical differences as well as other research cited in the introduction, is that it is more likely that Black students are being subjected to harsher
penalties for similar, or even less serious, infractions than those committed by
their White and Hispanic classmates.

Collectively, the results of this study suggest that a number of school factors
have a significant impact on suspensions and disciplinary referrals. From a policy
perspective, the most significant among them is academic disengagement. In this
study, once Black males became disengaged and involved in school crime, disciplinary referrals and truancy followed, which negatively affected their achievement
outcomes as measured by school grades. In addition to individual factors, the findings also suggest a combination of variables that create a specific path that leads
Black males to disproportionately receive school suspensions and disciplinary referrals. This research might be indicative of the relationship between racial discipline
disparities and academic disparities. The persistence of disproportionate punitive
discipline measures is detrimental to the academic performance of African American
males, specifically. If they are being suspended from school more frequently, they
are losing class time, instruction, and academic material and, subsequently, falling
further behind their peers in the academic experience. As mentioned earlier, this
increases the likelihood that these students will begin to engage in academic disiden-
tification as a protective factor against stereotype threat (Steele, 1992) and become
disengaged from the school environment. As the suspension-disengagement cycle
continues, students are more likely to drop out (Balfanz, Herzog, & MacIver, 2007).
By acknowledging the inverse relationship of academic engagement and disciplinary
referrals, education policy can work as an active agent to increase academic engagement, especially in African American males.

IMPLICATIONS FOR POLICY AND PRACTICE

- After considering the findings of this research study, future implications and plausible applications should be examined for the purpose of policy improvement. Educational policy should recognize the significant contribution of school engagement to school disciplinary outcomes by implementing strategies for improving student experiences and connections with school. This study found school disengagement to be the strongest predictor of suspension and disciplinary referrals across racial groups, and disciplinary referrals were found to be associated most with negative attitudes and dispositions toward school. Implementing school-based programs designed to promote positive schooling experiences and school connectedness, such as restorative justice (see Chapter 10), might promote higher levels of student engagement, which will in turn reduce suspensions and disciplinary referrals. In addition, strategies for improving school engagement and decreasing the number of disciplinary actions taken against males of color should seek to promote parental involvement, creation of a structured environment, schoolwide discipline programs, and the cultivation of mutual respect between teachers and students.

- Policymakers should recognize the impact of disengagement on truancy and the subsequent impact of truancy on achievement outcomes such as school grades. Whereas school disengagement was found to predict disciplinary referrals for all racial groups, Black males were the only group for which disengagement was also found to predict truancy. This study supports implementing school-based truancy prevention programs that target disengaged students and creating needed alternatives to suspensions based on minor violations such as truancy. Suspending a disengaged student who is not attending school regularly is only a temporary solution that fits the needs of the school which further hinders the student academically. The areas of engagement that are particularly important to address in these programs are related to increasing student effort and motivation to participate in the educational process by coming to class on time and completing assignments. Raising levels of engagement can potentially prevent problems of truancy, which can in turn prevent low achievement outcomes. The findings of this study also suggest that in order to prevent truancy and low levels of academic achievement, schools, administrators, and policymakers must consider the underlying factors that contribute to school disengagement, such as disparate access to the most effective teachers, negative school culture, and perceived unfairness in school disciplinary practices.

- Because Black males who are more likely to be suspended exhibit higher levels of hopelessness and lower positive self-worth, counseling and mental health services at the school to mitigate disciplinary referrals should be strengthened. Students often misbehave because of treatable mental health and adjustment problems, including depression, attention deficits, and acute stress and trauma reactions. Coping resources at the school, including counselors, social workers, and recreational therapists, can improve student behavior and reduce suspensions and disciplinary referrals.

- Educational policymakers need to emphasize discipline policy connected to the educational mission and that does not focus on frequent punishment and removal from school, which only exacerbates academic disengagement. Further, racial biases in instruction and racial inequities in enforcing school disciplinary measures must be addressed. This can be done in part through tracking of disciplinary referrals and the development of criteria used to determine the use of disciplinary measures. Stark racial differences were found in suspensions and disciplinary referrals among the racial groups in this study. Consistent with the findings of Morrison, Peterson, O'Farrell, and Redding (2004), policymakers should consider implementing systems of regular and consistent monitoring and analysis of disciplinary referrals to improve on precision, accuracy, fairness, and equity in the application of disciplinary measures.

NOTE

This study was completed with support from the Congressional Black Caucus Foundation and Open Society Institute Campaign for Black Male Achievement. Address all related correspondence to itoldson@howard.edu.

REFERENCES

The American Civil Liberties Union. (n.d.). *School-to-prison pipeline*. Retrieved from https://www.aclu.org/school-prison-pipeline

Balfanz, R., Herzog, L., & MacIver, D. J. (2007). Preventing student disengagement and keeping students on the graduation path in urban middle-grades schools: Early identification and effective interventions. *Educational Psychologist, 42*(4), 223–235.

Christle, C., Nelson, C. M., & Jolivette, K. (2004). School characteristics related to the use of suspension. *Education & Treatment of Children, 27*(4).

Crosnoe, R., Johnson, M. K., & Elder, G. H. (2004). Intergenerational bonding in school: The behavioral and contextual correlates of student–teacher relationships. *Sociology of Education, 77*, 60–61.

Day-Vines, N. L., & Day-Hairston, B. O. (2005). Culturally congruent strategies for addressing the behavioral needs of urban, African American male adolescents. *Professional School Counseling, 8*(3), 236–243.

Dupper, D. R., Theriot, M. T., & Craun, S. W. (2009). Reducing out-of-school suspensions: Practice guidelines for school social workers. *Children & Schools, 31*(1), 6–14.

Eitle, T. M., & Eitle, D. J. (2004). Inequality, segregation, and the overrepresentation of African Americans in school suspensions. *Sociological Perspectives, 47*(3), 269–287.

Furrer, C., & Skinner, E. A. (2003). Sense of relatedness as a factor in children's academic engagement and performance. *Journal of Educational Psychology, 95*, 148–162.

Gottfredson, M. R., & Hirschi, T. (1990). *A general theory of crime*. Stanford University Press.

Gregory, A., & Thompson, A. R. (2010). African American high school students and variability in be-
    havior across classrooms. *Journal of Community Psychology, 38*(3), 386–402.

Gregory, A., & Weinstein, R. S. (2008). The discipline gap and African Americans: Defiance or coop-
    eration in the high school classroom. *Journal of School Psychology, 46*(4), 455–475. doi:10.1016/j.
    jsp.2007.09.001

Hinojosa, M. S. (2008). Black–white differences in school suspension: Effect of student beliefs about
    teachers. *Sociological Spectrum, 28*(2), 175–193. doi:10.1080/02732170701796429

Jimerson, S. R., Anderson, G. E., & Whipple, A. D. (2002). Winning the battle and losing the war:
    Examining the relation between grade retention and dropping out of high school. *Psychology in
    the Schools, 39*(4), 441–457.

Johnston, L. D., Bachman, J. G., O'Malley, P. M., & Schulenberg, J. (2008). Monitoring the future: A
    continuing study of American youth (8th- and 10th-grade surveys), 2008. In *Inter-University
    Consortium for Political and Social Research.* Retrieved from http://www.icpsr.umich.edu/
    icpsrweb/ICPSR/studies/25422

Kaplan, D. S., Peck, M., & Kaplan, H. B. (1997). Decomposing the academic failure–dropout relation-
    ship: A longitudinal analysis. *Journal of Educational Research, 90,* 331–343.

Kesner, J. (2000). Teacher characteristics and the quality of the child–teacher relationship. *Journal of
    School Psychology, 28*(2), 133–149.

Kirk, D. S. (2009). Unraveling the contextual effects on student suspension and juvenile arrest: The
    independent and interdependent influences of school, neighborhood, and family social controls.
    Criminology, 47(2), 479–520. doi:10.1111/j.1745-9125.2009.00147.x

Krezmien, M. P., Leone, P. E., & Achilles, G. M. (2006). Suspension, race, and disability: Analysis of
    statewide practices and reporting. *Journal of Emotional & Behavioral Disorders, 14*(4), 217–226.

Losen, D. J., Gillespie, J., & Orfield, G. (2012). *Opportunities suspended: The disparate impact of dis-
    ciplinary exclusion from school.* Los Angeles, CA: Center for Civil Rights Remedies at the Civil
    Rights Project.

McConville, D. W., & Cornell, D. G. (2003). Aggressive attitudes predict aggressive behavior in middle
    school students. *Journal of Emotional & Behavioral Disorders, 11*(3), 179.

Mendez, L. M. R. (2003). Predictors of suspension and negative school outcomes: A longitudinal inves-
    tigation. *New Directions for Youth Development, 99,* 17–33.

Mickelson, R. A. (1990). The attitude-achievement paradox among black adolescents. *Sociology of
    Education, 63*(1), 44–61.

Morrison, G. M., Anthony, S., Storino, M., & Dillon, C. (2001). An examination of the disciplinary
    histories and the individual and educational characteristics of students who participate in an in-
    school suspension program. *Education and Treatment of Children, 24*(3), 276–293.

Morrison, G. M., Peterson, R., O'Farrell, S., & Redding, M. (2004). Using office referral records in
    school violence research: Possibilities and limitations. *Journal of School Violence, 3*(2/3), 39–61.
    doi:10.1300/J202v03n02_04

Osher, D., Woodruff, D., & Sims, A. E. (2002). Schools make a difference: The overrepresentation of
    African American youth in special education and the juvenile justice system. *Racial inequity in
    special education,* 93–116.

Reyes, M. R., Brackett, M. A., Rivers, S. E., White, M., & Salovey, P. (2012). Classroom emotional cli-
    mate, student engagement, and academic achievement. *Jounal of Educational Psychology, 104*(3),
    700–712.

Skiba, R., & Peterson, R. (1999). The dark side of zero tolerance. *Phi Delta Kappan, 80*(5), 372.

Skinner, E. A., & Belmont, M. J. (1993). Motivation in the classroom: Reciprocal effects of teacher
    behavior and student engagement across the school year. *Jounal of Educational Psychology, 85*(4),
    571–581.

Stearns, E., Moller, S., Potochnick, S., & Blau, J. (2007). Staying back and dropping out: The relation-
    ship between grade retention and school dropout. *Youth & Society, 38*(1), 29–57.

Steele, C. (1992). Race and the schooling of African-American Americans. *Atlantic Monthly, 269*(4),
    68–78.

Sugai, G., Sprague, J. R., Horner, R. H., & Walker, H. M. (2000). Preventing school violence: The use of office discipline referrals to assess and monitor school-wide discipline interventions. *Journal of Emotional & Behavioral Disorders, 8*(2), 94.

Tyler-Wood, T., Cereijo, M. V. P., & Pemberton, J. B. (2004). Comparison of discipline referrals for students with emotional/ behavioral disorders under differing instructional arrangements. *Preventing School Failure, 48*(4), 30–33.

Vavrus, F., & Cole, K. (2002). "I didn't do nothin'": The discursive construction of school suspension. *Urban Review, 34*(2), 87.

## CHAPTER 8

What Conditions Support Safety in Urban Schools?

The Influence of School Organizational Practices
on Student and Teacher Reports of Safety in Chicago

Matthew P. Steinberg, Elaine Allensworth, and David W. Johnson

Every child in America deserves a safe and healthy school environment, and it's
our job as educators, parents, and community members to ensure that happens.
—Arne Duncan, U.S. Secretary of Education[1]

School safety is a pressing issue in urban schools, yet we know little about why
schools serving students with similar backgrounds vary in safety. Using a unique
dataset on the Chicago Public Schools (CPS), we examine the internal and external conditions associated with students' and teachers' reports of safety, showing
that the social and organizational structures of schools mediate the external influences of crime, poverty, and human resources in students' residential communities. The quality of relationships among school staff, students, and parents helps
in particular to define safe schools in Chicago. Frequent use of suspensions, on
the other hand, is associated with less safe environments, even when comparing
schools serving students with similar backgrounds.

WHY SCHOOL SAFETY MATTERS

Students' and teachers' feelings of safety in schools influence the learning environment in numerous ways, often setting off a cascade of effects extending far beyond
the schoolyard.

Students' emotional well-being is, of course, intrinsically important. But
victimization also affects students' ability to function in school, adversely influ-
encing their self-efficacy, attitudinal and behavioral investments in education,

and the amount of time they dedicate to learning. Students who are victims of harassment attend school less frequently and feel less connected to and engaged in school. They in turn spend less time doing homework and participating in school activities, which ultimately has adverse effects on both cognitive and social growth (Bowen & Bowen, 1999; MacMillan & Hagan, 2004; Payne, Gottfredson, & Gottfredson, 2003). Victimization has also been linked to psychological and health problems and disrupted educational and occupational attainment, which in turn negatively affect a student's later economic status, including labor force participation, occupational status, and earnings (MacMillan & Hagan, 2004; Schreck & Miller, 2003).

Teachers too are affected by harassment and violence in schools, and unsafe school environments have adverse effects on their professional development and personal safety. Students who are physically or verbally abusive in the classroom divert teachers' attention away from teaching and prevent them from being able to teach effectively (Bowen & Bowen, 1999). Teachers are more likely to leave schools that have substantial student disciplinary problems, which further decreases those schools' capacity for effective instruction (Allensworth, Ponisciak, & Mazzeo, 2009; Payne et al., 2003; Smith & Smith, 2006).

School safety is a particularly pressing issue in urban public schools, where the incidence of violent episodes is almost 60% higher than in suburban schools and 30% higher than in rural schools. Disrespectful behaviors and threats are also more prevalent in urban schools, where the teachers are twice as likely as those at other schools to report that students verbally abuse and act disrespectfully toward them at least once a week and sometimes daily (Neiman & DeVoe, 2009). Although there are concerns about the safety of teachers and students, there are also increasing concerns that schools' disciplinary practices are excessive and might have harmful effects on students. In response, policymakers in some urban school districts, such as Chicago, New York, and Philadelphia, have made explicit attempts to limit school suspensions.

CONSIDERING EXISTING RESEARCH
ON SCHOOL SAFETY

Prevailing research suggests that students' feelings of safety at school and problems with peer relationships and bullying are influenced by a broad array of factors, including students' own attributes and the attributes of their schools, the adults with whom the students interact, the students' families, their neighborhoods, and the broader society. Community-level factors such as crime and poverty are strongly related to school safety but are not solely deterministic, as schools serving similar neighborhoods can have different degrees of safety (Bowen, Bowen, & Ware, 2002; Felson, Liska, South, & McNulty, 1994; Payne et al., 2003; Welsh, Greene, & Jenkins, 1999; Welsh, Stokes, & Greene, 2000).

However, there is little research on the ways the social-organizational structures of schools—the internal, school-based resources and the interactions among students, teachers, and parents—affect the safety climate in schools.

Several theories of organizational change suggest that the school learning climate is better when there are inclusive leadership and empowered stakeholders (Bryk & Schneider, 2002; Bryk, Sebring, Allensworth, Luppescu, & Easton, 2010; Sergiovanni, 2004). The importance of student–teacher relationships is also supported by sociological studies (Astor, Benbenishty, & Nuñez Estrada, 2009), showing that schools play an important role in transmitting to students values related to misconduct and violence—a student's violent and delinquent behavior is related to the values prevalent in the school (Felson et al., 1994)—and in helping students form social bonds with adults (Crosnoe, Johnson, & Elder, 2004; Payne et al., 2003). Stronger relationships between students and adults at school are associated with a lower likelihood of disciplinary problems (Crosnoe et al., 2004). Moreover, bullying is most common in the areas of schools that lack adult supervision, such as hallways, playgrounds, and lunchrooms, and evidence suggests that students feel most unsafe in those unsupervised places in and around schools (Steinberg, Allensworth & Johnson, 2011; Swearer, Espelage, Vaillancourt, & Hymel, 2010). Thus the extent to which students feel protected by their teachers and view their teachers as being supportive of their academic and social development can influence school safety.

This prior research suggests that school leadership and teachers' collaborative efforts and strong relationships with students are important mechanisms for mediating the influence of external factors on school safety. In this chapter, we confirm and extend these findings, using extensive data from the Chicago Public Schools. Specifically, we use data on school, community, and individual factors to empirically test the ways students' individual backgrounds interact with school and community factors to make students and teachers feel safe, or unsafe, at their schools.

EXAMINING SCHOOL SAFETY IN CHICAGO PUBLIC SCHOOLS

Our research breaks new ground by examining the extent to which school practices are related to school safety, relative to the students they serve. Policymakers and educators need to know what schools can do to improve safety in our schools, particularly in those serving students from neighborhoods with high levels of poverty and crime. We analyze a wide range of factors related to students' and teachers' feelings of safety at school—from those that cannot be shaped by policy and school practice (e.g., neighborhood characteristics), to those that can't be changed by school practice but might be affected by policy (e.g., school size and composition), to those that are potentially malleable through school practices—and design to answer the following questions:

- What community characteristics are most strongly associated with students' and teachers' feelings of safety at school, including (a) poverty, crime, and socioeconomic status in the neighborhood around the school and in students' residential neighborhoods, and (b) the extent of human and social resources in students' home neighborhoods?
- What school conditions are associated with school safety, including size, grade level, racial composition, and average entry-level achievement?
- How are the social-organizational characteristics of a school associated with school safety, including school leadership, teacher collaboration and support, school-family interactions, and student–teacher relationships?
- How are school discipline practices (e.g., suspension rates) associated with school safety?
- To what degree can strong social-organizational characteristics mediate the influence of adverse neighborhood conditions on students' and teachers' perceptions of school safety?

In our examination of the mechanisms through which a school may foster a safe learning environment, we incorporate in a series of quantitative analyses a variety of neighborhood, school, and student-level data from the Chicago Public Schools, as well as a rich set of survey measures on the organizational context of Chicago schools from the University of Chicago Consortium on Chicago School Research (CCSR).

Teacher and Student Surveys

We draw on survey data from the hundreds of schools that participated in the CCSR teacher and student surveys in the 2008–2009 academic year. Our teacher survey responses include 8,774 elementary school teachers (grades K–8) and 3,965 high school teachers (grades 9–12), representing 387 schools (319 elementary schools and 68 high schools). Our student survey responses include 65,007 elementary school students (grades 6–8) and 52,478 high school students (grades 9–12) from 524 schools (448 elementary schools and 76 high schools). Approximately 80% of students from our sample of schools come from economically disadvantaged backgrounds, as measured by receipt of free or reduced-price lunch. Approximately 60% of students are identified as African American and approximately 30% as Hispanic. Average elementary school enrollment is approximately 600 students; average high school enrollment is approximately 1,000 students.

School Safety Measures

School safety was measured by surveys conducted by CCSR of students in grades 6–12 and teachers in grades K–12 during the 2008–2009 school year. Students were surveyed about their general feelings of safety in and around the school, as well as the nature of interactions among students at school—for example, the degree to which peers are respectful or mean to each other. Teachers were asked about their perceptions of crime and disorder in their schools. In general, there is a very strong correspondence (correlation .80) between student and teacher reports of safety, which confirms that the surveys capture real differences in school safety, even though they are based on self-reports and different sets of survey questions.

There were considerable differences across the CPS in students' and teachers' perceptions of safety and disorder.[2] In one of the safer high schools, which is at the CPS system-wide average (includes both elementary and high schools) on the student safety measure, almost all students feel safe within the school building, and the vast majority feel safe coming and going to school. Teachers at this school report few problems with crime or violence—just occasional disorder in the hallways and some problems with theft, but few problems with classroom disorder, fights, or disrespect toward teachers. Most students say their peers get along well and care about each other, although only about half feel their peers are respectful to each other.

In a more typical CPS high school, the vast majority of students feel safe within the building, but there are problems outside the building. Half of the students are concerned about coming and going to school, and only about a third feel safe in the area just outside the school. Teachers report some problems with violent threats being made within the building, and many report problems associated with gang activity and fights. Furthermore, more than 60% of teachers report problems with disorder and disrespect.

In an unsafe CPS high school, which is two standard deviations below average on the student safety measure, students not only feel unsafe outside of the building, but as many as half feel unsafe in the hallways and bathrooms, and only 60% feel safe in their classrooms. Nearly all teachers report problems with robbery in the building, gang activity, fights, disorder, and disrespect, and three quarters of teachers report that students have threatened them with violence. Interactions between students and teachers are frequently hostile and mutually disrespectful—the majority of students say their peers don't get along and look out just for themselves, put each other down, and don't treat each other with respect.

School Organization Measures

Prior research and theory suggest four broad domains of a school's social-organizational structure that could potentially affect the climate of safety: school leadership, teacher collaboration and support, school–family interactions, and student–teacher relationships. We used multiple measures to study each of these social-organizational domains, creating each measure through multiple survey items. School leadership was studied through measures of teacher influence, the principal's instructional leadership, program coherence, and teacher–principal trust. There are four measures of teacher collaboration and support—collective responsibility, orientation to innovation, socialization of new teachers, and teacher–teacher trust. For school–family interactions, we used a measure of teacher–parent trust. Student–teacher relationships were measured by asking students questions about personal support from teachers and student–teacher trust.

School Context and Student Background Data

CPS school administrative files provide information on schools' racial composition, enrollment size, percentage of low-income students, and grade level. CPS student administrative files provide data on students' test scores and achievement.

We measured neighborhood crime, socioeconomic status, and poverty using data from the 2000 U.S. Census and Chicago Police Department records. For a detailed description of how these factors are measured, see the full report on the Civil Rights Project website (http://tinyurl.com/JanCRPconference) and Steinberg et al. (2011).

How We Analyze the Data

Our aim is to understand the ways community and school factors collectively relate to students' and teachers' feelings of safety in their schools. We begin with quantitative analyses that show the correlations of a large array of schools' compositional, structural, and organizational features with the three measures of safety. These correlations show which features of schools are independently most strongly related to school safety. We then examine the factors in combination to determine which are most directly related to school safety. Although we begin with the contribution of factors outside the control of the schools—for example, the community contexts and the neighborhoods in which students reside—we focus on what the internal factors tell us about how schools' contextual, structural, and social-organizational features are related to students' and teachers' reports of safety (see the online version of this chapter for further details at http://tinyurl.com/JanCRPconference).

OUR FINDINGS

As one would expect, schools serving a large percentage of students from high-poverty and high-crime neighborhoods and that have few human and social resources tend to feel less safe than schools serving more advantaged students. However, our findings reveal that the ways adults in the school building interact with each other, with parents, and with students can create school environments that feel safe, despite challenging environmental influences. Indeed, about one quarter of the differences in safety across schools can be attributed to school-based factors, rather than to student background or neighborhood factors.

What community characteristics are most strongly associated with students' and teachers' feelings of safety at school? Crime and poverty explain a substantial proportion of the differences in safety across schools. Specifically, crime in the neighborhood around the school explains 29% of the variation in student reports of safety and peer interactions across schools, whereas poverty around the school explains 25% of the variation. Similarly, crime in the neighborhood around the school explains 27% of the variation in teacher reports of crime and disorder across schools, whereas poverty around the school explains 21% of the variation. In contrast, crime and poverty in students' home neighborhoods explain approximately one third of the differences in students' and teachers' feelings of safety, and nearly half of the differences across schools in the quality of peer interactions.

Thus school safety is strongly defined by the characteristics of a school's student population—who attends the school and the neighborhoods in which they live. Peer interactions in particular are less supportive and respectful in schools with a greater percentage of students from high-poverty, high-crime neighborhoods.

What school conditions are associated with school safety? Generally speaking, elementary schools are safer than high schools. However, while there are marked differences in safety between the middle grades and high school grades, safety at a school is much more strongly influenced by where the school is located and the backgrounds of the students who attend it than by the grade levels it serves.

It is difficult to disentangle school racial composition from neighborhood characteristics such as crime and poverty. Almost all schools serving students from neighborhoods with the highest levels of crime and poverty have a majority of African American students. However, our analysis did show large differences in safety relative to schools' racial composition. Students attending schools that serve predominantly African American students on average feel much less safe and report less positive peer interactions than students at other schools. Teachers at these schools also report substantially less safe environments. The biggest difference in safety between African American schools and others is in the quality of peer interactions; African American students are especially unlikely to say their peers treat each other with respect.

The schools that are the safest in all three aspects of safety are those that are majority White and Asian. Schools that are predominantly Latino fall in between. However, most schools with a substantial proportion of White and Asian students serve students from neighborhoods with low or very low crime rates. Predominantly Latino schools tend to serve students from neighborhoods with average levels of crime and poverty.

Though school safety is strongly related to students' neighborhood characteristics, it is even more strongly related to the academic skills of the students served by the school, including the average prior achievement levels of students who enter in the middle grades or high school. On average, students in Chicago who attend schools that enroll higher-achieving students report feeling safer at school than students in schools serving students with lower academic skills. In fact, school achievement by itself explains approximately half of the differences in student reports of overall safety; teacher reports of crime and disorder; and quality of interactions among peers at both the elementary and high school levels.

One interpretation of this relationship might be that achievement is higher because safer schools better enable students to concentrate on learning. Other research has shown that schools are more likely to show test score improvement if they have safe learning climates (Bryk et al., 2010). However, in this case, school achievement level is measured by students' incoming test scores at the beginning of 9th grade for high school reports, and at the end of 5th grade for students in grades 6–8.

Another explanation of why the relationship between school achievement and school safety is stronger than the relationship of crime or poverty with safety involves the degree to which students are attached to school: High-achieving students tend to be engaged in learning and feel successful academically, whereas students with low levels of achievement are less likely to be engaged academically and more likely to feel frustrated by their school performance (Newmann, Wehlage, & Lamborn, 2002; Singh, Granville, & Dika, 2002). This in turn makes lower-achieving students more likely to act out and less likely to respond to academic punishments. Indeed, the salience of academic consequences for misbehavior might be minimal for students who are already poorly engaged in learning: If a student does not care about school, suspension might not be a powerful deterrent (Kazdin, 2000). Students living in high-poverty and high-crime neighborhoods are particularly vulnerable and likely to experience disruption—such as high rates of residential instability—and thus are likely to exhibit both low academic achievement and more behavioral problems. This is consistent with evidence that the greatest benefit to CPS students of selecting a higher-achieving school rather than a neighborhood school is the decreased likelihood of getting into trouble with the police (Cullen, Jacob, & Levitt, 2003).

Although school safety is strongly related to the characteristics of the students served, these characteristics do not completely determine a school's level of safety. Indeed, we found large differences in safety among schools serving similar types of students. For example, CPS schools serving students from neighborhoods with the highest crime rates—approximately two standard deviations above the mean—ranged from some of the very least safe (two standard deviations below the mean safety level) to others that were much safer than average, at about one standard deviation above the mean (around the 66th percentile of safety among all CPS schools). There also are schools that serve students from very low-crime neighborhoods that are less safe than the average CPS school, despite serving more advantaged students. Schools serving students from neighborhoods with average levels of crime vary quite dramatically in how their students report the level of safety. Some are among the safest schools in CPS (at the 99th percentile), whereas others serving students from neighborhoods with identical levels of crime are among the least safe (at the 10th percentile). We found that schools' social-organizational structures explain some of these differences.

How are the social-organizational characteristics of a school associated with school safety? Each feature of a school's social-organizational structure—leadership, teacher collaboration, school–family interactions, and student–teacher relationships—is significantly associated with school safety. Meaningful school–family interactions show particularly strong associations with school safety. Both students and teachers feel safest in schools where teachers view parents as partners in their children's education. These associations are so strong that they far outweigh the associations of neighborhood crime and poverty with safety; in fact, they are at least as strong as the association between safety and school achievement level.

School leadership and teacher collaboration are also associated with safer environments, as represented by the relationship between collective responsibility and teacher influence and school safety. The more teachers take responsibility for the whole school and work together, rather than just focusing on their individual classrooms, the safer those teachers feel. Moreover, the more teachers are involved in school decisionmaking, the safer the environment for both teachers and students. Safety is also greater when programs and instruction are coordinated, as indicated by the relationship between safety and program coherence.

Of course, the patterns observed could exist because it is easier to have strong relationships and good organizational structures in schools that serve more advantaged student populations. In other words, it is possible that the relationships themselves do not promote safety—they simply occur naturally in schools already inclined to be safe, based on their student population. To examine the degree to which school organizational structure is associated with school safety, after statistically controlling for the characteristics of the students served by the school and the school structure, our model (see Tables 6–8 in the website report, http://tinyurl.com/JanCRPconference) predicts school safety with variables from each component of a school's organizational structure, as well as the variables for school and community context. Because variables representing specific organizational features in schools (e.g., leadership, teacher collaboration) are correlated with each other, we aggregate the CCSR survey measures into composite measures. Each composite measure is standardized across the sample of schools.

Once we consider the four aspects of a school's organizational structure (leadership, teacher collaboration, school–family interactions, and student–teacher relationships), approximately 80% of the differences in safety across schools, as reported by students and teachers, are explained. Thus school organizational factors help explain why schools with very similar students can have very different outcomes when it comes to safety, and these factors lead to almost all of the differences in school safety that can be explained—only 20% remain unexplained in each measure of school safety.

What stands out in these models is the importance of positive and constructive relationships among students and teachers and teachers and families. Even after controlling for neighborhood poverty and crime, school structure (school level and enrollment), and the composition of students served by the school (race and academic achievement), we found that school–family interactions are significantly associated with safety, particularly teachers' feelings about crime and disorder at the school. Similarly, student–teacher relationships emerged as the strongest organizational feature associated with students' reports of peer interactions, and they are also as important as school–family partnerships to students' overall feelings of safety. Students feel safer and feel that their peers are more respectful when they have trusting, supportive relationships with teachers.

Can high-quality relationships make up for differences across schools in the types of students they serve? To examine this, we compared safety in schools that were highly disadvantaged but had strong personal relationships to schools that were advantaged but had weak relationships. We first divided schools into low-, middle-, and high-advantage groups based on socioeconomic characteristics, including the level of crime, poverty, and human and social resources in students' home neighborhoods, as well as the level of academic achievement in the school. We then created a composite of the quality of school-based relationships by combining the school-level values of the school–family interactions and student–teacher relationships constructs into one measure. We divided schools based on whether they had high-, average-, or low-quality relationships. Schools with low-quality relationships are approximately half a standard deviation or more below the mean level of school-based relationships, and schools with high-quality relationships are approximately half a standard deviation or more above the mean. For each combination of school advantage and quality of relationships (e.g., low-advantage/low-quality relationships, low-advantage/average-quality relationships, etc.), we compared the three measures of safety. Figure 8.1 summarizes the findings for student reports of safety.

Our findings support the conclusion that safety is greater in schools with high-quality relationships among students, teachers, and families. This holds true across all three indicators of school safety. What is particularly notable is the extent to which high-quality relationships between students and adults can make up for socioeconomic disadvantage. In particular, schools that serve the least advantaged students—those who live in neighborhoods with high levels of crime and poverty and few human and social resources, and who attend lower-achieving schools—but that have high-quality relationships are as safe, on average, as the most advantaged schools with weak relationships. Statistical tests confirmed that low-advantage schools with high-quality relationships are as safe as high-advantage schools with low-quality relationships. This holds true for student reports of safety, teacher reports of crime and disorder, and student reports of peer interactions.

How are school discipline practices associated with school safety? Are punitive school responses to safety also associated with student and teacher reports of safety? Suspensions are a response to school staff's perceptions of a threat and

Figure 8.1. Student Reports of Safety by School Advantage and Relationships

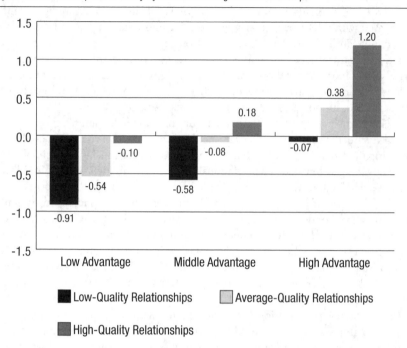

Notes: The values reported are the mean level of school safety as reported by students in standard deviation units. A school's level of advantage is a composite measure that includes crime, poverty, and the extent of human and social resources in students' home neighborhoods and the academic achievement of the school. A school's quality of relationships depends on the quality of its school–family interactions, as perceived by teachers, and student–teacher relationships, as perceived by students.

concerns about safety; they reflect which schools struggle the most with these is-sues. Given that there are strong associations among neighborhood context, school context, and school safety, we looked to see whether the relationship between sus-pension rates and feelings of safety persisted after controlling for neighborhood and school characteristics. Controlling for differences in community and school context, schools with higher suspension rates have lower levels of safety, based on reports by students and teachers.

Although we are not claiming a causal connection, this finding suggests that high suspension rates do not sufficiently address the problems that schools face— schools with high suspension rates are still less safe than others that serve students with similar backgrounds in similar neighborhoods. At worst, this suggests that suspensions themselves can aggravate problems with safety. This latter perspec-tive is consistent with research by others that shows schools with more severe suspension and zero-tolerance policies often have a higher level of student fear

(American Psychological Association Zero Tolerance Task Force, 2008). Through their disciplinary practices, schools serving students from high-crime/high-poverty neighborhoods might unwittingly be exacerbating their low levels of safety.

SUMMARY AND POLICY IMPLICATIONS

As might be expected, crime and poverty in students' residential neighborhoods are strongly associated with school safety. Neighborhoods with high crime and poverty tend to have fewer human and social resources available to instill a sense of safety in students as they travel between home and school, and as they manage conflicts with peers.

Demographics matter, but they need not determine a school's level of safety. As noted, schools serving very similar kids can have very different levels of safety. Inside the school building, the mutually supportive relationships that students and their parents have with teachers are a critical element in determining school safety for both students and teachers. Much of what accounts for the large differences in school safety among schools in Chicago is the ways parents, teachers, and students work together. Schools are safer when teachers view parents as supportive partners in their children's education. When students feel that their teachers care about their learning and overall well-being and listen to them, students and teachers alike report safer school environments. Strong relationships between teachers and students can mediate the degree to which conflicts with peers inside or outside of school interfere with students' behavior within the school. Teachers who know their students well are more aware of emerging problems and understand the people involved. This gives them a better opportunity to prevent problems from occurring and to keep them from escalating.

To put these differences into perspective, a school serving students with few advantages—with low incoming achievement levels and many students from neighborhoods with high rates of poverty and crime—would be unlikely to ever be considered a very safe school, regardless of the quality of relationships within the school. However, if that school had strong relationships among parents, teachers, and students, it would be more likely to become a school where most students feel safe within the school, despite some problems with fights and disrespect. Furthermore, a school that serves relatively advantaged students might have the opportunity to provide a very safe environment for students, but to do so it would have to develop and maintain strong relationships among parents, teachers, and students. If not able to do this, its students and teachers would be more likely to report feeling a substantial, if not overwhelming, threat to safety.

In contrast, punitive measures are less likely to instill a sense of safety than measures that foster respect and trust. High suspension rates do not show any benefit to students' or teachers' feelings of safety at school, and they might even have an adverse effect on school climate by aggravating distrust between students and adults. A focus on building relationships, rather than simply exacting punishment, is consistent with recent guidance for improving school climate and discipline issued by the U.S. Department of Education (U.S. Department of Education, 2014). It is vitally important, particularly in schools serving the most impoverished neighborhoods with the highest crime rates—where the student population tends to be 100% African American—that school staff have sufficient time and resources to develop effective school safety and discipline strategies, and to develop structures that support collaborative relationships with students and their families.

Our findings suggest that, in schools with significant safety concerns, staffing levels need to be sufficient to keep teachers and other staff members from feeling overwhelmed so they can develop positive relationships with each other, and with students and their families. Faculty and staff in very low-achieving schools must have the skills to manage conflict, and the time and resources to manage disruptive acts and violent threats strategically, so that students, their parents, and teachers themselves can work together productively. These findings also suggest that district and school leaders need to be strategic about building internal school structures that encourage productive dialogue between adults and students. Schools do not choose which students they serve, but the ways they set up interactions with parents, respond to conflicts between students, and build collaboration among staff members can do much to determine the climate in which students and teachers do their work.

NOTES

The full text of this report, including appendices, may be found on our website, http://tinyurl.com/JanCRPconference. The authors thank Jennifer Moore for editorial assistance.

1. Source: U.S. Department of Education (http://www.ed.gov/news/press-releases/us-department-education-awards-more-328-million-promote-safe-schools-healthy-stu)

2. See the full report for a summary of teacher and student reports of safety at three CPS high schools.

REFERENCES

Allensworth, E., Ponisciak, S., & Mazzeo, C. (2009). *The schools teachers leave: Teacher mobility in Chicago Public Schools.* Chicago, IL: Consortium on Chicago School Research.

American Psychological Association Zero Tolerance Task Force. (2008). Are zero tolerance policies effective in schools? An evidentiary review and recommendations. *American Psychologist, 63,* 852–862.

Astor, R. A., Benbenishty, R., & Nuñez Estrada, J. (2009). School violence and theoretically atypical schools: The principal's centrality in orchestrating safe schools. *American Educational Research Journal, 46,* 423–461.

Bowen, N. K., & Bowen, G. L. (1999). Effects of crime and violence in neighborhoods and schools on the school behavior and performance of adolescents. *Journal of Adolescent Research, 14,* 319–342.

Bowen, N. K., Bowen, G. L., & Ware, W. B. (2002). Neighborhood social disorganization, families, and the educational behavior of adolescents. *Journal of Adolescent Research, 17,* 468–490.

Bryk, A. S., & Schneider, B. L. (2002). *Trust in schools: A core resource for improvement.* New York, NY: Russell Sage Foundation.

Bryk, A. S., Sebring, P. B., Allensworth, E., Luppescu, S., & Easton, J. Q. (2010). *Organizing schools for improvement: Lessons from Chicago.* Chicago, IL: University of Chicago Press.

Crosnoe, R., Johnson, M. K., & Elder, G. H., Jr. (2004). Intergenerational bonding in school: The behavioral and contextual correlates of student-teacher relationships. *Sociology of Education, 77*(1), 60–81.

Cullen, J. B., Jacob, B. A., & Levitt, S. D. (2003). *The effect of school choice on student outcomes: Evidence from randomized lotteries* (National Bureau of Economic Research working paper series no. 10113). Cambridge, MA: National Bureau of Economic Research.

Felson, R. B., Liska, A. E., South, S. J., & McNulty, T. L. (1994). The subculture of violence and delinquency: Individual vs. school context effects. *Social Forces, 73*(1), 155–173.

Kazdin, A. E. (2000). *Behavior modification in applied settings* (6th ed.). Pacific Grove, CA: Brooks/Cole.

Macmillan, R., & Hagan, J. (2004). Violence in the transition to adulthood: Adolescent victimization, education, and socioeconomic attainment in later life. *Journal of Research on Adolescence, 14,* 127–158.

Neiman, S., & DeVoe, J. F. (2009). *Crime, violence, discipline, and safety in U.S. public schools: Findings from the school survey on crime and safety: 2007–08* (NCES 2009–326). Washington, DC: U.S. Department of Education, Institute of Education Sciences, National Center for Education Statistics.

Newmann, F. M., Wehlage, G. G., & Lamborn, S. D. (2002). The significance and sources of student engagement. In F. M. Newmann (Ed.), *Student engagement and achievement in American secondary schools* (pp. 11–39). New York, NY: Teachers College Press.

Payne, A. A., Gottfredson, D. C., & Gottfredson, G. D. (2003). Schools as communities: The relationships among communal school organization, student bonding, and school disorder. *Criminology, 41,* 749–777.

Schreck, C. J., & Miller, J. M. (2003). Sources of fear of crime at school: What is the relative contribution of disorder, individual characteristics, and school security? *Journal of School Violence, 2*(4), 57–79.

Sergiovanni, T. J. (2004). *The lifeworld of leadership: Creating culture, community, and personal meaning in our schools.* San Francisco, CA: Jossey-Bass.

Singh, K., Granville, M., & Dika, S. (2002). Mathematics and science achievement: Effects of motivation, interest, and academic engagement. *The Journal of Educational Research, 95,* 323–332.

Smith, D. L., & Smith, B. J. (2006). Perceptions of violence: The views of teachers who left urban schools. *The High School Journal, 89*(3), 34–42.

Steinberg, M., Allensworth, E., & Johnson, D. W. (2011). *Student and teacher safety in Chicago Public Schools: The roles of community context and school social organization.* Chicago, IL: Consortium on Chicago School Research.

Swearer, S. M., Espelage, D. L., Vaillancourt, T., & Hymel, S. (2010). What can be done about school bullying? Linking research to educational practice. *Educational Researcher, 39*(1), 38–47.

U.S. Department of Education. (2014). *Guiding principles: A resource guide for improving school climate and discipline.* Washington, DC: Author.

Welsh, W. N., Greene, J. R., & Jenkins, P. H. (1999). School disorder: The influence of individual, institutional, and community factors. *Criminology, 37*(1), 73–115.

Welsh, W. N., Stokes, R., & Greene, J. R. (2000). A macro-level model of school disorder. *Journal of Research in Crime and Delinquency, 37,* 243–283.

## CHAPTER 9

Where Should We Intervene?

Contributions of Behavior, Student, and School
Characteristics to Out-of-School Suspension

Russell J. Skiba, Choong-Geun Chung, Megan Trachok,
Timberly Baker, Adam Sheya, and Robin Hughes

Attention continues to increase at the national level concerning the overuse of exclusionary discipline in response to student behavior, particularly with respect to the overrepresentation of African American students in out-of-school suspension (OSS[1]). The issue has been highlighted in national reports (e.g., Council of State Governments, 2011; Losen & Skiba, 2010), research studies (Bradshaw, Mitchell, O'Brennan, & Leaf, 2010), and policy (U.S. Department of Justice, 2011). In such a climate, national attention naturally shifts to the question of where we should put limited resources in order to reduce such disparities most effectively.

Research can be helpful in determining where policymakers and practitioners can intervene in reforming school discipline by identifying factors that do and do not contribute to high and disparate rates of OSS. Data-based investigations have been useful in ruling out factors that do not contribute significantly to disparities, such as poverty or student misbehavior, but we know less about what does contribute to rates of school suspension and disproportionality in suspension.

The research described in this chapter simultaneously examined types of student infraction, student demographic characteristics, and school characteristics in order to identify key points in intervening to reduce both rates of OSS and ubiquitous racial/ethnic disparities in that consequence. Student characteristics, such as a poverty background or a tendency to engage in more seriously disruptive behavior, are commonly cited as primary reasons for high rates of suspension and for racial disparities in suspension. In this investigation, however, we found that OSS is not due only to student behavior and student characteristics but also to characteristics of the school. For racial disparities in OSS in particular, the results were even more striking: School characteristics, including principal's attitudes toward discipline, were among the strongest factors associated with racial disparities in out-of-school discipline. Thus, in seeking to reduce racial disproportionality in school discipline, an emphasis on changing school practices through attention to principal leadership, improved achievement, and reducing bias might be more important than a focus on behavioral or individual characteristics.

WHAT DO WE KNOW ABOUT CONTRIBUTING FACTORS?

The path from student misbehavior to OSS is by no means straight and invariable: Whether a student action leads to being excluded from school through OSS depends on a number of factors, including the type of behavior the student engaged in, the student's race or gender, the teacher's level of tolerance, and the perspective of those administering school discipline. Racial disparity in discipline is similarly complex. We know from previous research that the characteristics of infractions, students, and schools all contribute to school discipline outcomes.

Types of Behavioral Infraction

Previous research points to a number of key factors in the relationship between student behavior and OSS. First, as a student's behavior becomes more severe, it is more likely to result in more serious consequences such as OSS and expulsion (Skiba et al., 2011), yet the behaviors that present the greatest threat to safety, such as assault or possession of firearms or drugs, occur relatively infrequently as compared to minor and moderate types of misbehavior (Robers, Zhang, & Truman, 2012). Research shows that suspension tends to be used indiscriminately for a wide range of behaviors, including infractions such as disobedience and disrespect, defiance, attendance problems, and general classroom disruption (Gregory & Weinstein, 2008). Thus the vast majority of school suspensions occur in response to minor and moderate misbehaviors that do not threaten the safety of the school community.

Students' Nonbehavioral Characteristics

Regardless of their behavior, some groups of students are more likely to be suspended than others. Boys are suspended and expelled more often than girls (e.g., Raffaele Mendez, Knoff, & Ferron, 2002; Skiba, Michael, Nardo, & Peterson, 2002; Wu, Pink, Crain, & Moles, 1982). Students with a background of poverty are also suspended at a higher rate (Christle, Nelson, & Jolivette, 2004; Raffaele Mendez et al., 2002; Wu et al., 1982), even when controlling for rates of aggressive student behavior (Petras, Masyn, Buckley, Ialongo, & Kellam, 2011).

Race appears to be the strongest and most consistent nonbehavioral predictor of school discipline (e.g., Petras et al., 2011; Raffaele Mendez et al., 2002; Skiba et al., 2002; Wu et al., 1982). African American students are overrepresented in disciplinary outcomes ranging from office referrals (Bradshaw et al., 2010), to OSS (Eitle & Eitle, 2004), to expulsions resulting from zero-tolerance policy (Tailor & Detch, 1998).

It often has been assumed that disciplinary disparities are primarily the result of poor students of color engaging in higher rates of disruptive behavior, but the evidence to date has not supported that belief. Race consistently predicts suspension and expulsion even after statistically controlling for factors related to poverty (see, e.g., Wallace, Goodkind, Wallace, & Bachman, 2008; Wu et al., 1982). There also is no evidence that Black students in the same schools and districts engage in higher rates of misbehavior to merit their higher rates of school discipline. African American students have been found to be referred to the office more frequently than White students for less objective behaviors, such as disrespect and excessive noise (Skiba et al., 2002), and for behaviors that have less to do with safety than with minor disruption or defiance/noncompliance (Gregory & Weinstein, 2008).

School Contributions

Behavioral and student characteristics are far from the only factors that influence the likelihood that a student will be suspended; school characteristics also play an important role. Teachers' attitudes, tolerance, and skill in classroom management all influence the rate of office disciplinary referrals (Morrison, Anthony, Storino, & Dillon, 2001), so it is not surprising that disparities in discipline begin at the classroom level (Gregory & Weinstein, 2008; Skiba et al., 2011).

An administrator's perspective on school discipline also strongly influences whether a student will receive an OSS. Schools' differing rates of discipline and expulsion seem to be due in part to differences in principals' attitudes toward discipline (Advancement Project/Civil Rights Project, 2000; Mukuria, 2002). A comprehensive study of the relationship of principals' attitudes and disciplinary outcomes (Skiba, Edl, & Rausch, 2007) that surveyed 325 principals on their attitudes toward zero-tolerance, suspension and expulsion, and violence prevention strategies found a broad range of perspectives on school discipline. More important, however, is that OSS rates were lower, and the use of alternative preventive measures more frequent, at schools whose principals believed that suspension and expulsion are unnecessary in a positive school climate. Finally, the evidence suggests that African American students often receive harsher or longer punishments than White students for the same behavior in the case of both minor (Skiba et al., 2011) and more serious infractions (Nicholson-Crotty, Birchmeier, & Valentine, 2009).

Other school characteristics, including the school climate and proportion of Black enrollment, also appear related to a school's overall rate of exclusionary discipline. School climate can serve as either a protective factor that reduces the likelihood of suspension, or a contributing factor that increases racial disparities in discipline (Mattison & Aber, 2007). Regardless of the level of misbehavior and delinquency, schools with a higher Black enrollment have been found to have a higher rate of exclusionary discipline, court actions, and zero-tolerance policies (Welch & Payne, 2010). Poverty at the school level also contributes to rates of discipline, but not always in the expected direction. Although suspension rates are clearly higher in poor urban districts (Nicholson-Crotty et al., 2009), the gap between Black and White suspension rates is as great or greater in richer suburban districts (Eitle & Eitle, 2004; Wallace et al., 2008).

WHAT DRIVES SUSPENSION AND EXPULSION?

The use of OSS and racial disparity in its application are not driven simply by student behavior but by a complex interaction of the types of behavior exhibited, student characteristics independent of their behavior, and the characteristics of schools and their administrators. Our aim in this research was to study these three levels simultaneously in order to identify which are most predictive of OSS, and which contribute the most to racial/ethnic disparities in suspension. Identifying the strongest predictors of OSS might be extremely important in guiding policy and practice decisions regarding where to put limited intervention resources in discipline reform efforts.

Overview of the Research

Our basic database consisted of the entire set of records of student school disciplinary incidents from the State of Indiana Suspension and Expulsion database for the school year 2007–2008, which included 43,320 students at 730 schools. Organized by incidents of in-school suspension (ISS), OSS, and expulsion for all public schools in the state, the database included a total of 102,203 in- and out-of-school suspensions. We supplemented these data with those available from other state databases in order to describe student, teacher, and school demographics associated with each incident.

In order to assess the perspectives of principals on school discipline, we adapted the Disciplinary Practices Survey (Skiba et al., 2007), a survey designed to provide data on a broad range of principals' attitudes toward the process of school discipline.[2] Principals were asked to rate their agreement with statements reflecting various attitudes about the purpose, process, and outcomes of school discipline. They also rated the frequency with which they used a number of preventive disciplinary strategies (e.g., bullying prevention, conflict resolution, metal detectors) in their schools. Previous analyses of this measure found that principals' perspectives on school discipline separated them into two distinct groups or clusters: One group was more likely to endorse the use of suspension, expulsion, and zero-tolerance, and the other was more favorable toward using preventive approaches to minimize school exclusion.

Analyzing the Data

We examined the relative contribution of specific incidents, student characteristics, and school variables to the severity of school punishment using the multivariate statistical technique known as hierarchical linear modeling (HLM; Raudenbush, Bryk, & Congdon, 2004). This study analyzed only administrative decisions made at the office level once a student was referred to the office—that is, whether a student sent to the office would be given an OSS rather than in-school exclusion. As noted, we explored three categories of variables: the type of infraction that led to the punishment, personal characteristics of the student that were unrelated to their behavior, and characteristics of the school.

Type of Infraction. The first variable we examined was the contribution of various infractions that led to each incident of suspension. There were 17 categories that students were suspended for in the state database; these were regrouped into four categories: use/possession, fighting/battery, moderate infractions, and defiance/disruption. This portion of the analysis answered the question: To what extent does the severity of behavior predict the decision to assign an OSS rather than an in-school suspension?

Student Characteristics. Second, we looked at student characteristics that were independent of behavior, including gender, eligibility for free and reduced-price lunch (as an indicator of poverty), and race (Black or White). This part of the analysis answered the question: To what extent do a student's demographic characteristics predict the likelihood of being suspended out of school?

School Characteristics. Finally, we explored the extent to which characteristics specific to each school helped predict whether a student received an OSS. School characteristics included the proportion of African American students enrolled in the school, average years of experience among the school's teachers, the percentage of students in the school eligible for free or reduced-price lunch, the percentage of students who passed in math and English on the state accountability exam, and the principal's perspective on school discipline. As noted, the principal's perspective was measured through the Disciplinary Practices Scale, which classified principals into two groups: those favorable to prevention, and those more inclined toward suspension, expulsion, and zero-tolerance. This portion of the analysis answered the question: To what extent do characteristics of the school itself, including the principal's perspective on discipline, determine the choice of an in-school or out-of-school suspension?

WHAT DID WE LEARN?

Characteristics of the Infractions, Students, and Schools

Tables 9.1 and 9.2 present data for variables at the levels of infraction and student characteristics. The infraction data presented in Table 9.1 support the notion that more severe offenses lead to more severe consequences. Although defiance/disruption/other is the most frequently occurring infraction, students who participated in fighting/battery appear to be more likely to receive an OSS, whereas use/possession, the least common infraction, appears to be most often associated with expulsion. Table 9.2 describes the demographic characteristics for the students in this study: 68.6% of students were male, slightly more than half received free or reduced-price lunch, and 76.3% were White.

In terms of the third level of variables, school characteristics, the mean percentage of Black students enrolled in the schools was 7.9, the average number of years of teacher experience in these schools was 15, the mean percentage of students receiving free or reduced-price lunch was 38.7, and the percentage of students passing math and English in ISTEP testing was 65.3. Principals were somewhat more likely to support suspension and expulsion than preventive alternatives: 57.1% expressed beliefs that placed them in a group supporting the use of suspension and expulsion, whereas 42.9% indicated support for preventive alternatives.

Multiple Factors Contribute to Suspension and Expulsion Decisions

This research looked at one part of the complex process of school discipline—the decision whether to give a student who was referred to the office an OSS or ISS. Reviewing findings across three levels—type of behavior, student's nonbehavioral characteristics, and characteristics of the school the student attends—showed that those administrative decisions are determined by multiple factors operating simultaneously.

How Does Type of Infraction Affect the Likelihood of OSS?

Analysis at this level showed that the type of infraction the student engages in contributes significantly to whether a student is suspended out of school: More serious behavior results in more serious punishment. A student using or possessing a weapon or drugs (the least common infraction) was over seven times more likely to be suspended out of school than a student engaging in more minor misbehavior. These findings are consistent with previous research in showing that the most reliable predictors of more serious school consequences are the more serious, less frequently occurring infractions.

Table 9.1. Descriptive Statistics for Data Used in HLM Analyses, Level 1 Variables

Level 1: Incident	ISS		OSS		Expulsion		Total	
Type of Infraction	Number	Percentage of Incidents	Number	Percentage of Incidents	Number	Percentage of Incidents	Number	Percentage of Incidents
Use/possession	692	16.8%	2,795	68.0%	626	15.2%	4,113	100%
Fighting/battery	3,630	26.7%	9,727	71.6%	227	1.7%	13,584	100%
Moderate infractions	4,513	41.8%	6,138	56.8%	155	1.4%	10,806	100%
Defiance/disruption/ other	45,757	60.3%	28,951	38.1%	1,234	1.6%	75,942	100%
Total	54,592	52.3%	47,611	45.6%	2,242	2.1%	104,455	100%

Table 9.2. Descriptive Statistics for Data Used in HLM Analyses, Level 2 Variables

Level 2: Student		Number	Percentage of Students
Gender	Male	29,712	68.6%
	Female	13,608	31.4%
SES	Free or reduced-price lunch	23,125	53.4%
	None	20,195	46.6%
Race	Black	10,251	23.7%
	White	33,069	76.3%

Do Student Characteristics Predict the Likelihood of Suspension?

Our findings also showed that there is much more to the decision to assign an OSS than simply the type of behavior the student engaged in. Race, gender, and socioeconomic status all independently affect the probability of OSS. Among student characteristics, race was the strongest predictor of OSS. We found that Black students were significantly more likely to receive an OSS rather than an ISS than White students, and males more likely to receive an OSS than females. Students eligible for free or reduced-price lunch were slightly more likely to receive an OSS than noneligible students.

It is important to note that, in any multivariate analysis across levels, each variable's contribution to the outcome is unique and independent of other variables. Thus, in this analysis, the significant contribution of both poverty *and* race means that Black students are more likely to be suspended out of school *above and beyond* any effects due to poverty. Nor are racial differences in the decision to apply an OSS rather than an ISS due to the type of infraction in which the student engaged. Even after controlling for a range of infractions, from minor disruption to use and possession of drugs or weapons, African American students are significantly more likely to receive serious punishment. These data join a wealth of previous findings that a student's race plays a role in determining the severity of punishment whether the student is rich or poor or being punished for minor or more serious misbehavior.

How Do School Characteristics Contribute to OSS?

Finally, the characteristics of schools themselves help determine the severity of punishment, above and beyond the type of infraction the student engaged in or the student demographic characteristics. Results at the school level indicated that students are more likely to receive OSS than ISS in schools whose principals believe that suspension and expulsion are an inevitable and important part of school discipline. In schools whose principals are more oriented toward prevention, students were significantly less likely to receive OSS. Finding that the principal's attitude toward discipline strongly affects the rate of suspension at a school is not unexpected, but those data are extremely important in terms of intervention (see Implications).

The results of the current analyses were consistent with recent studies that have found that the percentage of Black enrollment in a school is a strong and consistent predictor of school suspension (Welch & Payne, 2010). In the current study, attending a school with a higher percentage of Black students is among the strongest predictors of OSS, after only use/possession and assault, in how well it predicted OSS. It is somewhat striking that attending a school with more Black students increases a student's risk of OSS nearly as much as involvement in drugs, weapons, or assault.

Students at schools with higher average achievement levels were significantly less likely to be suspended out of school. Just as higher academic achievement is a protective factor for individuals, a school's ability to maintain high overall achievement is a protective factor for students attending that school. Because these results control for student demographic characteristics, they suggest that, regardless of the economic level of the students served in a school community, schools that are able to raise their academic achievement will also see improvements in school discipline outcomes. Neither a school's rate of students eligible for free and reduced-price lunch nor average years of teacher experience was significant in predicting the likelihood of OSS.

The Important Influence of School Factors on Racial Disparities

Factors that determine the degree of racial disparity in discipline might be different from the factors that predict overall rates of discipline; thus we also specifically examined contributions to Black disproportionality in OSS. In these analyses, racial disparities in the administration of OSS were not accounted for by the severity of student infraction or level of student poverty. However, when school-level variables, including principal's perspectives on discipline, percentage of Black enrollment, and school achievement, were introduced into the equation, the contribution of individual student race to the likelihood of OSS was reduced to nonsignificance. This demonstrates that racial disparities in OSS are best explained not by student behavior or poverty status but by a range of school-level factors, including the principal's perspective on discipline. Put simply, attending a school with lower average achievement, more Black students, or a principal who supports zero-tolerance and school exclusion puts Black students at greater risk for OSS regardless of behavior or poverty status.

A common explanation for such disparities relies on what Valencia and Solarzano (1997) term "deficit thinking"—that is, inequitable treatment is viewed as being caused by the characteristics or behavior of the marginalized population themselves. This research, however, in no way supported the deficit model; racial disparities remained significant regardless of the type of behavior or extent of individual poverty. It was school characteristics, including the principal's attitude toward discipline, that best explained racial disparities in the use of OSS.

IMPLICATIONS: SCHOOLS HAVE THE POWER
TO CHANGE THEIR DISCIPLINARY OUTCOMES

These findings—that school characteristics are among the predictors of OSS in general and among the strongest predictors of racial disparities—join other chapters in this volume in arguing that schools have the power to change their disciplinary outcomes. In particular, the findings of this research suggest a focus on three areas: the power of the principal, the importance of considering bias as a contributing factor, and the integral relationship of achievement and student behavior.

The Power of the Principal to Change Disciplinary Practices

This is not the first time it has been demonstrated that principals' perspectives have a significant influence on decisions to use exclusionary discipline, but this research extends previous findings by showing that principals' perspectives are a key predictor of racial disparities in discipline. If schools and school districts wish to change their disciplinary outcomes, it will be critical to ensure that school leaders are aware of, and supported in, the use of alternative disciplinary approaches that have been successful in reducing the use of punitive and exclusionary school discipline.

Fortunately, a number of school- and classroom-wide interventions have been shown to be effective in improving school discipline or school climate and seem to have potential for reducing disproportionality in suspension and expulsion (Osher, Bear, Sprague, & Doyle, 2010). These interventions appear to focus on three aspects of school discipline and school climate. First, effective interventions seek to build and strengthen relationships and classroom interactions among students, faculty, and administration. González analyzed school data from an implementation of restorative conferences and found that, over a 7-year period, participating schools reduced both their overall rate of suspension and their racial/ethnic disparities in suspension (see Chapter 10). Second, structural changes in school disciplinary systems, such as schoolwide positive behavior supports (see Chapter 14) or the use of threat assessment procedures (see Chapter 12), have been shown to reduce the use of exclusionary discipline, although it is not yet clear whether such procedures are sufficient in and of themselves to eliminate racial/ethnic disparities in discipline. Finally, social–emotional learning programs might improve student behavior and school climate by teaching students the emotional regulation and interpersonal skills they need to succeed in school and society. Over the course of 3 years, the Cleveland Metropolitan School District implemented a social–emotional learning program in conjunction with student support teams and planning centers. They found that referrals for suspendable offenses were cut in half, out-of-school suspensions were reduced by 58.8%, and attendance improved (see Chapter 13).

Shifts in policy to support school leaders seeking to implement more effective and inclusive disciplinary practices are beginning to emerge at the district, state, and federal level. New policies enacted by the Los Angeles Unified School District recently removed "willful defiance" from the list of offenses that could be subject to suspension and encouraged administrators to broaden the responses of administrators when students are referred to the office (Jones, 2013). Schools in Broward County, Florida, implemented a variety of alternatives to exclusion, including counseling, community service, and anger management, and saw substantial reductions in school arrests from 2011 to 2012 (Alvarez, 2013). These changes are being supported by a number of state-level initiatives in Maryland, Florida, Texas, Ohio, and California, among others. At the federal level, the U.S. Justice and Education Departments have recently issued guidance that include recommendations regarding policies and practices to reduce rates of exclusionary discipline and improve school safety and climate (U.S. Department of Education and Department of Justice, 2014). Such initiatives will be most effective in changing practice to the extent that they pair (a) accountability measures that require a review of disaggregated discipline data with (b) training for school personnel in effective behavioral procedures that can reduce the need for suspension and expulsion.

Acknowledging and Addressing Bias

Among the most striking findings in this research, again consistent with previous findings (e.g., Welch & Payne, 2010), was the extent to which higher Black enrollment predicted a higher likelihood of more severe punishment. In both disadvantaged and more advantaged schools, regardless of the severity of the misbehavior students engage in, students are more likely to receive OSS than ISS in schools with a higher proportion of Black students.

Discussions about race and racial stereotypes are difficult and complex, creating a strong desire to avoid the topic (Pollock, 2008). Yet research has shown that racial stereotypes and implicit bias remain widespread in society in general (Cunningham, Nezlek, & Banaji, 2004) and in schools in particular (Ferguson, 2000; Howard, 2008). Such stereotypes might be particularly strong as they relate to Black males and their behavior. In a study that included interviews with school personnel to discuss their perceptions of disproportionality, one teacher commented, "Whenever we are having chronic behavior problems, it is a little Black boy—every time. We call them the Duwans. . . . They have a brother at home who dropped out at 16, and he gets to play Nintendo all day. Why should they try?" (Skiba et al., 2006, p. 1443). Just as stereotypes about academic ability can threaten academic achievement (Taylor & Walton, 2011), stereotypes and bias regarding behavior and race might well be expected to make remediation of disciplinary disparities more difficult. Recent research, however, has begun to demonstrate that it is possible to address and change levels of implicit bias. Participants in a 12-week instructional intervention showed a significant reduction in implicit bias after being encouraged to use specific strategies to reduce prejudice, such as stereotype replacement and increased opportunity for contact with individuals of other races/ethnicities (Devine, Forscher, Austin, & Cox, 2012).

The Relationship Between Achievement and Suspension

The results of this research suggest that, just as higher academic achievement is a protective factor for individuals, a school's ability to maintain high overall achievement is a protective factor for students attending that school. Across more or less disadvantaged schools and regardless of their racial/ethnic makeup, schools with higher average achievement place fewer students in OSS. Student behavior and academic outcomes are clearly inextricably related, Gregory, Skiba, and Noguera (2010) term the achievement gap and discipline gap "two sides of the same coin." Thus interventions that improve the quality of academic instruction and learning outcomes can have important outcomes in terms of improved student behavior and school climate (Scott, Nelson, & Liaupsin, 2001; also see Chapter 7). At the same time, schools that focus on the proactive development of a supportive school climate are likely to see academic benefits as well.

Limitations

Because the data for these analyses were drawn from a statewide database containing all incidents of school exclusion, the results are limited to administrative decisions concerning the seriousness of the punishment to be administered; the data contained no information about the contribution of earlier events in the disciplinary process, such as office referrals from the classroom. Given the significant contribution of classroom referrals to racial differences in school discipline (Skiba et al., 2011), estimates of racial and ethnic disparity in these data might well be lower than the actual disproportionality in OSS.

CONCLUSIONS

Our original hypothesis in this work—that the decision to apply out-of-school suspension rather in-school suspension is determined by a complex interaction of behavioral, student, and school-level variables—was supported. Type of infraction; race, gender, and to a certain extent socioeconomic status at the individual level; and percentage of Black enrollment, school achievement level, and principal's perspectives on discipline at the school level all contributed to the probability of a student being assigned an OSS. These data also continue to raise serious concerns about the extent to which race predicts exclusionary discipline. Racial disparities in OSS are ubiquitous and are likely to occur more frequently as Black enrollment increases, regardless of the level of student or school poverty or the seriousness of the infraction. The single most important finding from this analysis might well be that systemic school-level variables contribute to disproportionality in OSS more than either student behavior or individual characteristics. Thus those wishing to reduce racial disparities in discipline would be well advised to move away from a focus on variables such as family or community poverty that are out of a school's control, and instead seek to implement interventions that focus on relationships, structural reform, and emotional self-regulation.

NOTES

We gratefully acknowledge the generous support of the William T. Grant Foundation for this research through their Major Grants Program. Thanks are also due to Leigh Kupersmith for her diligent assistance with copy editing and formatting.

1. Although the original analyses for this chapter included description of both out-of-school suspension and expulsion in relation to in-school suspension, in the interest of space, the chapter describes only results comparing administrative decisions between in-school and out-of-school suspension.

2. In the interest of space, both the details of the Disciplinary Practices Survey and the technical details of the HLM modeling were minimized in this version of the paper. A more complete description of the analytical techniques and results of the analysis can be found in Skiba, Chung, Trachok, Baker, Sheya, and Hughes (2014).

REFERENCES

Advancement Project/Civil Rights Project. (2000). *Opportunities suspended: The devastating consequences of zero tolerance and school discipline.* Cambridge, MA: The Civil Rights Project at Harvard University.

Alvarez, L. (2013, December 3). Seeing the toll, schools revisit zero tolerance. *New York Times,* p. A1.

Bradshaw, C. P., Mitchell, M. M., O'Brennan, L. M., & Leaf, P. J. (2010). Multilevel exploration of factors contributing to the overrepresentation of Black students in office disciplinary referrals. *Journal of Educational Psychology, 102,* 508–520. doi:10.1037/a0018450

Christle, C., Nelson, C. M., & Jolivette, K. (2004). School characteristics related to the use of suspension. *Education and Treatment of Children, 27,* 509–529.

Council of State Governments Justice Center. (2011). *Breaking schools' rules: A statewide study of how school discipline relates to student's success and juvenile justice involvement.* Washington, DC: Author.

Cunningham, W. A., Nezlek, J. B., & Banaji, M. R. (2004). Implicit and explicit ethnocentrism: Revisiting the ideologies of prejudice. *Personality and Social Psychology Bulletin, 30,* 1332–1346.

Devine, P. G., Forscher, P. S., Austin, A. J., & Cox, W. T. L. (2012). Long-term reduction in implicit race bias: A prejudice habit-breaking intervention. *Journal of Experimental Social Psychology, 48,* 1267–1278.

Eitle, T. M., & Eitle, D. J. (2004). Inequality, segregation, and the overrepresentation of African Americans in school suspensions. *Sociological Perspectives, 47,* 269–287. doi:10.1525/S0P.2004.47.3.269

Ferguson, A. A. (2000). *Bad boys: Public school and the making of Black masculinity.* Ann Arbor, MI: University of Michigan Press.

Gregory, A., Skiba, R., & Noguera, P. (2010). The achievement gap and the discipline gap: Two sides of the same coin? *Educational Researcher, 39,* 59–68.

Gregory, A., & Weinstein, R. S. (2008). The discipline gap and African Americans: Defiance or cooperation in the high school classroom. *Journal of School Psychology, 46,* 455–475.

Howard, T. C. (2008). Who really cares? The disenfranchisement of African American males in pre K–12 schools: A critical race theory perspective. *Teachers' College Record, 110,* 954–985.

Jones, B. (2013, August 11). Back to school means big changes, challenges at LAUSD. *Los Angeles Daily News*. Retrieved from http://www.dailynews.com/20130811/back-to-school-means-big-changes-challenges-at-lausd

Losen, D., & Skiba, R. (2010). *Suspended education: Urban middle schools in crisis*. Birmingham, AL: Southern Poverty Law Center.

Mattison, E., & Aber, M. S. (2007). Closing the achievement gap: The association of racial climate with achievement and behavioral outcomes. *American Journal of Community Psychology, 40*(1), 1–12. doi:10.1007/s10464-007-9128-x

Morrison, G. M., Anthony, S., Storino, M., Cheng, J., Furlong, M. F., & Morrison, R. L. (2001). School expulsion as a process and an event: Before and after effects on children at-risk for school discipline. *New Directions for Youth Development: Theory, Practice, Research, 92*, 45–72.

Mukuria, G. (2002). Disciplinary challenges: How do principals address this dilemma? *Urban Education, 37*, 432–452. doi:10.1177/00485902037003007

Nicholson-Crotty, S., Birchmeier, Z., & Valentine, D. (2009). Exploring the impact of school discipline on racial disproportion in the juvenile justice system. *Social Science Quarterly, 90*, 1003–1018. doi:10.1111/j.1540-6237.2009.00674.x

Osher, D., Bear, G. G., Sprague, J. R., & Doyle, W. (2010). How can we improve school discipline? *Educational Researcher, 39*(1), 48–58. doi:10.3102/0013189X09357618

Petras, H., Masyn, K. E., Buckley, J. A., Ialongo, N. S., & Kellam, S. (2011). Who is most at risk for school removal? A multilevel discrete-time survival analysis of individual- and context-level influences. *Journal of Educational Psychology, 103*(1), 223–237. doi:10.1037/90021545

Pollock, M. (Ed.). (2008). *Everyday antiracism: Getting real about race in schools*. New York, NY: The New Press.

Raffaele Mendez, L. M., Knoff, H. M., & Ferron, J. M. (2002). School demographic variables and out-of-school suspension rates: A quantitative and qualitative analysis of a large, ethnically diverse school district. *Psychology in the Schools, 39*, 259–277. doi:10.1002/pits.10020

Raudenbush, S. W., Bryk, A. S., & Congdon, R. T. (2004). *Hierarchical linear and nonlinear modeling*. Chicago, IL: Scientific Software International.

Robers, S., Zhang, J., & Truman, J. (2012). *Indicators of school crime and safety: 2011* (NCES 2012-002/NCJ 236021). Washington, DC: U.S. Department of Education, National Center for Education Statistics, and U.S. Department of Justice, Bureau of Justice Statistics, Office of Justice Programs.

Scott, T. M., Nelson, C. M., & Liaupsin, C. J. (2001). Effective instruction: The forgotten component in preventing school violence. *Education and Treatment of Children, 24*, 309–322.

Skiba, R. J., Chung, C. G., Trachok, M., Baker, T., Sheya, A., & Hughes, R. L. (2014). Parsing disciplinary disproportionality: Contributions of infraction, student, and school characteristics to out-of-school suspension and expulsion. *American Educational Research Journal, 51*, 640-670.

Skiba, R., Edl, H., & Rausch, M. K. (2007, April). *The Disciplinary Practices Survey: Principal attitudes towards suspension and expulsion*. Paper presented at the annual meeting of the American Educational Research Association, Chicago, IL.

Skiba, R. J., Horner, R. H., Chung, C.-G., Rausch, M. K., May, S. L., & Tobin, T. (2011). Race is not neutral: A national investigation of African American and Latino disproportionality in school discipline. *School Psychology Review, 40*(1), 85–107.

Skiba, R. J., Michael, R. S., Nardo, A. C., & Peterson. R. (2002). The color of discipline: Sources of racial and gender disproportionality in school punishment. *Urban Review, 34*, 317–342.

Skiba, R. J., Simmons, A., Ritter, S., Kohler, K., Henderson, M., & Wu, T. (2006). The context of minority disproportionality: Practitioner perspectives on special education referral. *Teachers College Record, 108*, 1424–1459.

Tailor, H., & Detch, E. R. (1998). *Getting tough on kids: A look at zero tolerance*. Nashville, TN: Tennessee Office of Education Accountability, Comptroller of the Treasury.

Taylor, V. J., & Walton, G. M. (2011). Stereotype threat undermines academic learning. *Personality and Social Psychology Bulletin, 37*, 1055–1067.

U.S. Department of Education/Department of Justice .(2014). U.S. Departments of Education and Justice release school discipline guidance package to enhance school climate and improve school discipline policies/practices. Washington, DC: Author. Retrieved from http://www.ed.gov/news/press-releases/us-departments-education-and-justice-release-school-discipline-guidance-package/

U.S. Department of Justice. (2011). *Attorney General Holder and Secretary Duncan announce supportive school discipline initiative.* Retrieved from http://www.ojjdp.gov/enews/11juvjust/110721.html

Valencia, R. R., & Solarzano, D. (1997). Contemporary deficit thinking. In R. R. Valencia (Ed.), *The evolution of deficit thinking: Educational thought and practice* (pp. 183–210). Washington, DC: Falmer Press.

Wallace, J. M. Jr., Goodkind, S. G., Wallace, C. M., & Bachman, J. (2008). Racial, ethnic and gender differences in school discipline among American high school students: 1991–2005. *Negro Educational Review, 59,* 47–62.

Welch, K., & Payne, A. A. (2010). Racial threat and punitive school discipline. *Social Problems, 57,* 25–48. doi:10.1525/SP.2010.57.1.25

Wu, S. C., Pink, W. T., Crain, R. L., & Moles, O. (1982). Student suspension: A critical reappraisal. *The Urban Review, 14,* 245–303. doi:10.1007/BF02171974

SPECIFIC REMEDIES FOR CLOSING THE DISCIPLINE GAP

Even policymakers convinced of the need for change might be reluctant to change course without a clear and specific direction. "Study as we go" is maybe a reasonable enough direction for those who find the status quo untenable, but most policymakers want to know that the new direction will also be better before they seek reforms. In this case, *better* is defined as not merely reducing suspension rates for students, generally, but finding less discriminatory alternatives. Simply put, the chapters in Part II describe in great detail distinct policies and practices that districts can pursue instead of what they are doing today. In each chapter, particular attention is given to whether the policy or practices described reduce racial and ethnic disparities. Great efforts were made to ensure that these chapters would demonstrate to policymakers that there are concrete approaches to school discipline reform that do in fact reduce racial disparities. To this end, the chapters in this part provide an unblinking analysis of potential remedies. The part begins and concludes with two anecdotal stories from administrators who provide an on-the-ground sense of the benefits of pursuing alternatives to out-of-school suspension. The first three chapters describe remedies with the strongest evidence base in terms of reducing disciplinary exclusion and closing the racial discipline gap. Some of the most impressive findings are in Chapter 10, which presents González's 6-year study of the implementation of restorative practices in Denver's public schools.

Each of the chapters in Part II includes empirical analyses based on established scientific methods. Because it is important that policymakers not lose touch with the human perspective on education reform, we introduce Part II via a brief personal story from Karen Brocker, assistant principal of the Silverado middle school in California, who is making efforts to close the discipline gap at her school using restorative practices. The following section is from her point of view.

ON THE TRANSFORMATIVE PROPERTY OF INCORPORATING RESTORATIVE PRACTICES INTO THE DISCIPLINE PROCESS IN THE MIDDLE SCHOOL[1]

In 2004, I took the job as assistant principal at Silverado Middle School thinking I would transform the traditional role of an AP as a disciplinarian into one that focused on teaching and learning. I would be proactive and work with students before they got into trouble and had to be sent out of class. But from the first day I started, I found students sitting on the bench outside my office. They were all out of class, missing out on learning, waiting for me to assign a consequence for something they did.

> Ten years ago, a girl chewed gum at our school. She got a detention. She did not serve the detention, so she was assigned Saturday School. She did not serve Saturday School, so she was suspended for a day.

> Ten years ago, two boys got into a fight in the hallway. The boys were sent home for 2 days after a quick call to parents. There was no further follow-up. Within a few weeks, both were in the office again for another fight.

Chew gum, get suspended. Get in a fight, get suspended. Clearly, something was wrong with the way we dealt with discipline at Silverado Middle School. State-level data showed that our school had suspension and expulsion numbers that exceeded national norms. In fact, suspension and expulsion numbers were sky high throughout the Napa Valley Unified School District.

By 2007, the District responded to these troubling data by refocusing efforts to deal with behavioral issues and training staff in a research-based positive behavioral intervention program, including a focus on restorative practices. They also committed to providing ongoing support so that, today, every school site in the district has worked to transform site behavior policies and discipline practices from consequence based to restoration and restitution based.

The most recent data, from the 2012–2013 school year, show Silverado Middle School's suspension and expulsion rates at an all-time low. Students still chew gum, but they are asked to spit the gum out and reminded of school rules. They might do a public service announcement or post signs to remind others of the rule, or they might help clean up during lunch.

Students also still get into fights, and though they might be sent home to cool down for an afternoon or a day, they come back sooner and begin the work of learning to resolve conflict nonviolently and to repair any harm done to others.

> Last week a girl threw the wrapper from her cookie on the ground during lunch. After reviewing the expectation that all students and staff keep the

campus clean, she is given a chance to spend 10 minutes picking up trash in the quad during lunch rather than getting a 30-minute detention. She chooses to clean up, and soon returns to talking with friends.

Last year, two boys got into a fight after pushing each other in the hallway. The boys each told their side of the story, and parents were called. No one was hurt, so everyone agreed that both boys would spend that afternoon and the next morning working on repairing the harm done to each other and restoring balance on the campus. The boys wrote apologies and participated in conflict mediation with the counselor. They spent breaks and lunch together for 2 weeks, learning more about each other. They created a poster that encouraged students to talk it out rather than fighting and had their picture taken together. Neither of the boys has had a fight or any major discipline issue since.

Now, in my 10th year as an assistant principal, I truly believe that positive behavioral intervention and restorative practices have been the key to reducing Silverado Middle School's suspension and expulsion rates. I also believe that they are why those students who in the past would be sitting on the bench outside my office waiting for me to assign a consequence for their behavior are no longer there. They are in class, where teachers are teaching and students are learning.

NOTE

1. The editor of this volume submitted a call for stories detailing alternatives to exclusionary discipline. Karen Brocker, assistant principal at Silverado Middle School, composed this piece demonstrating the effects of restorative justice practices at her school.

## CHAPTER 10

Socializing Schools

Addressing Racial Disparities in Discipline
Through Restorative Justice

Thalia González

Restorative justice as an approach to improving the school learning environment and student behavior is based on three core principles: repairing harm, involving stakeholders, and transforming community relationships (Macready, 2009; Morrison, 2003, 2007; Zehr, 2003). Since the first documented use of restorative justice in schools, its advocates have promoted it as an alternative to zero-tolerance and punitive exclusionary discipline. As interviews with administrators, teachers, parents, students, and school resource officers in the Denver Public Schools have revealed, the impact of restorative practices is not simply an academic idea but a practice for transforming the community:

> Restorative justice serves our classroom because students are no longer alienated by the discipline process, but rather affirmed in their feelings and coached on how to act on those feelings in a constructive way. Students are taught how to behave, not punished for breaking rules they never learned.
> *2nd/3rd Grade Math/Science Teacher, CASA*

In recent years, diverse models of restorative justice have been implemented in schools across the United States to address increasing concerns about the significant negative impact of exclusionary discipline, particularly for African American and Latino students (Skiba et al., 2011). Research showing that punitive discipline and zero-tolerance policies have resulted in a significant increase in suspensions and expulsions for all students has also documented the alarmingly disproportionate rates at which African American and Latino students experience discipline (Gregory, Cornell, & Fan, 2011; Skiba et al., 2011). Such experiences have far-reaching negative implications, from academic underperformance to increased risk of antisocial behavior and entry into the school-to-prison pipeline.

International studies of restorative justice practices in schools provide significant evidence of its positive outcomes for students, teachers, parents, and community members (Morrison, 2007). No similar study has been conducted in the United
States, until now. This longitudinal study on the impact of restorative justice in
Denver Public Schools (DPS) is the first conducted in an urban school district in the
United States. This multiyear examination of the implementation of school-based
restorative justice practices across several school sites is based on an unusually rich
combination of empirical and qualitative data allowing for comprehensive analysis.

The findings presented in this chapter are based on a case study analysis of
DPS conducted from 2008 to 2013, and on data collected by DPS from 2006 to
2013. Data are drawn from observations, open-ended interviews, and secondary
analyses of empirical discipline data from DPS at both the district and school
levels. The findings provide educational policymakers with five key consider-
ations. First, the systemic implementation of restorative justice at the school and
district levels, coupled with the reform of discipline policies, can play a key role
in addressing disproportionality in discipline outcomes. Second, the positive impact of restorative practices not only addresses disproportionate discipline but
also can be correlated with increased academic achievement. Third, the implementation of restorative practices should be aligned with clear short-, medium-,
and long-term goals, beginning with a small pilot phase and transitioning to
widespread adoption. Fourth, the implementation of restorative practices will
be different in every district, as it is not simply about adding another program
to a teacher's classroom or disciplinarian's protocols but about institutional-
izing practices that facilitate microinstitutional changes that are responsive to
the needs of individuals and communities. Fifth, the most effective approach to
implementing restorative practices is a comprehensive continuum model that
can have transformative effects within an individual school community and also
be part of districtwide implementation.

RESTORATIVE JUSTICE IN SCHOOLS

The broad aim of restorative justice is to develop educational policies and practices that are more responsive and restorative to the needs and concerns of the school
community (Morrison, 2007). Restorative justice models contribute to the goal of
education by emphasizing accountability, restitution, and restoration of a school
community. Restorative justice values a deliberative process because it facilitates
mutual understanding, problem solving, and expressions of remorse, compassion,
apology, and forgiveness, which might lead to reparative agreements and promote
feelings of respect, peace, and satisfaction. As qualitative data have revealed, these
feelings contribute to the social capital of a school community and thus should be
viewed as positive outcomes of the practice:

Restorative justice has been a powerful practice to use because it aligns with not only my beliefs as a teacher, but my hopes for the future of my students. ... Working with my students in a restorative way means [producing] a generation of students who are productive members of my community and society and not students who become community members of the prison system. *3rd/4th Grade Intervention Teacher, CASA*

The underlying assumption of restorative justice is that students who commit delinquent or offensive acts are breaching the social contract between them and the school community. That social contract cannot be restored if the breaching party is absent—that is, if the school's first and most frequent response is to ban the offender from the community. The inclusive community-based framework of restorative justice lies in sharp contrast to exclusionary discipline policies. As it has no restorative component, it is not surprising that disciplinary exclusion fails to correct student misbehavior and often leads to increased student suspensions, poor academic achievement, a loss of reputation among peers, social isolation, psychological problems, and ultimately, juvenile delinquency (Skiba et al., 2011). Restorative practices emphasize the importance of relationships, which is also at the heart of several other promising interventions for reducing the discipline gap.

Restorative justice is often perceived as a particular way for a school community to respond to a student who has caused damage or harm to a person or property. As the DPS case study illustrates, the practice of restorative justice in schools can be much more. In the most effective schools, the integration of a continuum model aims not only to restore harms to the community but also to build social capital, improve academic performance, and promote a safer school environment. A continuum model entails the incorporation of diverse practices, ranging from brief informal teacher–student exchanges to formal conferences to address misbehavior and resulting consequences. This model provides educators with a more comprehensive set of tools to address the wide range of issues and offenses schools regularly face. In DPS, the continuum model,[1] which includes frequent proactive restorative exchanges, affective statements, questions, informal conferences, large group circles, and conferences, has been found to have the greatest impact.

Other studies of restorative justice also suggest that a comprehensive continuum model is likely to be highly effective, as it is designed to increase student engagement and transform the entire school environment (Morrison, 2007; Morrison, Blood, & Thorsborne, 2005; Wachtel, 2001). Although this study was not designed to compare the outcomes of different models of restorative justice, the qualitative analysis does suggest that greatest benefits are achieved when schools employ the practices they find to have the greatest impact.

EXAMINING RESTORATIVE JUSTICE
IN DENVER PUBLIC SCHOOLS

This study provides a descriptive analysis of the integration and implementation of school-based restorative justice practices in Denver Public Schools since 2003. Empirical data used in this study include data collected by DPS beginning in 2003. In 2006, DPS administered surveys and questionnaires and conducted interviews with DPS employees who were engaged in the pilot implementation of restorative justice. In 2009 I began conducting qualitative interviews at North High School (NHS), George Washington High School, Montbello High School, and in 2011, Cole Arts and Sciences Academy (CASA). Interview subjects included students, teachers, staff members, community members, administrators, and DPS restorative justice practitioners. Observations of restorative mediations conferences and circles occurred from 2009 to 2013. Data also were drawn from the observations of participants in more than 1,300 restorative justice cases, the development and practice of training restorative justice coordinators in DPS, and the implementation of discipline systems oriented to comprehensive restorative justice at NHS and CASA.

As findings in Table 10.1, Figure 10.1, and Figure 10.2 indicate, between 2006 and 2013 DPS reduced the district's overall suspension rate from 10.58% to 5.63%, as well as the suspension rates for each subgroup. Although racial disparities in the district still must be addressed, suspension rates for African Americans fell 7.2 percentage points during this period, the largest reduction in absolute terms, which contributed to the narrowing of the racial discipline gap depicted most clearly in Figure 10.2. Most notable is that the African American/White gap decreased by almost 4 percentage points, from nearly a 12-point gap in 2006 to just over an 8-point gap in 2013. Both Latinos and Whites saw reductions in their rates, whereas the Latino/White gap also decreased.

The impact of restorative justice was especially significant at some schools. At CASA, suspension rates for all African American students decreased 14 points, from 16.89% in 2011–2012 to 2.86% in 2012–2013, after schoolwide implementation of restorative practices. At Abraham Lincoln High School (ALHS), the suspension rate for African American male students in 2006–2007 was 24.4%; by 2009–2010 it had decreased 18 points, to 6.25%. The use of restorative practices also affected the suspension rates for Latino male students at ALHS, which decreased over 5 points during those years, from 11.67% to 6.38%. At NHS, the overall suspension rate, which was 14.12% in 2006, fell over 8 points by 2012–2103, to 5.91%. The suspension rate for African American male students at NHS fell almost 15 points during the same period, from 19.35% to 4.55%.

Table 10.1. Total Suspensions, Enrollment, and Suspension Rates by Race (2006–2013)

Year	Total Unduplicated Suspensions	Enrollment	DPS Suspension Rate	African American Suspension Rate	Latino Suspension Rate	White Suspension Rate
2006–2007	7,090	66,960	10.58%	17.61%	10.18%	5.88%
2007–2008	6,739	67,324	10%	16.46%	10.16%	4.62%
2008–2009	6,432	72,005	8.93%	14.79%	8.81%	3.78%
2009–2010	5,944	76,090	7.81%	15.20%	8.68%	2.94%
2010–2011	5,969	78,354	7.62%	14.90%	7.35%	2.95%
2011–2012	5,515	81,392	6.78%	12.70%	5.90%	2.83%
2012–2013	4,751	84,424	5.63%	10.42%	4.74%	2.28%

Figure 10.1.Suspension Rates by Race (2006–2013)

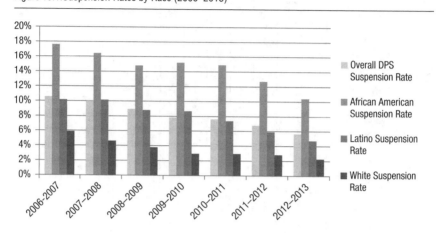

Figure 10.2.Racial Gap in Suspension Rates (2006–2013)

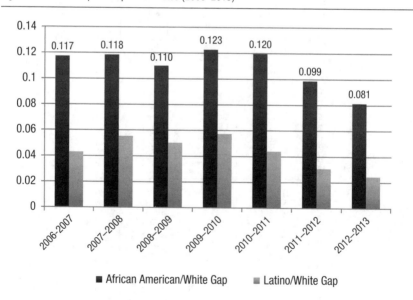

THE IMPLEMENTATION OF RESTORATIVE JUSTICE
IN DENVER'S PUBLIC SCHOOLS

The implementation of restorative practices in DPS began as an intervention response to the rapid rise in suspensions and expulsions; from 2001 to 2005, the number of out-of-school suspensions (OSS) rose from 9,846 to 13,487. Implementation of restorative practices began in 2003 with a single-year pilot project at Cole Middle School (CMS). In 2006, DPS embarked on a multischool project, targeting schools with the highest rates of racial disproportionality in discipline. In late 2007, DPS established district-level processes to support practices developed at the early school sites to facilitate more effective implementation in additional schools. In 2009, DPS reoriented restorative justice from a model of intervention to one of prevention. DPS now regards restorative justice as a districtwide practice that promotes positive change in the school culture at all levels.

Since 2006, DPS has adopted both bottom-up and top-down strategies that provide key models for urban school policymakers. At the district level, restorative justice has benefited from having continued central office support. At the individual school level, restorative justice has benefited from having dedicated principals, deans, school resource officers, teachers, and parents who are committed to alternative responses to misbehavior and conflict. Furthermore, the implementation of restorative justice in Denver could not have occurred without a sustained partnership with the community-based organization, Padres y Jóvenes Unidos. Padres y Jóvenes Unidos's campaigns for racial justice and educational equity have created accountability for DPS (González, 2011). Further, Padres y Jóvenes Unidos has provided significant input into the development of effective and culturally responsive discipline models.

After 10 years of employing restorative approaches and practices, the key lesson DPS learned is that districts must approach implementation through a model that can be adapted to individual communities and contexts. As the DPS experience illustrates, restorative justice is not a "one-size-fits-all" process and thus should be implemented as part of a comprehensive multilevel response to behavior problems and conflict. As the data suggest, by adopting a continuum model, DPS was able to reduce racial disparities in school discipline every year for each racial group, even in the earliest stages of implementation. Moreover, schools using restorative justice practices often saw a positive impact on school safety. For example, from 2006 to 2008, NHS averaged more than 50 fights per year; by 2010 that number had declined to 10 or 12. Other schools, as discussed below, experienced significant academic gains as they implemented restorative practices.

2003–2004: Cole Middle School Restorative Justice Pilot

In spring 2003, DPS adopted a 1-year pilot project at Cole Middle School. The CMS pilot was a community-based restorative justice initiative implemented by VORP of Metro Denver and funded by the Office of Juvenile Justice and Delinquency Prevention. The selection of the school was simple: CMS was notorious for having the largest number of suspensions, tickets, and arrests in the district. As a VORP of Metro Denver community organizer noted, "[Cole] was stereotyped as a 'gang factory' where teachers would see students fighting in the hall and close their door instead of intervening."

Models of practice at CMS included both victim offender mediation and large group circles. Victim offender mediation required responsible and affected parties to sit together and work through an issue to repair the negative effects of a behavior, hold the responsible party accountable, and empower victims to advocate for their needs. Large group circles at CMS were used to address the concerns of several conflicting parties or situations in which many individuals and parties shared responsibility.

Data reported by VORP of Metro Denver indicate that, in spring 2003, 11 of 14 cases of fighting were referred to restorative intervention, and restorative agreements were reached in each instance. Given these successes and the positive impact on school culture, restorative justice was integrated into the CMS discipline protocols in fall 2004 and used as an alternative to suspensions and police citations in specific cases. In December 2004, VORP of Metro Denver reported that 95 students were referred to restorative justice in lieu of suspensions; 84% of these students signed restorative agreements for conflicts ranging from "trash talk" to physical altercations. By the end of the pilot, police citations had declined by 86% and suspensions by over 40%. VORP reported that more than 200 students had been referred to restorative justice and more than 80 agreements were signed and honored. In spring 2004, the school was awarded the DPS Outstanding Safe School Award.

While the CMS project was a 1-year pilot, the results provided DPS administrators in the Office of Prevention and Intervention Initiatives (OPII) the opportunity to seek support from the Colorado Department of Education to begin a multiyear implementation of restorative justice.

2006–2009: Development of Multischool Restorative Practices

In 2006, DPS began whole-school implementation of restorative justice programs at North High School and its three feeder middle schools: Skinner Middle School, Horace Mann Middle School, and Lake Middle School. These schools represented 10% of the DPS secondary school students (2,599). Like CMS, all four schools were identified as high need, as they had some of the district's highest number of suspensions, tickets, and arrests. In 2007, implementation was expanded to include Abraham Lincoln High School, Rishel Middle School, and Kunsmiller Middle School.

Data from each school suggested positive disproportionality outcomes. For example, all four of the initial pilot schools showed a consistent decrease in expulsions, from 23 in 2005–2006 to 6 in 2007–2008 (Baker, 2008). In 2008–2009, 1,235 students were referred to the restorative justice program, and a total of 223 cases were resolved without out-of-school suspension (Baker, 2009). Eleven additional cases resulted in reduced suspension time (Baker, 2009). As Table 12.1 indicates, overall suspensions declined by 5,400 during this period.

During this time, OPII refined the restorative justice models and developed short- and long-term strategies for districtwide implementation. Adopting a new approach to implementation, OPII hired full-time restorative justice coordinators in each new pilot school. Consistent with prior research findings, OPII believed that developing close relationships among the restorative justice coordinator, school resource officer, teachers, and administrators was essential to implementation success. As the qualitative analysis has revealed, this approach was critical to the positive transition from one-dimensional models of practice to a comprehensive continuum model, including formal and informal restorative practices.

Consistent with a continuum approach, models of practice at each school varied. At NHS, for example, restorative dialogues, preventive classroom circles, mediations, conferences, group conferences, and student-led circles were all used in a continuum of practice. ALHS focused on more traditional student mediation to address student conflicts, both before and after incidents. SMS adopted a model similar to NHS but limited the use of restorative practices to certain offenses specifically defined within the discipline matrix. Though each approach varied, all were consistent in adopting a restorative approach and promoting whole-school implementation. Although different practices were implemented, focusing on each school community's unique needs, three core practices emerged: restorative justice dialogues, restorative conferencing, and restorative circles. The use of each restorative practice aligned with the specific issue and its impact on individuals and the school community.

In DPS, a restorative dialogue is a one-on-one conversation between two members of the school community, such as a teacher and a student, guided by restorative justice questions. Such interventions are used when the student behavior correlates with the first step of the discipline ladder. For example, restorative mediations are used when both parties bear equal responsibility for an incident (e.g., a fight). A restorative conference occurs when a third party, such as a restorative justice coordinator, facilitates a conference between two parties. The conference is structured to allow facilitated dialogue, in which the parties take turns answering basic restorative questions until an agreement is reached.

Restorative conferences are similar to dialogues but occur when responsibility for an incident is shared unequally between parties, such as bullying. During a restorative conference, the third-party facilitator works to correct an imbalance of power between the parties and create a structure to protect the victim. Restorative circles, defined as group conferences in other settings, are used for incidents involving multiple parties. Restorative circles are implemented in a similar manner to restorative conferences in that each party takes turns answering basic restorative questions. In contrast to a two-party restorative conference, participants are arranged in nonadversarial positions and answer questions in the order in which they are sitting. In DPS, restorative circles also include members of the school community who were indirectly affected by an incident. Restorative circles are most commonly used in classrooms to support learning outcomes, set boundaries, and develop positive relationships. As such, their use is directly linked to managing curriculum, pedagogy, and behavior. The following narrative captures the transformative nature of restorative practice:

> In 2011, several 9th-grade football players became involved in throwing each other into dumpsters at the end of the day. At some point, they decided to begin to intimidate and grab other students who were not willing participants, and throw them in. These students felt harassed and intimidated by this process. After their parents found out this was happening, they called the school, irate about their children's experience. Instead of responding in a punitive manner, the school discipline team decided to begin with a restorative circle involving all the students. The restorative justice coordinator chose a circle so that a larger community could be involved with the discipline process. The circle included football players who had thrown other students in the dumpster, football players not involved but aware of the actions of their teammates, students who were thrown in the dumpsters, the school dean (disciplinarian), a guidance counselor, the school social worker, the school resource officer, and the principal. During the circle, participants used restorative justice to guide their dialogue. They talked about what happened, how it affected the students who were thrown in the dumpster against their will, the larger school community, their parents, school personnel, and the reputation of the football team. The students and adults worked together to build empathy and understand the full impact of such adolescent behavior. When it came time to address accountability, the football players owned up to what they had done and how it could have been perceived as bullying or harmful to other students. The nonparticipating football players expressed their disappointment in being bystanders and their failure to show leadership in what they knew were poor choices. The school personnel took responsibility for the lack of supervision and their failure to educate the students about the potential dangers of unwanted physical behavior. When asked how to fix the situation, the football players volunteered to miss the homecoming game to demonstrate how seriously they took their behavior. Several also volunteered to speak at a class meeting about their behavior, apologize to the school community, apologize to the individual students, and make it clear that this behavior would not happen again.

This narrative exemplifies the implementation experience in DPS. Although the circle required participants to meet for only about 45 minutes, the impact on the school community lasted beyond 2011. In fact, the school principal noted, "If we had not done restorative justice, there would have been more incidents this year. By making a public commitment to everyone in the circle, these students took it seriously and felt accountable to more than just a small group of adults who punished them." Furthermore, had the school employed a retributive approach to discipline the offending students, who were predominantly Latino and African American male students, they would have faced OSS for 3 to 5 days and potential police citations. Moreover, as qualitative analysis has revealed, these students would have been less likely to accept responsibility for their actions or to engage in activities to promote a safer school community. By using restorative justice, school officials were able to foster the development of healthy, meaningful, and safe peer-to-peer relationships.

In addition to developing sustained restorative practices in the pilot schools, the OPII began to revise the DPS discipline policy to formally incorporate restorative principles into all discipline processes. The OPII recognized that, without a formal districtwide shift from retributive practices, implementing a sustained restorative justice program would be challenging. The process of revising the discipline policy was key to the successful implementation of restorative justice, from the early pilot stages to becoming a normalized disciplinary practice in DPS.

2007–2013: Districtwide Expansion of Restorative Practices and Policies

Several interconnected occurrences supported the eventual transformation of restorative justice in DPS from an isolated program to a districtwide philosophical and values-based approach and practice. These included the 2008 discipline policy reform, the creation of a practitioner-based restorative justice training to support implementation in additional schools, increased community accountability, reorganization of and increased support from the central district office, a districtwide focus on disproportionality and equity, and the 2013 revised Intergovernmental Agreement between the Denver Public Schools and the Denver Police Department. Furthermore, the OPII developed new structures for guaranteeing consistency and transparency in data collection to document student behavior and the restorative practices used.

The 2008 revisions to the DPS discipline policy included several key changes. The policy explicitly sanctioned restorative justice as an intervention strategy focused on the "opportunity to learn from their [students'] mistakes, and re-engage the student in learning." In fact, the policy identifies the use of restorative justice interventions as "problem solving interventions done 'with' the offender, in contrast to different administrative interventions all involving some degree of removal, done 'to' the offender" (Policy JK-R, 2008). Moreover, the policy states that disciplinary practices in DPS will "address the needs of the student who engaged in the misconduct, the needs of those who were affected by the misconduct, and the needs of the overall school community."

The policy locates these restorative justice efforts within the context of addressing disproportionality:

> Efforts shall be made to eliminate any racial disparities in school discipline. Staff members are specifically charged with monitoring the impact of their actions on students from racial and ethnic groups or other protected classes that have historically been over-represented among those students who are suspended, expelled, or referred to law enforcement. (Policy JK-R, 2008)

The policy also states, "schools should minimize the use of out-of-school suspensions, recommendations for expulsion, and referrals to law enforcement, to the extent practicable while remaining consistent with state statute, local ordinances, and mandatory reporting laws." As discussed above, restorative justice practices at NHS were often used in lieu of suspensions or in conjunction with reduced suspension time. Moreover, OSS were limited under the revised policy to be consistent with restorative practice, and if "previous interventions have not been successful, the principal or principal's designee may consider the use of an in-school suspension of 1-3 days or a one-day out-of-school suspension" (Policy JK-R, 2008).

By grounding disciplinary practices within a restorative rather than a retributive framework, schools have been able to impact disproportionality and foster positive school culture more effectively. For example, before the 2008 revisions, OSS was assigned for 3 to 5 days following a severe misbehavior, such as a fight. Under the revised policy, schools opted to assign shorter OSS in conjunction with employing restorative practices when students reentered school. Consider NHS, where the average OSS decreased from 3 days to less than 1 day beginning in 2006. Interviews at NHS revealed that this practice also changed the character of suspension. Under the prior policy, the tone when the student returned to the community was adversarial. By using a more restorative approach, students were prepared on their return to begin a process to resolve the issue at hand.

As the qualitative data reflect, this process ultimately allowed the school to change its culture and its approach to discipline, and to heal staff–student relationships. Administrators, teachers, and students at NHS have all attributed the change in culture to the use of restorative practices to create accountability and promote meaningful relationships. Although quantitative data cannot capture the interpersonal experiences, suspension rates declined at NHS from 14.12% to 5.91% by 2012–2013.

In 2009, DPS also began revising the teacher-evaluation systems, increasing accountability for punitive disciplinary responses, and implementing leadership development. In addition to these internal reforms, the OPII began a comprehensive districtwide training focused on implementation of individualized restorative justice practices under the revised discipline policy. As interviews with teachers revealed, there was a high demand for restorative justice trainings specifically for teachers to promote positive academic experiences and behaviors. The trainings were developed by restorative justice coordinators and emphasized an individualized approach to restorative practices for school communities.

In 2009, additional trainings were offered two to three times a year and were attended by school disciplinarians, administrators, and mental health professionals. By 2011, an average of 500 people, including teachers, parents, and students, attended monthly restorative justice trainings. DPS continues to experiment with best practices and ways to offer this training to deepen and improve restorative justice practices. In 2012–2013, 75% of Denver schools reported having at least one person trained in restorative justice facilitation and that they were using restorative justice practices to address discipline in their school.

In 2011, DPS reorganized the OPII into the Department of Mental Health and Assessment in Student Services. This reorganization led to key changes, which further developed districtwide restorative justice practices. Most important, restorative justice implementation shifted from the intervention and prevention model of individual school practitioner to a team of mental health support specialists engaged in whole-school implementation. The goal of the teams is to create equitable disciplinary outcomes through a range of practices. At the center of all of these practices are restorative principles.

In addition to the internal changes supporting this holistic implementation, in 2013 the Denver Police Department and DPS reached an agreement that clarified the role of school resource officers (Intergovernmental Agreement, 2013). The agreement refines and limits the role of the school resource officers and specifically delineates DPS's commitment to restorative justice rather than punitive discipline. The agreement also establishes increased due process protections for students and parents, requires school resource officers to meet regularly with community groups, and requires school resource officers be trained in restorative justice, child and adolescent development, and conflict de-escalation.

As DPS continues to implement restorative justice in its schools, it is clear that the use of restorative approaches should not be viewed as a "program." Instead, the whole-district implementation reflects a paradigm shift that views restorative justice as another tool to effectively educate students. DPS thus considers conflict or misconduct not as an opportunity to suspend or expel but to teach and learn by promoting connections and positive communities. One NHS teacher's reflection captures this idea:

> When other teachers ask me why I use restorative justice with my students, my answer is simple. It changes how my students learn. . . . It used to be that we would try to push conflict outside the classroom door by suspending or removing a student in some way, but that does not resolve the conflict, it just makes it worse when that same student walks back through your door.

DENVER PUBLIC SCHOOLS AS A MODEL
FOR IMPLEMENTING RESTORATIVE JUSTICE

Many positive outcomes have been realized in Denver, but the implementation of restorative justice in the district is far from over. As it moves forward, the long-term DPS vision focuses not only on sustainability but on striving for greater equity in its educational and disciplinary practices, and on developing deeper relationships within the community. In this context, DPS is committed to continued collaboration with diverse stakeholders to develop effective top-down and bottom-up strategies to address racial disproportionality, build social capital, promote school engagement, and improve academic performance.

The experience in Denver provides valuable insights for policymakers seeking to implement restorative justice as an alternative to racially disproportionate disciplinary practices. Schools seeking to address disproportionality in discipline through restorative justice should envision a 4- to 6-year implementation plan that focuses on six key areas: (1) establishing specific reasons for implementation and buy-in from key members of the school community; (2) developing a clear institutional vision with short-, medium-, and long-term goals; (3) creating a responsive, effective, and adaptive practice; (4) adopting a districtwide disciplinary policy and discipline practices that integrate restorative justice; (5) developing school-based discipline practices that promote a whole-school approach rather than a program-based model; and (6) investing in a continuous system of growth and professional development for all members of the school community.

Finally, it should be noted that between 2009 and 2013 DPS showed a steady and substantial increase in the percentage of students scoring proficient or above on statewide tests in reading, writing, and math in all grades tested (3–10), with the exception of grade-8 reading. In 2013, the district made overall gains from 2009 of 4 percentage points in reading, 7 points in math, 6 points in writing, and 9 points in science. Furthermore, the average ACT scores in DPS increased from 15.4 to 17.6. On-time graduation rates also increased, from 46.4% (2009) to 51.8% (2010). During the same time, high school dropout rates decreased from 11.1% (2006) to 6.4% (2010). This trend is consistent with other studies showing that, after controlling for poverty and other factors, lower suspending districts had higher test scores. There is no question that, during a period of significantly reducing the use of suspension in DPS, gains were made in academic achievement in all subjects in nearly every grade. These gains might be merely coincidental or the result of changes in other policies, but this academic growth should allay fears that reducing suspensions will create a chaotic and less productive learning environment. Although this study of DPS did not put the hypothesis to the test, it seems plausible that by reducing the discipline gap Denver also reduced the achievement gap.

NOTES

The author would like to recognize Benjamin Cairns for his substantial contributions and collaboration on this project since 2009. Without his commitment to the research, capturing the diverse experiences in Denver would not have been possible.

1. Prior research on restorative practices in DPS provides a more detailed description of the continuum model (González, 2011, 2012).

REFERENCES

Baker, M. L. (2008, August 31). *DPS restorative justice project executive summary 2007–2008.* Denver, CO: Denver Public Schools.

Baker, M. L. (2009, September 16). *DPS Restorative Justice Project: Year Three. Year end report 2008–2009.* Denver, CO: Denver Public Schools.

Denver Public Schools. (2008, August 21). *Policy JK-R—student conduct and discipline procedures.* Retrieved from http://ed.dpsk12.org:8080/policy/FMPro?-db=policy.fp3&-format=detail. html&-lay=policyview&File=JK&-recid=32967&-find=

Denver Public Schools & Denver Police Department. (2013). *Intergovernmental agreement concerning the funding, implementation, and administration of programs involving police officers in schools.* Retrieved from http://b.3cdn.net/advancement/e746ea2668c2ed19b3_urm6iv28k.pdf

González, T. (2011). Restoring justice: Community organizing to transform school discipline policies. *U.C. Davis Journal of Law and Policy 15*, 1–36.

González, T. (2012). Keeping kids in schools: Restorative justice, punitive discipline, and the school to prison pipeline. *Journal of Law and Education 41*, 281–335.

Gregory, A., Cornell, D., & Fan, X. (2011). The relationship of school structure and support to suspension rates for black and white high school students. *American Educational Research Journal, 48*, 904–934.

Macready, T. (2009). Learning social responsibility in schools: A restorative practice. *Educational Psychology in Practice, 25*, 211–220.

Morrison, B. E. (2003). Regulating safe school communities: Being responsive and restorative. *Journal of Educational Administration, 41*(6), 690–704.

Morrison, B. E. (2007). *Restoring safe school communities.* Sydney, Australia: Federation.

Morrison, B. E., Blood, P., & Thorsborne, M. (2005). Practicing restorative justice in school communities: The challenge of culture change. *Public Organization Review, 5*, 335–357.

Skiba, R. J., Horner, R. H., Chung, C.-G., Rausch, M. K., May, S. L., & Tobin, T. (2011). Race is not neutral: A national investigation of African American and Latino disproportionality in school discipline. *School Psychology Review, 40*(1), 85–107.

Wachtel, T. (2001). Restorative justice in everyday life: Beyond the formal ritual. *Reclaiming Children and Youth: The Journal of Strength-Based Interventions, 12*(2), 83–87.

Zehr, H. (2003). *The little book of restorative justice.* Intercourse, PA: Good Books.

## CHAPTER 11

The Promise of a Teacher Professional Development Program in Reducing Racial Disparity in Classroom Exclusionary Discipline

Anne Gregory, Joseph P. Allen, Amori Yee Mikami,
Christopher A. Hafen, and Robert C. Pianta

Racial disparities in school discipline and student achievement are interconnected. Teachers need support in their efforts to raise the achievement level of historically underperforming student groups and to reduce the likelihood that they will exclude such students from classroom instruction for disciplinary reasons. This kind of support can be provided effectively through professional development programs. In this chapter we provide an empirical examination of a teacher professional development program that has been shown to improve student achievement. We present the first study of the program's effect on lowering the use of exclusionary discipline for all students, and especially for African American students—a group that research by Skiba et al. (Chapter 9) and Finn and Servoss (Chapter 3) shows are the most likely racial group to be excluded from class for subjective and minor offenses such as disruption and disobedience (Gregory & Weinstein, 2008).

The My Teaching Partner (MTP) professional development program has a comprehensive focus on improving how teachers and students interact by enhancing emotional, organizational, and instructional supports—three domains of support that are closely tied to student engagement in classroom activities. A fundamental premise of the program is that improving teacher–student interactions and increasing student engagement can produce a range of positive student outcomes. It should be noted that the program is not focused primarily on reducing suspensions.

Research has shown that engaging and motivating teachers can prevent students from disrupting class in the first place. When students do act up, these teachers are able to diffuse disruptive and disobedient behavior quickly, without relying on an office discipline referral that excludes a student from the classroom. Engaging, motivating teachers also foster students' academic progress by providing dynamic instruction, a well-organized flow of activities, and attention to individual students' needs. This might be especially beneficial for African American students, who historically have had less access to high-quality learning environments than other racial groups.

The MTP coaching model for training teachers uses the Classroom Assessment Scoring System (CLASS) to foster teacher reflection and improvement in the domains of emotional support, classroom organization, and instructional support. The coaching was originally developed for prekindergarten and early elementary classrooms and has been shown to be effective (Pianta, 2011; Pianta et al., 2003; Pianta, Mashburn, Downer, Hamre, & Justice, 2008). The secondary school model (MTP-S), which was developed for training middle and high school teachers, is the focus of the analysis in this chapter.

For training secondary teachers, coaches use the CLASS to provide teachers with regular and rigorous feedback about their behavior in the classroom and their interactions with students. Despite the model's record of success in improving student performance on academic tests (Allen, Pianta, Gregory, Mikami, & Lun, 2011), this study is the first to test whether this intensive training program reduces teachers' reliance on exclusionary disciplinary approaches in the course of fostering more productive learning environments.

THE SUSTAINED, FOCUSED, AND RIGOROUS APPROACH OF MY TEACHING PARTNER–SECONDARY

Efforts to build teacher capacity usually take the form of single-session professional development workshops. These workshops generally have little follow-up (Darling-Hammond, Chung Wei, Andree, Richardson, & Orphanos, 2009; Klingner, 2004), although the evidence suggests that the single-session approach does not produce changes in teacher practice (Darling-Hammond et al., 2009). Policymakers and educators have called for more sustained programs that are integrated into school hours (Darling-Hammond et al., 2009; Pianta, 2011).

The My Teaching Partner model is one such sustained approach. Central to this training program is a focused and rigorous process in which teachers and their assigned coaches reflect on video recordings of the teacher's instruction using the CLASS throughout the school year. Each video leads to a multistep coaching cycle in which the coach examines the video and isolates examples of teacher behavior that falls within three overarching domains: emotional support, classroom organization, and instructional support (Pianta & Hamre, 2009; Pianta, Hamre, Hayes, Mintz, & LaParo, 2007). Within the three domains are 10 observable dimensions (e.g., positive climate, negative climate, teacher sensitivity). The aim of this training program is to improve teacher–student interactions by altering teachers' behavior in each of these dimensions. Table 11.1 describes each dimension in the version used for training middle and high school teachers (Allen et al., 2013).

In each coaching cycle, the MTP coaches use video clips to direct the teachers' attention to moments in the classroom when they had high-quality interactions with students, as well as to behaviors that could be altered in their future instruction to improve one of the dimensions. The teachers then view the clips and answer written prompts to help in their observation of how their interactions did or did not align with the dimensions. The coaches communicate with the teachers one on one via phone or computer to discuss their feedback and observations. Together they develop individual action plans to build on teachers' strengths and address challenges. They identify strategies for implementing new behaviors that target a particular dimension in their future instruction.

Table 11.1. Theoretical Model of the Classroom Assessment Scoring System-Secondary (CLASS-S)

Domain	Dimensions	Description
Emotional Support	Positive climate	The emotional tone of the classroom (e.g., warmth and connection among teachers and students)
	Teacher sensitivity	The teacher's responsiveness to academic and social/emotional needs of students
	Regard for adolescent perspectives	The extent to which the teacher offers leadership, autonomy, and content relevance to students
Classroom Organization	Behavior management	Teacher's use of effective methods to encourage desirable behavior and redirect misbehavior
	Productivity	The teacher's management of time to maximize instruction
	Negative climate	The level of expressed negativity (e.g., irritability, frustration, anger)
Instructional Support	Instructional learning formats	The teacher's provision of interesting, varied lessons, and materials
	Content understanding	The depth of lesson content and integration of facts, skills, concepts, and principles
	Analysis and inquiry	The degree to which the teacher facilitates higher level thinking skills, problem solving, and metacognition
	Quality of feedback	The provision of feedback that expands or extends learning and understanding

One recent randomized controlled trial with 78 middle and high school teachers and over 1,400 of their students (22% of whom were African Americans) showed that teachers who were coached and trained using the MTP-S program (MTP-S teachers) made improvements over control teachers who received no coaching or training. Improvements were made in the dimensions of positive classroom climate, teacher sensitivity, teacher regard for adolescent perspectives, instructional learning formats, and analysis and inquiry (Allen et al., 2011). Outside observers found that MTP-S teachers' patterns of relating with students were characterized by warmth and responsiveness to students' academic, social, and emotional needs. They engaged their students in a developmentally appropriate way that allowed for student leadership, autonomy, and collaboration with peers. They facilitated student engagement using novel materials and a variety of teaching strategies and activities. Finally, they pushed students to engage in higher-order thinking and problem solving with appropriately challenging material.

The randomized controlled trial of the MTP-S training program also demonstrated positive changes in students. After 1 year of the program, the students of MTP-S trained teachers had higher scores on the end-of-course standardized state exam than the students in the nontrained (control) teachers' classrooms (Allen et al., 2011). The higher scores equate an average increase in student achievement from the 50th to the 59th percentile. The MTP-S training was also associated with increases in observed student engagement (Gregory, Allen, Mikami, Hafen, & Pianta, 2013) and positive peer interactions (Mikami, Gregory, Allen, Pianta, & Lun, 2011). Findings in the three outcome studies held for all teachers in the intervention, no matter the racial composition of the classroom, the percentage of classroom students who qualified for free or reduced-priced meals (a proxy for low-income status), or the number of low-achieving students in the classroom at the start of the year. Given that the findings held across these different classrooms with a diverse group of students, MTP-S appears to have universal benefits for students' achievement, engagement, and prosocial peer relations.

IMPROVING TEACHER–STUDENT INTERACTIONS TO LEVERAGE CHANGE IN DISCIPLINE PRACTICES

Many teachers rely on exclusionary discipline when they react to perceived student misbehavior. This is particularly pronounced with African American students (Gregory & Thompson, 2010). Exclusionary discipline occurs when teachers issue discipline referrals and send students to the administration office for perceived misbehavior. Administrators will typically assign a punishment, usually in the form of suspension (in school or out of school), which results in the student missing instructional time (Skiba, Michael, Nardo, & Peterson, 2002). Lost instruction time can accrue, making it harder for students to keep up with their peers in coursework (Scott & Barrett, 2004). Moreover, excluding a student from class can initiate a harmful and escalating negative pattern of student–adult interaction and contribute to students' psychological disengagement from schooling, which often culminates in their dropping out of school altogether (see Chapters 1 and 4). The frequency with which teachers use exclusionary discipline is not trivial (see Chapters 3 and 13). One study showed that teachers in a school with 3,000 enrolled students excluded students from the classroom for perceived misbehavior more than 2,000 times in a single semester. Noteworthy is the fact that 70% of the exclusionary discipline was applied to African American students, who comprised 38% of the student body (Gregory, Nygreen, & Moran, 2006). The overrepresentation of African American students in classroom exclusion directly feeds into the better known and well-documented disparities in out-of-school suspensions (Skiba et al., 2002).

There are strong theoretical reasons to believe that if training programs could effectively improve how teachers interact with adolescents by providing enhanced emotional, organizational, and instructional supports, they would reduce teachers' reliance on exclusionary discipline. The benefits of improved teacher–student interactions might be particularly important for teachers and their African American students, given the clear indications that their classroom interactions with one another need to be improved (see Chapter 7).

To be more specific, African American students tend to receive less support and more unfair treatment from their teachers than do White students (Sheets, 1996; Meehan, Hughes, & Cavell, 2003). Many teachers view African American students as more defiant and disruptive and may tend to apply harsher disciplinary consequences to their perceived misbehavior (e.g., Bradshaw, Mitchell, O'Brennan, & Leaf, 2010). A program that specifically aims to improve interactions might reduce the likelihood that mutually held negative perceptions and serious conflicts between teachers and students would lead to students' exclusion from class and possible suspension. In other words, if teachers and students have stronger relationships and more engaging instruction, negative interactions might be prevented in the first place (see Chapter 8). When a student breaks classroom rules, stronger relationships could increase the likelihood that disputants give each other the benefit of the doubt and disrupt any preconceived notions or unconsciously held stereotypes (see Chapter 10). With trust and good will between teachers and students, conflict could be diffused and cooperation enhanced (Gregory & Ripski, 2008).

OVERVIEW OF THE RESEARCH

For the current study, teachers and students participated in a randomized controlled trial to rigorously examine the effects of MTP-S on student discipline. Below, we describe participants, measures, and the data analytic plan. Then, we report the descriptive and statistical results of the analyses.

Participating Students and Teachers. Teacher participants in this study came from five middle and high schools in a midsized city in the southeastern region of the United States. The schools' percentages of low-income students ranged from 20% to 40%, as measured by those who qualified for free and reduced-priced meals. The schools' African American student enrollment ranged from 40% to 79% of the student body.

In August 2010, 95 teachers from the five schools were randomly assigned to either the control condition or the MTP-S program for 2 years of coaching. Program teachers received a 1-day introductory workshop, followed by coaching cycles every 2 weeks, all of which targeted a focal classroom for each teacher—as a rule, the lowest-level course they taught for which standardized tests were given. Control teachers were given only "business as usual" inservice training, and their lowest-level courses also were the target of the data collection. The 979 participating students were racially and ethnically diverse: 59% African American, 30% White, 8% Hispanic, and 3% Asian.

Thirty-nine teachers were in the program condition and 43 in the control condition ($N = 82$). The teachers in each group had the same average age and years of experience, and the two groups were nearly identical in terms of racial and gender composition. Classroom composition was similar for both groups as well, comprised on average of two thirds African American students and one third low-income students. In sum, there were no statistically significant differences between the control and intervention groups.

Measures of Teacher Characteristics. Teachers completed surveys about their own characteristics and the characteristics of their focal classroom. The analyses controlled for these characteristics, called teacher covariates, which included teacher gender, race, years of teaching experience, and course subject area. By so doing, we learned whether the MTP-S training had an effect on exclusionary discipline above and beyond what might be attributed to these covariates.

We also wanted to ascertain whether the effect MTP-S had on exclusionary discipline held for teachers regardless of their course subject area. If it did, it would corroborate previous findings showing that MTP-S benefitted student achievement regardless of the classroom subject area (Allen et al., 2011). For analytic purposes, we grouped teachers into two areas—math/science (45%) and English/humanities (55%). The duration of the teachers' focal classroom varied from a semester to a full school year, which we accounted for in our analyses.[1] Finally, we included the percentage of African American students in the classroom as a covariate in all analyses. This was based on the finding that racial composition has been linked to suspension rates. Specifically, some studies suggest that the racial gap in suspensions is higher in schools that have higher percentages of African American students (see Gregory, Cornell, & Fan, 2011; also see Chapter 9 of this book).

Measures of Student Characteristics. Controlling for a wide array of student characteristics allowed us to identify whether the training program had an impact on teachers' use of exclusionary discipline with African American students as compared to other students. The study specifically controlled for the known risk factors for students' receiving such discipline, including a student being male, low achieving, and low income (e.g., Wallace, Goodkind, Wallace, & Bachman, 2008).[2] We also included students' prior performance on the Standards of Learning, which are end-of-course exams in a subject similar to the MTP-S teachers' subjects (e.g., math, science, English).[3]

Measure of School Disciplline. We obtained school records for the participating students who received exclusionary discipline in the focal classrooms during the year of the study. This meant that a student had received an office discipline referral for perceived misbehavior from the project teacher's classroom. Teachers applied exclusionary discipline mostly for reasons related to disrespect, disruption, and fighting or bullying. When a teacher applies such discipline, the student typically leaves the classroom and meets with an administrator who determines the punishment (e.g., suspension).

Data Analytic Plan. Using data from the first year of MTP-S coaching, we applied well-established statistical techniques to increase the rigor of the findings (see online conference paper for methodological details, http://tinyurl.com/JanCRPconference). Our analyses took into account the aforementioned student and teacher characteristics. Results from the statistical models answered (a) whether an African American student was more likely than a non–African American student to be given exclusionary discipline in the program teachers' classrooms or in the control teachers' classrooms, and (b) whether the program teachers tended to use less exclusionary discipline with all students than the control teachers.

It is important to note that we decided to compare the application of exclusionary discipline to African American students to that of all other students, which included White, Hispanic, and Asian students. This decision was based on the small percentage of Hispanics (8%) and Asians (3%) in the sample. That said, we reran analyses comparing only African American and White students, and the magnitude of the effects was similar to the results presented. In addition, some teachers in both the intervention and the control conditions had very few students participating. Thus, whether these teachers referred their one or two participating students might not reflect their larger referral pattern with the numerous other students in their focal classroom (see online conference paper for a discussion of methodological limitations, http://tinyurl.com/JanCRPconference). That said, when we excluded the teachers with low numbers, our findings were similar. Moreover, detecting the effects of MTP-S on exclusionary discipline with such a small sample was remarkable, and it offers hope that it would hold up in future replications with larger samples.

MY TEACHING PARTNER–SECONDARY EFFECTS ON EXCLUSIONARY DISCIPLINE

On average, 13.7% of participating African American students and 5.1% of all other participating students in the control teachers' classrooms received at least one exclusionary discipline referral—a difference of nearly 9 percentage points. In the program teachers' classrooms, 6% of participating African American students and 5.8% of all other participating students received at least one exclusionary discipline referral—just 2/10ths of a percentage point, not a significant difference. Equally important is that the referral rate for African American students in the control group was nearly 8 points higher than the rate for African American students in the intervention group. There was only a minimal difference—less than 1 percentage point—between the non–African American students in the control group and their counterparts in the intervention group.

PROGRAM EFFECTS ACCOUNTING FOR CLASSROOM, TEACHER, AND STUDENT CHARACTERISTICS

Statistical models showed that the program effects took a positive direction among all student groups (the African American students and non–African American students) when accounting for a range of classroom, teacher, and student characteristics (see Table 11.2; for more detail, see online conference paper, http://tinyurl.com/JanCRPconference). In other words, the effects taking a positive direction suggested that no group in the intervention classrooms was worse off in terms of receiving exclusionary discipline, as shown in Figure 11.1. That said, when other factors were taken into account in the statistical analyses, the program had the strongest beneficial effects for African American students. The probability of disciplinary exclusion was slightly lower for non–African students in the intervention group, although not statistically significantly lower than the control group.

African American students had a similar probability of receiving exclusionary discipline as their fellow students in the intervention classrooms. In contrast, the gap between African American and other students persisted in the control classrooms; for example, African American students were more than twice as likely as other students to receive exclusionary discipline. It is important to note that the statistical models isolated the effects of the program on student race, given the model's rigorous controls. This means African American students who had equivalent achievement, income, and gender in an intervention classroom had a lower probability of experiencing exclusionary discipline than in the control classroom.

Table 11.2. Relation of the My Teaching Partner Program to African American Student Discipline Rates

	b	CI	OR[c]
Main Effects[a]			
Teacher race (0–AA[d], 1–Not AA)	−.09	[−.25, .03]	0.97
Years teaching	.02	[−.12, .13]	1.0
Subject (math/science–0, English/humanities–1)	.09	[−.09, .24]	1.04
Teacher scheduling (0–block, 1–traditional)	.16*	[.02, .29]	1.56
Percentage of AA students in classroom	.11	[−.03, .26]	1.06
Student gender (0–female, 1–male)	.18*	[.04, .33]	1.59
Student prior achievement	−.11	[−.26, .04]	0.96
Student free or reduced-rate lunch (0–not qualify, 1–qualify)	.08	[−.07, .32]	1.02
Student race (0–not AA, 1–AA)	.32**	[.10, .32]	2.07**
MTP intervention group (0–control, 1–intervention)	−.28**	[−.47, −.24]	0.51**
Interactions			
Student race x MTP intervention group[e]	−.16*	[−.30, −.02]	

Notes: a. Student outcome = exclusionary discipline by teacher (0 = no referral; 1 = 1 or more exclusionary discipline referrals); b. The estimates are for predictors when they were entered as a block; c. OR = odds ratio; d. AA = African American; e. The estimate is a cross-level interaction term in Hierarchical General Linear Modeling, which accounts for nested data with dichotomous outcomes. Table 11.2 displays the Hierarchical General Linear Modeling estimates for predictors when they were entered as a block. If the estimate for a predictor is statistically different from 1.00, then the 95% Confidence Interval (CI) does not contain 1.00. We also calculated odds ratios using the exponentiated logistic regression coefficients. To interpret the odds ratio, if the estimate is larger (or smaller) than 1.00, it depicts the increase (or decrease) in the chance of receiving exclusionary discipline for a unit increase (or decrease) on the scale of the predictor. For example, an estimate of 2.0 means that, for each unit increase in the predictor, the risk of exclusionary discipline doubles.

Figure 11.1. Intervention Group and Likelihood of Exclusionary Discipline as a Function of Student Race (AA = African American)

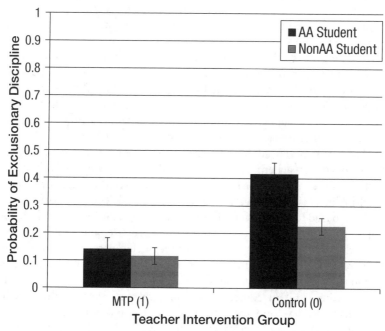

IMPLICATIONS OF PROGRAM EFFECTS FOR SCHOOL DISCIPLINE

This is one of the few randomized controlled studies to demonstrate a teacher professional development program's promise in reducing the racial discipline gap. We have confidence in this finding because (a) we used an experimental design and assigned teachers randomly to either the intervention or the control condition, and (b) the two teacher groups were comparable at the start of the intervention. The research-based MTP-S approach also is known to improve instruction and has no anticipated negative consequences. Although the findings should be replicated with larger samples before this particular training program can be regarded as "proven effective," the policy implications of these promising findings should not be ignored. Current disciplinary approaches in school—namely, the widespread use of suspension as a punishment—are largely ineffective (American Psychological Association Task Force, 2008), and alternatives should be explored. Thus the MTP research–based approach is a highly promising practice for reducing racial disparities with known benefits for improving instruction and no anticipated negative consequences. Interventions that work directly with teachers on strengthening teacher–student interactions through enhanced emotional, organizational, and instructional supports using a video-recorded coaching model might have the power to shift the longstanding racial disparity in the use of exclusionary discipline.

The MTP program is driven by theory and research that can help explain why the evaluation showed reductions in teachers' use of exclusionary discipline. Multiple studies have reported associations between students' sense of social connection and outcomes ranging from higher achievement scores to greater student engagement to more positive academic attitudes (e.g., for a review see National Research Council, 2004; also see Chapters 7 and 8 of this book). Moreover, at-risk adolescents report that having a close and supportive relationship with a teacher is key in distinguishing those who succeed in school from those who do not (Resnick et al., 1997). When relationships function well, the resulting increase in motivation to comply with basic school norms also appears likely to lead to a reduction in problematic behavior (Bryant, Schulenberg, Bachman, O'Malley, & Johnston, 2000). Pianta, Hamre, and Stuhlman (2002) conclude that, for adolescents, the dimensions of closeness, connection, and affiliation are critical features of classroom interactions. Moreover, when teachers are trained through MTP-S to better integrate opportunities for higher-level problem solving, student choice, leadership, and peer sharing, their students are more likely to develop trust with them and feel more motivated to engage in the material. This would increase the positive interactions between African American students and their teachers and prevent negative interactions that could culminate in exclusionary discipline.

Like MTP, training that attempts to increase teachers' skill in attending to students' social and emotional cues and needs might also help teachers individuate their students and disrupt explicit stereotyping or implicit bias. Sociopsychological research has shown that implicit negative attitudes can be triggered by racial stimuli, such as images of darker skinned faces, which might lead teachers to make more punitive decisions (Graham & Lowery, 2004). A recent meta-analysis showed that implicit bias predicts behavior, particularly behavior characterized by the differential treatment of dissimilar individuals (Greenwald, Poehlman, Uhlmann, & Banaji, 2009). By individuating and personalizing relationships with African American students, this program could disrupt unconscious attitudes that affect disciplinary decisionmaking. In the classroom, highly sensitive teachers might have greater contextual understanding when they "read" students' behavior or attempt to diffuse uncooperative behavior. Research and theory support this line of reasoning. A recent intervention with undergraduate students suggested that individuation is one of a menu of successful cognitive strategies to reduce implicit bias (Devine, Forscher, Austin, & Cox, 2012). Teachers getting to know their students authentically also has been identified as a way to strengthen trust with students of color (Aronson, 2008).

SUMMARY AND RECOMMENDATIONS FOR POLICY AND PRACTICE

Public education reformers seek recommendations for changes to education policy that are backed by strong empirical evidence of improved outcomes for students. Most consider a randomized controlled trial to meet the "gold standard" of rigorous evidence. We found that teachers receiving training used less exclusionary discipline with their students than teachers not in the program. We also found that the training significantly reduced exclusionary discipline more for African American students than for others. These findings have important relevance to policymakers seeking evidence for interventions that have the potential to close the school discipline gap, even though researchers agree that these findings will be much stronger and persuasive if they are corroborated by future research conducted in other districts. The program might have changed how African American adolescents and adults interacted in specific classrooms, which ultimately reduced the likelihood of African American students being negatively perceived as disruptive or defiant and disproportionately issued exclusionary discipline.

Policymakers need guidance in determining the types of teacher training programs that are worthy of investment. MTP-S provides one choice, but others that are successful at improving student engagement and student–teacher relationships might also be effective. This suggests that policymakers and administrators must carefully scrutinize teacher support programs to ensure they include a sustained, focused, rigorous, and comprehensive approach. Moreover, they need to identify programs that have a high yield for the investment. Our findings suggest that programs such as MTP-S can effect change in a range of student outcomes. The empirically supported impact of MTP-S includes improved interactions among peers, improved student engagement with academic tasks, and improved performance on standardized achievement tests. With another positive outcome added to the list—teachers' reduced use of exclusionary discipline—policymakers can see that sustained teacher training programs that help close the school discipline gap are not only real and viable but also can contribute to improved academic outcomes.

NOTES

1. Fifteen percent of teachers instructed students for long class periods each semester and changed students at midyear ("block" teachers.) In contrast, a majority of teachers (85%) taught the same students for shorter class periods over the whole school year ("traditional" teachers).

2. Student eligibility for free and reduced-priced meals was used as a proxy for family low-income status. The meal program is offered to families with incomes up to 185% of the federal poverty line, and eligibility is used in research to reflect students' low-income status (Harwell & LeBeau, 2010).

3. The Commonwealth of Virginia Standards of Learning standardized testing system has demonstrated good reliability and validity (Hambleton et al., 2000).

REFERENCES

American Psychological Association Task Force. (2008). Are zero tolerance policies effective in schools? An evidentiary review and recommendations. *American Psychologist, 63,* 852–863.

Allen, J. P., Gregory, A., Mikami, A. Y., Lun, J. Hamre, B., & Pianta, R. C. (2013). Observations of effective teacher–student interactions in secondary school classrooms: Predicting student achievement with the Classroom Assessment Scoring System Secondary. *School Psychology Review, 42,* 76–98.

Allen, J. P., Pianta, R. C., Gregory, A., Mikami, A.Y., & Lun, J. (2011). An interaction-based approach to enhancing secondary school instruction and student achievement. *Science, 333,* 1034–1037.

Aronson, J. (2008). Getting to know students as individuals. In M. Pollock (Ed.), *Everyday antiracism: Getting real about race in school* (pp. 67–69). New York, NY: The New Press.

Bradshaw, C. P., Mitchell, M. M., O'Brennan, L. M., & Leaf, P. J. (2010). Multilevel explorations of factors contributing to the overrepresentation of Black students in office discipline referrals. *Journal of Educational Psychology, 102,* 508–520.

Bryant, A. L., Schulenberg, J., Bachman, J. G., O'Malley, P. M., & Johnston, L. D. (2000). Understanding the links among school misbehavior, academic achievement, and cigarette use: A national panel study of adolescents. *Prevention Science, 1*(2), 71.

Darling-Hammond, L., Chung Wei, R., Andree, A., Richardson, N., & Orphanos, S. (2009). *Professional learning in the learning profession: A status report on teacher development in the United States and Abroad.* Dallas, TX: National Staff Development Council. Retrieved from www.nsdc.org

Devine, P. G., Forscher, P. S., Austin, A. J., & Cox, W. T. L. (2012). Long-term reduction in implicit race bias: A prejudice habit-breaking intervention. *Journal of Experimental Social Psychology, 48,* 1–12.

Graham, S., & Lowery, B. S. (2004). Priming unconscious racial stereotypes about adolescent offenders. *Law and Human Behavior, 28,* 483–504.

Greenwald, A. G., Poehlman, T. A., Uhlmann, E. L., & Banaji, M. R. (2009). Understanding and using the Implicit Association Test: III. Meta-analysis of predictive validity. *Journal of Personality and Social Psychology, 97,* 17–41.

Gregory, A., Allen, J. Mikami, A. Hafen, C. & Pianta. R. (2013). Effects of a professional development program on behavioral engagement of students in middle and high school. *Psychology in the Schools, 51,* 143–163.

Gregory, A., Cornell, D., & Fan, X. (2011). The relationship of school structure and support to suspension rates for Black and White high school students. *American Educational Research Journal, 48,* 904–934.

Gregory, A., Nygreen, K., & Moran, D. (2006). The discipline gap and the normalization of failure. In P. Noguera & J. Wing (Eds.), *Unfinished business: Closing the racial achievement gap in our schools* (pp. 121–150). San Francisco, CA: Jossey-Bass.

Gregory, A., & Ripski, M. (2008). Adolescent trust in teachers: Implications for behavior in the high school classroom. *School Psychology Review, 37,* 337–353. Retrieved from http://www.nasponline.org/publications/spr/abstract.aspx?ID=1959

Gregory, A., & Thompson, A. (2010). African American high school students and variability in behavior across classrooms. *Journal of Community Psychology, 38,* 386–402.

Gregory, A. & Weinstein, S. R. (2008). The discipline gap and African Americans: Defiance or cooperation in the high school classroom. *Journal of School Psychology, 46,* 455–475.

Hambleton, R. K., Crocker, L., Cruse, K., Dodd, B., Plake, B. S., & Poggio, J. (2000). *Review of selected technical characteristics of the Virginia Standard of Learning (SOL) assessments.* Richmond, VA: Commonwealth of Virginia Department of Education.

Harwell, M., & LeBeau, B. (2010). Student eligibility for a free lunch as an SES measure in education research. *Educational Researcher, 39,* 120–131.

Klingner, J. K. (2004). The science of professional development. *Journal of Learning Disabilities, 37,* 248–255.

Meehan, B. T., Hughes, J. N., & Cavell, T. A. (2003). Teacher-student relationships as compensatory resources for aggressive children. *Child Development, 74,* 1145–1157.

Mikami, A. Y., Gregory, A., Allen, J. P., Pianta, R. C., & Lun. J. (2011). Effects of a teacher professional development intervention on peer relationships in secondary classrooms. *School Psychology Review, 40,* 367–385.

National Research Council. (2004). *Engaging schools: Fostering high school students' motivation to learn.* Washington, DC: National Academies Press.

Pianta, R. C. (2011). *Teaching children well: New evidence-based approaches to teacher professional development and training.* Washington, DC: Center for American Progress.

Pianta, R. C., & Hamre, B. K. (2009). Conceptualization, measurement, and improvement of classroom processes: Standardized observation can leverage capacity. *Educational Researcher, 38,* 109–119.

Pianta, R. C., Hamre, B. K., Hayes, N., Mintz, S., & LaParo, K. M. (2007). *Classroom assessment scoring system—secondary (CLASS-S).* Charlottesville, VA: University of Virginia.

Pianta, R. C., Hamre, B. K., & Stuhlman, M. (2002). How schools can do better: Fostering stronger connections between teachers and students. In J. E. Rhodes (Ed.), *New directions for youth development: A critical view of youth mentoring* (pp. 91–107). San Francisco, CA: Jossey-Bass.

Pianta, R. C., Kinzie, M., Justice, L., Pullen, P., Fan, X., & Lloyd, J. (2003). *Web training: Pre-K teachers, literacy, and relationships. Effectiveness of early childhood program, curricula, and interventions.* Washington, DC: National Institute of Child Health and Human Development.

Pianta, R. C., Mashburn, A. J., Downer, J. T., Hamre, B. K., & Justice, L. (2008). Effects of web-mediated professional development resources on teacher–child interactions in pre-kindergarten classrooms. *Early Childhood Research Quarterly, 23,* 431–451.

Resnick, M. D., Bearman, P. S., Blum, R. W., Bauman, K., Harris, K. M., Jones, J., . . . Udry, J. R. (1997). Protecting adolescents from harm: Findings from the National Longitudinal Study of Adolescent Health. *Journal of the American Medical Association, 278,* 823–832.

Scott, T. M., & Barrett, S. B. (2004). Using staff and student time engaged in disciplinary procedures to evaluate the impact of school-wide PBS. *Journal of Positive Behavior Interventions, 6,* 21–27.

Sheets, R. H. (1996). Urban classroom conflict. Student–teacher perception: Ethnic integrity, solidarity, and resistance. *Urban Review, 28,* 165–183.

Skiba, R. J., Michael, R. S., Nardo, A. C., & Peterson, R. L. (2002). The color of discipline: Sources of racial and gender disproportionality in school punishment. *Urban Review, 34,* 317–342.

Wallace, J. M. Jr., Goodkind, S., Wallace, C. M., & Bachman, J. G. (2008). Racial, ethnic, and gender differences in school discipline among U.S. high school students: 1991–2005. *Negro Educational Review, 59,* 47–62.

## CHAPTER 12

Student Threat Assessment as a Method of Reducing Student Suspensions

Dewey Cornell and Peter Lovegrove

Severe acts of violence in schools are a serious concern, but they are relatively rare events that few schools will ever experience. In contrast, threats of violence are found in almost every school and pose a complex problem for our nation's schools (Borum, Cornell, Modzeleski, & Jimerson, 2010). The most recent national review (Robers, Kemp, & Truman, 2013) found that 7% of students in grades 9 through 12 reported being threatened or injured with a weapon on school property. In a separate study (Robers et al., 2013), 7% of teachers reported being threatened with injury by a student. Student threats are much more common than official records indicate. For example, a recent survey of 3,756 high school students found that 12% recalled being threatened at school in the previous 30 days, but only 26% of those threats were reported to school authorities (Nekvasil & Cornell, 2012). Most student threats are not considered serious; the dilemma for school authorities is to distinguish a serious threat from what might be nothing more than a joking comment or a fleeting expression of anger in order to avoid both underreacting and overreacting to student behavior. Unfortunately, school shootings can generate a climate of fear and concern that tilts school authorities toward overreaction.

When school authorities learn of a threat, they often apply a zero-tolerance model of discipline that typically involves immediately removing the offending student from school (American Psychological Association Zero Tolerance Task Force, 2008). A zero-tolerance approach means that all students receive a harsh consequence regardless of the seriousness of their intentions. Although suspension is intended as a corrective measure that motivates students to improve their behavior, there is abundant evidence that it does not achieve that purpose. Suspended students tend to engage in further misbehavior and are likely to be suspended again (Fabelo et al., 2011; Hemphill, Toumbourou, Herrenkohl, McMorris, & Catalano, 2006). School suspensions are consistently associated with negative academic outcomes, including disengagement, truancy, poor academic performance, and, ultimately, dropping out of school (Fabelo et al., 2011; Lee, Cornell, Gregory, & Fan, 2011; Skiba & Sprague, 2008). Because Black students are more likely to be suspended than White students (Wallace, Goodkind, Wallace, & Bachman, 2008), they disproportionately experience the negative consequences of this counterproductive discipline strategy.

Studies of school shootings by both the FBI (O'Toole, 2000) and the Secret Service (Fein et al., 2002) recommended that schools use a threat-assessment approach to prevent violence by distinguishing serious threats from those that pose no real danger. Threat assessment is a violence prevention strategy that begins with the evaluation of individuals who threaten to harm others, and is followed by interventions designed to reduce the risk of violence. A key aspect of threat assessment is its emphasis on considering the context and meaning of the student's behavior and taking action proportionate to the seriousness of the student's actions.

Consider a simple example. Even an explicitly threatening statement such as "I'm gonna kill you" must be considered in context. A student could make such a statement as a joke, as an expression of frustration with no intent to harm, or as an expression of intent to fight but not kill someone. Finally, in the most serious situation, the student might be planning and preparing to carry out a lethal attack. Those judging the severity of such a threat must consider the full circumstances. Although one can imagine ambiguous cases in which it is difficult to judge the seriousness of a threat, our experience is that school authorities can gather enough information to make a reasonable determination in the overwhelming majority of cases. This permits school authorities to avoid the one-size-fits-all approach of zero-tolerance, in which all students are automatically suspended from school regardless of the seriousness of their offense.

VIRGINIA STUDENT THREAT ASSESSMENT GUIDELINES

The Virginia Student Threat Assessment Guidelines (Cornell & Sheras, 2006) were developed as an alternative to the zero-tolerance approach to student threats of violence. In the adoption of these guidelines, a multidisciplinary team at each school is trained to use a standard procedure and a seven-step decision tree to evaluate the seriousness of a student's threatening behavior, and to take appropriate action based on that evaluation. However, the threat assessment does not stop when the seriousness of the behavior is determined; it includes an effort to intervene on the student's behalf to resolve whatever problem, conflict, or stressful situation underlies the threatening behavior. Most cases are resolved as "transient threats" that pose no serious danger to others, whereas the more serious "substantive threats" require a progressively more extensive assessment and intervention process. Our studies have consistently found that these cases are resolved without the threat being carried out, even in an urban school system serving a city with a high rate of violent crime (Strong & Cornell, 2008). On the contrary, we have found that threats resolved using the assessment method have resulted in improved student behavior and lower levels of bullying, along with a decrease in school suspensions (e.g., Cornell, Gregory, & Fan, 2011).

The threat assessment team typically consists of a school administrator, a school resource officer, and one or more mental health professionals. The team leader—usually the school administrator who handles disciplinary matters—calls on team members for help as needed, depending on the seriousness and complexity of the case. The school administrator can resolve some simple cases working alone, and in other cases he or she will want to engage a school counselor or other mental health professional to work with a student. In the most serious cases, a law-enforcement officer is consulted to determine whether a law-enforcement investigation and/or security measures are appropriate.

A threat assessment team takes a problem-solving approach to violence prevention that includes providing counseling and support services to resolve the conflict or difficulty that incited the threat, and working out a solution that allows the student to continue in school. The basic idea is that a student threatens violence because he or she is frustrated by a problem, such as a conflict with peers. One goal of the threat assessment process is to help the student deal with the problem so that there is no longer a need to make a threat. This approach to student threats reflects a broader shift in perspectives on preventing student misbehavior. It reduces reliance on punitive sanctions, such as school suspension, and puts greater emphasis on teaching students more effective ways to solve problems and choose appropriate behavior (Osher, Bear, Sprague, & Doyle, 2010). For this reason, threat assessment training might have a more generalized impact on school discipline and the use of suspension.

We recently conducted a randomized controlled study of threat assessment (for details of this study and a review of prior studies, see Cornell, Allen, & Fan, 2012). In this study, a single school division (what school systems are called in Virginia) agreed that 20 of its 40 schools would be randomly assigned to receive threat assessment training, and 20 would delay training for 1 year and serve as a control group. During 1 school year, 201 students in both groups of schools (100 in intervention schools and 101 in control schools) were identified as making threats of violence. The critical issue was how school authorities would respond to these threats and the extent to which they would rely on school exclusionary consequences such as suspension or transfer to a different school.

The Virginia Guidelines were designed to produce three outcomes that were assessed in this study: (1) use of counseling and mental health services to resolve conflicts, (2) involvement of parents in response to the threat, and (3) return of students to school without long-term suspension or alternative school placement. A potential fourth outcome was to examine whether the students carried out their threat of violence. However, as we found in our previous studies (Cornell et al.,

2004; Strong & Cornell, 2008), few students carried out their threats. Because only seven students were identified as carrying out their threat of violence in the present study, no group comparisons were undertaken.

For each hypothesized outcome, a series of logistic regression analyses compared the intervention and control students, after controlling for the effects of demographic variables (student gender, school level, and race) and severity of the threat. Students in schools using the Virginia Guidelines were approximately four times more likely than control students to receive counseling services, and students in the intervention group were about two-and-a-half times more likely to have the benefit of a parent conference. Students in the intervention group were about one third as likely to receive long-term suspension and one eighth as likely to receive an alternative school placement.

Intervention efforts typically do not have equivalent effects in all schools. Thus we examined differences in how well schools adopted the Virginia Guidelines (fidelity of implementation) and whether those differences were associated with student outcomes. The fidelity of school staffs' implementation of the threat assessment guidelines was assessed for the 20 intervention schools using a compliance scale based on the extent to which team members at each school attended threat assessment meetings, completed documentation forms, and reported that they used the threat assessment model. Higher compliance scores were associated with a 24% increase in the use of counseling services and a 25% lower rate of long-term suspensions.

NEW RESEARCH FINDINGS

This chapter summarizes new findings from two studies. The first was a follow-up analysis from the randomized controlled trial just described (Cornell et al., 2012). This analysis examined whether the positive findings from the initial analyses benefited both White and Black students. The second study examined the link between use of the Virginia Guidelines and school suspension rates in a much larger statewide sample of elementary, middle, and high schools. Here the main question was whether the positive effects on long-term suspensions that were observed in controlled studies would be observed in a large-scale implementation.

Randomized Controlled Trial

A new analysis was conducted on the 201 students from the 40 schools that participated in the randomized controlled trial (Cornell et al., 2012). The original study found that students who made threats of violence at schools using the threat assessment model were approximately one third as likely to receive long-term suspensions as students who made threats in the control schools. The purpose of this analysis was to determine whether the reduction in long-term suspensions and other positive outcomes were comparable for Black and White students (details available from the author). We found lower suspension rates for both Black and White students, and that both groups experienced comparable benefits.

Study of Statewide Suspension Rates

Previous studies found that high schools using the Virginia Guidelines had lower suspension rates than comparison high schools (Cornell et al., 2011; Cornell, Sheras, Gregory, & Fan, 2009). These studies also observed better student–teacher relations, less bullying, and a more positive school climate in schools that had adopted the Virginia Guidelines. This suggested that, when school authorities moved from a zero-tolerance approach to a threat assessment approach, there was the potential for a broader impact on all school discipline decisions, not just responses to threatening behavior. However, studies have not looked for similar effects in elementary and middle schools, nor have they examined whether these effects vary across schools with differing racial and socioeconomic composition.

The second study examined the scaled-up implementation of the Virginia Guidelines in Virginia public schools using a retrospective, quasi-experimental design. Over the past decade, an increasing number of Virginia school divisions have gradually adopted the Virginia Guidelines. The decision of whether or not to adopt them was made by school administrators in each local school division. Information about the Virginia Guidelines was disseminated largely through state conferences and meetings, and by informal reports of success that school administrators shared with one another. By school year 2011–2012, 1,141 schools representing 58% of Virginia's public schools reported using the guidelines. An important question is whether the schools that adopted the guidelines saw a reduction in school suspension rates. Unlike the randomized controlled trial, this study did not track the outcomes for individual students but instead examined schoolwide suspension rates to determine whether there was a generalized effect at the school level. A more detailed report of these results can be found in Virginia's annual safety audit report (Virginia Department of Criminal Justice Services, 2013).

The sample for this study consisted of 1,795 regular public schools in Virginia, including 1,157 (65%) elementary schools, 327 (18%) middle schools, and 311 (17%) high schools.[1] The demographic composition of the schools was 59% White, 25% Black, 9% Hispanic, 5% Asian, and 4% other groups. (For additional demographic information, see Table 12.1 in the online report., http://tinyurl.com/JanCRPconference)

Each year, all Virginia public school principals are required by law to complete an online school safety audit survey. In 2011, principals were asked first, "Does your school use a formal threat assessment process to respond to student threats of violence?" Those who answered "yes" were asked a follow-up question: "For your formal threat assessment process, do you follow the guidelines developed by the University of Virginia?" We compared 971 schools that reported using the Virginia Guidelines with all other schools, consisting of 381 who reported not using any type of threat assessment method and 443 using some other threat assessment model. Principals also reported how many years they had been using the Virginia Guidelines and whether their school staff had been formally trained in using them.

All public schools in Virginia are required to report their annual number of short-term (<10 days) and long-term (>9 days) suspensions.[2] Suspension rates vary considerably across schools, but they report on average 2 long-term suspensions and 83 short-term suspensions per year. We conducted a series of regression analyses to investigate the relations between the use of the Virginia Guidelines and the use of long- and short-term suspensions. These analyses controlled for the type of school (elementary, middle, or high), enrollment size, and the proportion of students eligible for a free or reduced-price meal. As a baseline measure of school misbehavior, the analyses also controlled for the total number of disciplinary infractions reported for the 2006–2007 school year.

The first research question was whether use of the Virginia Guidelines was associated with fewer school suspensions. Results indicate that schools using the guidelines had 19% fewer long-term suspensions than schools not using them, after controlling for school demographic measures. Use of the Virginia Guidelines was also associated with 8% fewer short-term suspensions.

The second research question was whether the period of time the Virginia Guidelines had been in use was associated with fewer long-term and short-term suspensions. These analyses were limited to the schools that used the Virginia Guidelines. A 1-year increase in the period of time a school had used the Virginia Guidelines was associated with a 16% reduction in long-term suspensions and a 5% reduction in short-term suspensions.

The third research question concerned whether schools that had formal staff training in the Virginia Guidelines showed a greater reduction in suspensions than schools using the Virginia Guidelines but without training. The analysis distinguished between those who reported using the Virginia Guidelines without training and those who reported using the Virginia Guidelines with training. Regression analyses found that suspension rates at schools using the Virginia Guidelines without training did not differ from those that were not using the guidelines, whereas schools that used the Virginia Guidelines with training experienced 22% fewer long-term suspensions and 10% fewer short-term suspensions than schools not using the guidelines.

The fourth research question concerned whether the lower suspension rates observed in schools using the Virginia Guidelines varied across schools with different proportions of White and minority students. This kind of analysis is useful in discerning whether there are differential effects between schools with high and low percentages of minority students. Skiba and colleagues (see Chapter 9) found that schools with a high percentage of minority students tended to have substantially higher suspension rates, and that both minority and nonminority students were more likely to be suspended in high-minority schools than in those with a lower percentage of minority students.

Our regression analyses examined the statistical interaction between use of the Virginia Guidelines and the proportion of White students in the school. We constructed six separate regression models using long-term and short-term suspensions as an outcome, and using three different measures of Virginia Guidelines use: (1) guidelines used and not used, (2) number of years using the guidelines, and (3) using the guidelines with and without formal training. We found that the significantly lower suspension rates observed in schools using the Virginia Guidelines did not differ across schools with different proportions of White and minority students.

A fifth research question concerned whether the lower school suspension rates were observed among both Black and White students. To undertake these analyses, the Virginia Department of Education provided us with a data file that contained a record of each school's suspensions disaggregated by race and gender. These data allowed us to calculate both short-term and long-term suspension rates for Black males, White males, Black females, and White females. Our initial analyses of these rates again revealed that schools using the Virginia Guidelines had lower suspension rates than schools not using them. However, the differences were significant only in the middle and high schools, not in the elementary schools. Both short-term and long-term suspension rates in elementary schools tend to be substantially lower than in middle or high schools, and many elementary schools have no long-term suspensions for the entire school year. In contrast, middle and high schools have similarly high suspension rates. Thus we focused our attention on a combined group of 663 middle and high school schools, of which 398 used the Virginia Guidelines and 265 did not.

Overall, the short-term suspension rate in schools using the Virginia Guidelines was 9.2 suspensions per 100 students, compared to 10.8 suspensions per 100 students in other schools. This represents a difference of approximately 15%. For long-term suspensions, the contrast was 3.6 suspensions per 1,000 students among schools using the Virginia Guidelines versus 4.8 per 1,000 among schools not using the Virginia Guidelines, a difference of approximately 25%. To put these results in perspective, a 15% decrease from the 62,942 short-term suspensions in Virginia secondary schools would mean that 9,441 fewer students received a short-term suspension. A decrease of 25% for the 3,060 long-term suspensions would mean that 765 fewer students received a long-term suspension.

As shown in Figure 12.1, short-term suspensions were lower in schools using the Virginia Guidelines for all four race-by-gender groups. The lower rates for White males, Black females, and White females were statistically significant, but the lower rate for Black males fell short of statistical significance ($p = .075$). As shown in Figure 12.2, the long-term suspensions rates were also lower in schools using the Virginia Guidelines for all four groups, but only the lower rate for Black males was statistically significant.

Figure 12.1. Short-Term Suspensions for Zero-Tolerance Versus Threat-Assessment Schools

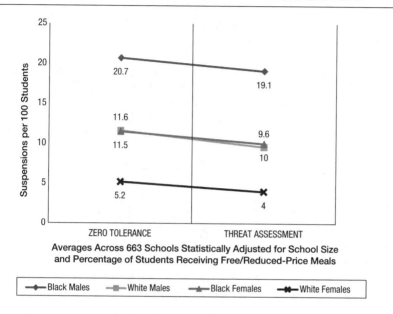

Figure 12.2. Long-Term Suspension Rates for Zero-Tolerance Versus Threat-Assessment Schools

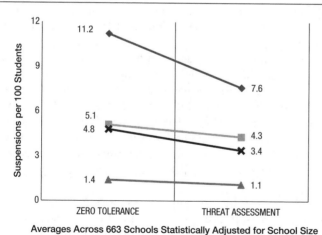

The racial disparity in suspension rates for Black and White students can be gauged as the difference between the two groups. For short-term suspensions, the racial disparity is similar in the two groups of schools for both males and females, although the overall suspension level is reduced. In the case of long-term suspensions, however, the disparity between White and Black males is notably lower in schools using the Virginia Guidelines. In schools using the guidelines, the disparity between White and Black males is 3.3 percentage points (7.6–4.3), as compared to 6.1 percentage points (11.2–5.1) in schools not using the guidelines. The difference between 3.3 and 6.1 was statistically significant ($p = .04$).

POLICY IMPLICATIONS

The new findings reported in this chapter build on previous studies that found that use of the Virginia Guidelines was associated with lower rates of school suspension (Cornell et al., 2011; Cornell et al., 2009).[3] The randomized controlled trial conducted in 40 schools produced strong evidence that the Virginia Guidelines can reduce long-term suspensions among students who have made a threat of violence. The statewide study found correlational evidence of lower rates of both long-term and short-term suspensions in schools that have adopted the guidelines. Together, these findings suggest that school authorities have a viable alternative to zero-tolerance methods of handling students who threaten violence. It seems possible for school authorities to take a problem-solving approach to resolve student threats without resorting to school suspension. This would enable schools to avoid the well-known negative consequences associated with suspension (APA Zero Tolerance Task Force, 2008).

Reducing the number of student suspensions for making threats of violence could not alone account for the statewide differences of 15% for short-term suspensions and 25% for long-term suspensions observed in secondary schools, because relatively few such students have been identified in the average school over the course of a school year. In one study, schools conducted an average of 5.4 threat assessments in 1 school year (Cornell et al., 2004), and in another study the average was 5.0 cases (Cornell et al., 2012). It appears that school authorities are using suspension less frequently for a wider range of student misbehavior, for which there are several possible explanations. For example, schools might be making other changes in their disciplinary practices at the same time, but we observed no such changes in our previous studies, including a randomized controlled trial (Cornell et al., 2012).

Another possibility is that the adoption of threat assessment has convinced school authorities to move away from zero-tolerance practices and put greater emphasis on resolving the problem or conflict that underlies a student's misbehavior. Our training studies provide some evidence to support this hypothesis. Before receiving threat assessment training, school personnel often support a zero-tolerance approach to school discipline and tend to overestimate the prevalence of homicidal violence in schools. Three studies have shown that training produced changes with statistically large effects in school personnel attitudes and knowledge about school violence (Allen, Cornell, Lorek, & Sheras, 2008; Cornell et al., 2012; Cornell et al., 2011). Notably, school personnel showed a lower commitment to zero-tolerance and consistently positive attitudes toward using the Virginia Guidelines after training. These changes were observed for school administrators (principals and assistant principals), as well as school-based mental health professionals (school psychologists, counselors, and social workers) and school-based law-enforcement and security officers.

A key issue for policymakers is the importance of educating school leaders about the negative consequences of school suspension and convincing them of the viability of alternatives to suspension as a disciplinary consequence. As Skiba and colleagues (see Chapter 9) conclude, principals' attitudes toward discipline play an important role in determining whether a student is suspended from school for a disciplinary infraction. Our findings show that schools using the Virginia Guidelines have lower suspension rates, and that longer use of the guidelines was associated with progressively lower suspension rates.

The quality of the guidelines' implementation is important, too. The randomized controlled trial found that schools with a higher quality of implementation had outcomes superior to schools using the model with lower-quality implementation (Cornell et al., 2012), and the statewide study found that schools that had formal training in the guidelines had lower suspension rates than schools that reported adopting the guidelines without formal training.

Skiba and colleagues (Chapter 9) observed that suspension rates tend to be highest in schools with high proportions of minority students, and that this effect was observed for both White and minority students, suggesting that school demographics have an influence on suspension rates. In this context, it is noteworthy that the present study found that the percentage of White students in the school did not affect the magnitude of differences between schools using the Virginia Guidelines and those not using them. This suggests that the Virginia Guidelines can be used with comparable effects in schools that have both high and low percentages of minority students. Our randomized controlled study found similar reductions in the suspension rates of both Black and White students, and the statewide correlational study found some evidence that the gap between Black and White males was reduced for long-term suspensions. Nevertheless, the strongest and most important finding was that suspension rates for Black students were reduced. Reductions in suspension rates are an important goal that has concrete benefits for minority students.

Virginia schools, as well as several thousand schools in more than a dozen other states, have chosen to adopt the Virginia Guidelines. Policymakers could learn from Virginia's experience, which could encourage more rapid adoption of threat assessment methods. The process in Virginia began with 35 schools that tested the new model in the 2001–2002 school year, and over a 10-year period it has reached more than 1,000 schools. Most of these schools were trained in 1-day workshops held by their school system. Many school divisions recognized the need to sustain use of the model by holding training sessions for new staff members in later years, and several of the largest school divisions developed their own training program with in-house trainers.

After the 2012 shooting at Sandy Hook Elementary School in Connecticut, the governor of Virginia established the Task Force on School and Campus Safety, which recommended that all public schools be required to establish threat assessment teams. This proposal was signed into law in 2013 (Virginia Code § 22.1-79.4). The Virginia state government then began to sponsor regional training workshops and a train-the-trainer program to expedite the process of implementing and maintaining threat assessment teams in all its state schools.

NOTES

1. Schools serving special populations, such as alternative, correctional, preschool, and technical schools, were not included in these analyses because their suspension policies and attendance requirements could not be appropriately compared to the other schools. However, threat assessment is used in many of these schools.

2. This information is available to the public on the Virginia Department of Education website: http://www.doe.virginia.gov/statistics_reports/.

3. In 2013, the Virginia Student Threat Assessment Guidelines were recognized as an evidence-based program in the National Register of Evidence-Based Programs and Practices (NREPP; http://www.nrepp.samhsa.gov/ViewIntervention.aspx?id=263). This is an important milestone in light of the movement in American education to adopt evidence-based practices. NREPP is a scientific review process operated by the Substance Abuse and Mental Health Services Administration of the U.S. Department of Health and Human Services.

REFERENCES

Allen, K., Cornell, D., Lorek, E., & Sheras, P. (2008). Response of school personnel to student threat assessment training. *School Effectiveness and School Improvement, 19,* 319–332.

American Psychological Association Zero Tolerance Task Force. (2008). Are zero tolerance policies effective in the schools? An evidentiary review and recommendations. *American Psychologist, 63,* 852–862. doi:10.1037/0003-066X.63.9.852

Borum, R., Cornell, D., Modzeleski, W., & Jimerson, S. (2010). What can be done about school shootings? A review of the evidence. *Educational Researcher, 39,* 27–37. Retrieved from http://scholarcommons.usf.edu/cgi/viewcontent.cgi?article=1533&context=mhlp_facpub

Cornell, D., Allen, K., & Fan, X. (2012). A randomized controlled study of the Virginia Student Threat Assessment Guidelines in grades K–12. *School Psychology Review, 41,* 100–115.

Cornell, D., Gregory, A., & Fan, X. (2011). Reductions in long-term suspensions following adoption of the Virginia Student Threat Assessment Guidelines. *Bulletin of the National Association of Secondary School Principals, 95,* 175–194.

Cornell, D., & Sheras, P. (2006). *Guidelines for responding to student threats of violence.* Longmont, CO: Sopris West.

Cornell, D., Sheras, P., Gregory, A., & Fan, X. (2009). A retrospective study of school safety conditions in high schools using the Virginia Threat Assessment Guidelines versus alternative approaches. *School Psychology Quarterly, 24,* 119–129.

Cornell, D., Sheras, P., Kaplan, S., McConville, D., Douglass, J., Elkon, A. et al. (2004). Guidelines for student threat assessment: Field-test findings. *School Psychology Review, 33,* 527–546.

Fabelo, T., Thompson, M. D., Plotkin, M., Carmichael, D., Marchbanks, M. P. III, & Booth E. A. (2011). *Breaking schools' rules: A statewide study of how school discipline relates to students' success and juvenile justice involvement.* New York, NY, and College Station, TX: Council of State Governments Justice Center and Texas A&M University Public Policy Research Institute. Retrieved from http:// www2.mysanantonio.com/PDFs/Breaking_Schools_Rules_embargo_final_report.pdf

Fein, R. A., Vossekuil, B., Pollack, W. S., Borum, R., Modzeleski, W., & Reddy, M. (2002). *Threat assessment in schools: A guide to managing threatening situations and creating safe school climates.* Washington, DC: U.S. Department of Education, Office of Elementary and Secondary Education, Safe and Drug-Free Schools Program and U.S. Secret Service, National Threat Assessment Center.

Hemphill, S. A., Toumbourou, J. W., Herrenkohl, T. I., McMorris, B. J., & Catalano, R. F. (2006). The effect of school suspensions and arrests on subsequent adolescent antisocial behavior in Australia and the United States. *Journal of Adolescent Health, 39,* 736–744. doi:10.1016/j.jadohealth.2006.05.010

Lee, T., Cornell, D., Gregory, A., & Fan, X. (2011). High suspension schools and dropout rates for black and white students. *Education and Treatment of Children, 34,* 167–192.

Nekvasil, E., & Cornell, D. (2012). Student reports of peer threats of violence: Prevalence and outcomes. *Journal of School Violence, 11,* 357–375.

Osher, D., Bear, G. G., Sprague, J. R., & Doyle, W. (2010). How can we improve school discipline? *Educational Researcher, 39,* 48–58.

O'Toole, M. E. (2000). *The school shooter: A threat assessment perspective.* Quantico, VA: Federal Bureau of Investigation, National Center for the Analysis of Violent Crime.

Robers, S., Kemp, J., & Truman, J. (2013). *Indicators of School Crime and Safety: 2012* (NCES 2013-036/NCJ 241446). Washington, DC: National Center for Education Statistics, U.S. Department of Education, and Bureau of Justice Statistics, Office of Justice Programs, U.S. Department of Justice.

Skiba, R., & Sprague, J. (2008). Safety without suspensions. *Educational Leadership, 66,* 38–43.

Strong, K., & Cornell, D. (2008). Student threat assessment in Memphis city schools: A descriptive report. *Behavioral Disorders, 34,* 42–54.

Virginia Department of Criminal Justice Services. (2013). *The 2012 Virginia school safety audit survey results.* Richmond, VA: Author.

Wallace, J. M., Goodkind, S., Wallace, C. M., & Bachman, J. G. (2008). Racial, ethnic, and gender differences in school discipline among U.S. high school students: 1991–2005. *Negro Educational Review, 59,* 47–62.

## CHAPTER 13

Avoid Quick Fixes

Lessons Learned From a Comprehensive Districtwide Approach to Improve Conditions for Learning

David M. Osher, Jeffrey M. Poirier, G. Roger Jarjoura, and Russell C. Brown

Schools, districts, and communities struggle to address the needs of economically disadvantaged students, many of whom attend schools where the staff is overwhelmed by students' unmet needs (Kendziora & Osher, 2009) and where neither staff nor students receives the supports necessary to meet high behavioral and academic standards (Osher, Sandler, & Nelson, 2001). An extensive body of research demonstrates the importance of safe, orderly, and supportive schools (Osher, Dwyer, Jimerson, & Brown, 2012; Osher et al., 2007; Osher & Kendziora, 2010), yet urban schools often have poor conditions for learning (CFL) that affect student attendance, behavior, and achievement. Schools with poor learning conditions often struggle to maintain order and safety, and many frequently suspend or expel students to control the environment (Borum, Cornell, Modzeleski, & Jimerson, 2010; Osher, Bear, Sprague, & Doyle, 2010). This control-oriented approach is particularly pervasive in urban schools that serve large numbers of students of color, whose lives often are characterized by the adversities of poverty and racism (Gregory, Skiba, & Noguera, 2010).

Positive CFL include emotional connectedness to and support from caring adults and peers, social and emotional competence among peers, and academic engagement (Osher & Kendziora, 2010). However, many school districts concerned about safety prioritize investing in security hardware and school police rather than learning conditions. The Cleveland Metropolitan School District (CMSD) long experienced challenges to school safety and thus had a history of investing heavily in security. In recent years, however, the district has changed its strategy, instead prioritizing efforts to promote better teaching and provide greater supports, which enables students to improve their social competence, behavior, and academic growth.

Our research of CMSD's efforts, including the challenges the district has faced in their implementation, found that CFL can be improved and that alternatives to punishment and exclusion can be developed at the same time safety is improving. The CMSD experience and the research findings described in this chapter demonstrate that, if they want to improve discipline, increase learning opportunities, and improve student well-being, policymakers and school leaders can be more effective if they look beyond "quick fixes" to school safety issues. Such quick fixes include zero-tolerance policies, armed police in schools, and an overreliance on metal detectors. The research is rooted in an extensive body of research that demonstrates the importance of safe and orderly schools, particularly for children who experience the adversities of poverty (Cornell & Mayer, 2010; Osher & Kendziora, 2010).

The results of Cleveland's alternative approach refute the belief that "soft" youth disciplinary measures cannot work in urban districts. As of the 2013–2014 school year, the majority of CMSD students are students of color, and more than 80% are Black or Latino; in 52 of the district's 99 schools, students of color make up more than 90% of the student body; and 100% of CMSD's students receive free lunch at school.

This chapter examines CMSD's efforts to improve CFL over a 5 year period. These efforts were undertaken in response to a districtwide audit conducted for CMSD by the American Institutes for Research (AIR) in 2007–2008 to assess the district's strengths and weaknesses in creating positive CFL (Osher et al., 2008). Beginning in the 2008–2009 school year, CMSD adopted a three-tiered public health approach that included universal prevention, early intervention, and individualized interventions. The approach was designed to address the impact the high number of risk factors in the community and schools had on school safety and order, to reduce the number of out-of-school suspensions (OSS), and to improve attendance and CFL districtwide.

This chapter focuses on four districtwide efforts CMSD has undertaken to improve student social competence, behavior, and other outcomes: (1) planning that uses data on CFL; (2) implementing the Promoting Alternative Thinking Strategies (PATHS) social and emotional learning (SEL) program in prekindergarten to grade 5; (3) establishing student support teams to review students' needs and connect them to appropriate resources; and (4) opening planning centers as an alternative to in-school suspension to prevent an escalation of negative student behavior and reduce OSS. Our research led to conclusions about the collective effects of these efforts on safety, order, and other conditions for learning. The chapter addresses the following:

1. What changes in student attendance, behavior, and CFL were evident between 2008 and 2011?
2. What changes in elementary students' social and emotional competence, attention, and aggression occurred between 2010 and 2012?

3. Do these outcomes and perceptions vary by student characteristics (e.g., race/ethnicity)?

4. To what extent are improvements in student behavior and student reports of CFL associated with the quality of the implementation of the three interventions?

The research draws on 5 years of data from surveys of student perceptions of CFL, along with data on academic achievement, attendance, discipline, and safety. It suggests that implementing a three-tiered, data-driven public health approach is effective and that there is a strong relationship between implementation quality and outcomes. A full description of this research and its theoretical and research foundations, along with more detailed findings and technical notes, are available on the Civil Rights Project website (Osher, Poirier, Jarjoura, Brown, & Kendziora, 2013). This research (along with other literature) has important implications for policy and practice. Hence, we conclude the chapter with six recommendations: (1) assess factors contributing to disparities in school safety and discipline, (2) develop school capacity to reduce disciplinary disparities, (3) expand the collection and use of data on nonacademic conditions in schools, (4) apply tiered approaches, (5) implement evidence-based social and emotional learning, and (6) broaden investment in "humanware."

CLEVELAND'S DISTRICT CONTEXT AND INTERVENTIONS

The Cleveland Metropolitan School District had an estimated 41,000 students that were approximately 68% Black, 15% White, and 13% Latino during the 2011–2012 school year. Research (Osher et al., 2008) has documented the following risk factors for poor discipline and violence in CMSD:

- Reactive, punitive, and inconsistent approaches to discipline at home and in school.
- High levels of long-term poverty, which increases the likelihood that children will arrive at school with inadequate relationships and self-regulatory skills.
- Lead poisoning and lead effect rates between 17% and 21%, which is higher than most other U.S. cities and over eight times the national average. This toxicity puts students at risk for academic problems and antisocial behavior.
- Poor CFL in schools. Compared to Chicago, for example, where the same survey was administered, Cleveland students felt less safe, less supported by teachers, and viewed their fellow students as having poorer social and emotional competencies.

- High levels of student engagement in risky and aggressive behavior. For example, according to CMSD's 2004 Youth Risk Behavior Survey of students in grades 9–12, significantly more students (43.7%) reported being in a physical fight during the 12 months prior to taking the survey than was reported at the national level (33.0%), and 22.5% of males and 13.1% of females reported that they carried a weapon to school some time during the 30 days prior to taking the survey. Similar percentages for fighting were reported by students in grades 7 and 8.
- In many schools, students' mental health needs overran the school's capacity to help them. In such schools, the behavior of students with unaddressed mental health needs draws disproportionate staff attention. Staff members then experience the school as being out of control and focuses on responding to rather than preventing "fires," and on punishing students rather than preventing poor behavior.

Considering the extent of these risk factors, the success of CMSD's most recent interventions is remarkable.

Cleveland started to address these concerns after a student who had been suspended for fighting came to school with a gun, shot two adults and two students, and then killed himself. The city's first response was to invest $3.4 million in metal detectors and $3.7 million in new security officers, which in the words of a city council member "demonstrate[d] that the district is finally getting tough on crime in the schools." However, Cleveland did not stop there. Its leaders, who distinguished between hardware and "humanware," commissioned an American Institutes for Research (AIR; www.air.org) audit to assess the quality and sufficiency of existing health and human services provided to CMSD students.

Based on the audit's recommendations, Cleveland implemented the following strategies:

- Use data on a small number of metrics to build a climate for change, sustain it over multiple years, refine the interventions, and enhance the district's approach to improving student outcomes and well-being.
- Support the ability of schools, agencies, and staff to systematically implement proven, high-quality practices and programs.
- Use data for planning, monitoring, and evaluation.
- Employ a three-tiered approach to build conditions and capacities to learn and teach.
- Eliminate ineffective or counterproductive practices and behaviors.

CMSD notably sustained this implementation process during a period of revenue loss, school closures, declining enrollment, staff layoffs, and the retirement of the chief executive officer. The sustained effort reflected a high level of administrative, union, and community support, and a school board committed to the effort.

The district's chief academic officer was actively involved in this work. He assigned leadership for this work to a humanware executive committee, which included student support services managers; representatives of the chief of security, who actively supported this work; and members of the teachers union, all of whom helped design and operationalize the interventions.

From the beginning, Cleveland committed to systemic and universal implementation across the district, which might have helped sustain and extend the effort through tough times. Certain schools were the first adopters, and their staffs embraced the new ideas and readily understood the underlying principles that framed the new approach. Others did not initially embrace or understand the underlying logic of the approach, and some passively resisted the new expectations. The following is a brief description of the three key interventions CMSD implemented.

UNIVERSAL SOCIAL AND EMOTIONAL LEARNING IN ELEMENTARY SCHOOLS

Social and emotional learning includes acquiring and mastering skills to recognize and manage emotions, develop care and concern for others, establish positive relationships, make appropriate decisions, and handle challenging situations effectively (Elias et al., 1997). Cleveland chose to implement SEL first at the primary school level due in part to limited resources, but also because the return on investment is greater when intervention occurs early. After a planning process that involved teachers and their union, as well as community agencies and pupil services professionals, CMSD selected Promoting Alternative Thinking Strategies (PATHS), an empirically validated program that had been implemented successfully in schools that were demographically similar to Cleveland's (Wright, Lamont, Wandersman, & Osher, in press). The PATHS curriculum, delivered by classroom teachers, is divided into three units: self-control, feelings and relationships, and interpersonal cognitive problem solving. PATHS teaches students to understand, regulate, and express their emotions, to recognize the feelings of others and relate others' experiences to their own, to develop empathy, and to understand how the behaviors of others can affect their own emotions.

CMSD trained pre-K through grade-2 teachers in PATHS, with plans to implement the program in 2009–2010; it did the same with grade 3–5 teachers in 2010–2011. Coaching was an important part of the implementation strategy, but Cleveland's financial constraints meant the district could hire only half the recommended number of coaches, had to delay their hiring, and could not rehire coaches for 2011–2012. Nevertheless, PATHS became part of the education of many elementary school students via a coherent districtwide implementation strategy.

Student Support Teams

Interventions require a referral process that can respond to students' needs in a timely, coordinated, and effective manner. In 2008–2009, CMSD implemented a planning model for students who exhibit early warning signs of academic, behavioral, or emotional challenges. Twenty-six national organizations and an expert panel convened at the request of President Clinton to address the warning signs of school violence vetted this model (Dwyer, Osher, & Warger, 1998; Dwyer & Osher, 2000). CMSD replaced a cumbersome special education planning process, which focused on eligibility rather than on consultation and referral, with student support teams (SSTs) in each school. The purpose of the SSTs was to address students' problems and warning signs in a timely manner and to help students succeed and achieve in school.

The SSTs met weekly to discuss students' academic problems and issues such as tardiness, poor behavior, and other challenges hindering students' success in school. Each SST included three staff members: a building administrator, a qualified teacher, and a student support staff member (e.g., school social worker). The team used prereferral interventions and coordinated with community agencies that provided students with intensive, school-based, coordinated mental health services. Teachers, principals, other school staff members, external agency partners, parents, or students themselves could make referrals. The referral was assigned to the school staff member with the most knowledge of the student's needs and strengths (for the SST guidelines and meeting protocol, see Osher et al., 2013).

Challenges to implementation have included a high level of need at some schools, which contributed to backlogs in handling SST referrals. In addition, layoffs of social workers reduced the number of professionals with mental health expertise. CMSD tried to address this decreased capacity by producing training materials, providing training, and monitoring quality through the central office.

Planning Centers

CMSD replaced ineffective in-school suspensions with planning centers that employed SEL learning strategies. These strategies, which used PATHS concepts in K–8 schools, focused on students completing their academic work and learning to manage their emotions. The planning center instructional aides (PCIA) who formerly staffed in-school suspension rooms assumed the role of a supportive resource instead of disciplinarian and gatekeeper. The planning centers were implemented in 2010–2011, which included training for 135 PCIAs on their roles in the planning center model, understanding behavior, and de-escalation strategies.

The planning center represented a fundamental reorientation from punitive and exclusionary disciplinary approaches to more learner-centered ones. This meant focusing on student needs, providing a place for upset students to cool down, and using protocols and resources to help students learn self-discipline.

Students were referred as needed to SSTs for additional support. They also could refer themselves to a planning center, which acknowledges that students might recognize the need to "escape" a problematic situation and go to a safe, supportive environment. All PCIAs had a copy of the PATHS "problem-solving sheet" and were encouraged to use it as they worked with students. Some high schools also used PATHS strategies and materials related to good decision making.

The district addressed a number of challenges in implementing planning centers. One in particular was the requirement for a center staff that included a teacher, social worker, and school psychologist, or a behavior specialist with several years of experience in behavioral support programming. CMSD did not have the resources to provide this, so the paraprofessionals who had managed in-school suspension rooms received intensive training from CMSD and were redeployed to staff the centers, with support from clinical staff.

The planning centers were the last stop before a student was removed from the building and the first stop when a student returned from being suspended or involuntarily transferred. This generally included a 15-minute assessment between the PCIA and the student, which was an important part of transitioning suspended students or new enrollees. By helping to increase acceptable behavior and decrease unacceptable behavior, PCIAs helped prepare students to return to their classroom learning environment by applying de-escalation and social problem-solving techniques; teaching alternative behaviors, social skills, and anger management; applying safety techniques and providing intensive interventions for aggressive behaviors; and working with students' families.

CHANGES IN STUDENT OUTCOMES AND THEIR ASSOCIATION WITH INTERVENTION IMPLEMENTATION QUALITY

The following research takes into account CMSD's efforts over a 5-year period to improve students' school experience. These efforts addressed gaps identified in AIR's 2008 districtwide audit, which assessed students' needs regarding connectedness, safety, support, and other CFL. Building from baseline information on these conditions and examining implementation of the interventions put in place following the audit (PATHS, planning centers, SSTs), we used our analysis of multiple years of data to answer the four core questions listed in our introduction.

What Changes in Student Attendance and Behavior Were Evident?

According to attendance and out-of-school suspension data, Cleveland's efforts have been fruitful, although results were tempered by the impact of deficits:

- The attendance rate districtwide increased 1.5 percentage points over the 3-year period.

- The number of suspensions reported by CMSD schools declined from an average of 233.1 incidents per school in 2008–2009 to 132.4 in 2010–2011.
- This decrease in the average number of suspensions included statistically significant reductions in the following categories:

> Disobedient/disruptive behavior (131.8 reduced to 73.9)
> Fighting/violence (54.5 reduced to 36.4)
> Harassment/intimidation (12.8 reduced to 5.6)
> Serious bodily injury (13.3 reduced to 5.8)

- After 2 years, the extreme ends of the distribution for violent incidents changed. Most important was that there were 86 fewer incidents per year among schools in the 90th percentile.
- Out-of-school suspensions also decreased nearly 60% districtwide over the 3-year period, from 21,119 during the 2008–2009 school year to 8,694 in 2010–2011.

How Do Disciplinary Outcomes Vary by Student Race/Ethnicity and Sex?

Research suggests that although race-neutral approaches might reduce the absolute risk of exclusionary discipline, they might not eliminate disparities (Skiba & Horner, 2011). Analyses of the most currently available disciplinary data from the U.S. Department of Education's Office for Civil Rights (OCR) provide more specific details about behavioral outcomes and how student subgroups experienced exclusionary school discipline during CMSD's 2009–2010 school year—the halfway point for most of our research. While there have been positive changes overall, these data suggest disparities in exclusionary discipline for Black and Latino students remain. This is not surprising, though, as these disparities were not targeted as part of CMSD's strategy.

As we consider the range from the less serious to the more serious responses (i.e., in-school suspension, to only one OSS, to more than one OSS), the disproportion of Black and Latino students increases as the severity of the response increases. These data also show disparities in exclusionary school discipline based on sex, with Black female and Latina students experiencing greater disparities than their White peers.

Although these disparities are included for the 2009–2010 school year, they suggest a problem that other studies have also identified. For example, race-neutral processes that lower the number of disciplinary incidents might reduce the base rate for disciplinary actions and the harm caused by suspension and expulsion, but they do not reduce disparities in discipline. Research on positive behavioral interventions and supports provides an example of this (Skiba & Horner, 2011), as do studies of disparities in special education placement and other areas that might be affected by implicit bias and a lack of understanding of behaviors grounded in students' cultural backgrounds (Osher et al., 2012).

What Changes in Conditions for Learning in Grades 5–12 Were Evident?

The AIR Conditions for Learning Survey has been administered annually since 2008 to students in grades 5 through 12. We analyzed the survey data from the 2008–2009 to the 2012–2013 school year. Overall conditions improved over this period for students in all grades. As expected, there was variation between schools and individual students. The following changes of 5 percentage points or more were evident:

Academic Challenge. Twenty-six percent of schools showed an increase in the percentage of students who reported having an "adequate" or "excellent" academic challenge; 9% showed a decline.

Peer Social–Emotional Competence. Twenty-one percent of schools showed improvement in the percentage of students who reported peer social and emotional competence as "adequate" or "excellent," whereas 21% showed a decrease.

Student Support from School Staff. Twenty-one percent of schools showed an increase in the percentage of students who reported receiving "adequate" or "excellent" student support, compared to 10% that showed a decline.

Safe and Respectful Climate. Twenty-two percent of schools reported an increase in the percentage of students who reported "adequate" or "excellent" conditions of safety and respect, whereas 25% reported a decline. This was particularly evident for students in grades 5–8.

Analyses of subscales created from the CFL survey's "safe and respectful climate" scale suggest that students were aware of the effects of the aforementioned changes in student behavior between the 2008–2009 and 2011–2012 school years:

- Students in grades 5 through 8, particularly male, Latino, and White students, reported worrying less about violence and seeing fewer incidents of student bullying over the 3-year period.
- Students in grades 5 through 8, particularly Black students, reported they were feeling safer over time. No significant difference was found for students in grades 9 through 12.
- Fewer males agreed with statements that students in the school were prepared to fight. This was particularly true for males in grades 5 through 8.

Finally, CFL scores have an important relationship with academics and attendance. We found that higher CFL scores were associated with higher results on the Ohio Department of Education Performance Index (PI), which indicates how well students perform on the Ohio Achievement Tests in grades 3 through 8 and the Ohio Graduation Test in grade 10. The 3 years of CFL scores were associated with 62% of the changes in high school PI scores and 30% of elementary PI scores. Also, taking student attendance into account along with CFL scores improved our ability to predict PI scores.

CMSD has continued to face challenges, including students experiencing homelessness (2,800 in 2012), 18 school closings in 2011, and a high level of student mobility (over 33% in 2012). These challenges might have contributed to the increased number of suspensions during the 2011–2012 and 2012–2013 school years. However, the statistical association between CFL and academics has remained consistently strong through 2012–2013, and has increased for elementary schools.

How Did Elementary Students' Social Competence Change?

AIR conducted an evaluation of PATHS in CMSD during the 2010–2011 and 2011–2012 school years (Faria, Kendziora, Brown, & Osher, 2012). Teachers in prekindergarten through grade 5 completed surveys in the fall and spring of both school years, rating the social and emotional competence, attention, and aggression of a random sample of students in their classrooms. In 2010–2011 we observed significant improvement from fall to spring for social competence and attention but did not see a significant change in aggression. In 2011–2012, we replicated our findings for social competence and attention but saw a significant increase in aggression between fall and spring. The findings for teacher-rated aggression were consistent with results from prior studies (e.g., Kendziora & Osher, 2009) that documented normative increases in aggression from fall to spring. However, the increase in aggression was smaller in classrooms with more effective PATHS implementation.

To What Extent Were Student Outcomes Associated With Intervention Implementation Quality?

Implementation quality is key to determining whether evidence-based interventions improve student outcomes. Successful implementation depends not only on effective intervention models but on districts' and schools' organizational capacity and support, as well as staff buy-in, training, coaching, and monitoring. Teachers often do not commit to a new approach until they master it and tangibly experience the effects. This is not easy for teachers who lack the time or support to master the new approach. By support we refer to a commitment from the leadership, which was available in CMSD at the highest levels but not always from principals. Teacher support must also address factors that facilitate change, such as timely access to reliable and effective training, and ongoing coaching, quality improvement, and assurance processes for course correction along the way, and reinforcement of positive changes among colleagues and students. CMSD's progress in developing these components has been slow, due to its organizational culture, capacity, and economic constraints.

Principals' self-reported data on implementation (low, medium, high) from the 2011–2012 school year suggest an association between the decline in the number of suspensions and the quality of the implementation of the humanware strategies. For schools rated as implementing a medium or high level of PATHS, we found a statistically significant decrease from 2008–2009 to 2010–2011 in the number of behavioral incidents in each of five categories: (1) total incidents, (2) disobedient/disruptive behavior, (3) fighting/violence, (4) harassment/intimidation, and (5) serious bodily injury. Changes in disciplinary incidents as of spring 2012 in schools with a medium or high level of implementation of these three interventions included the following:

- For schools with medium- or high-level PATHS implementation, the number of disciplinary incidents decreased an average of 35.9%.
- For schools with medium- or high-level SST implementation, the number of disciplinary incidents decreased an average of 49.1%.
- For schools with a medium or high level of planning center implementation, the number of disciplinary incidents decreased an average of 51.4%.

Students in schools where principals rated the implementation quality of these three interventions as high also had higher perceptions of safety in these schools. Furthermore, where students indicated on the CFL survey scale whether their school peers are often threatened, bullied, and teased, more positive results were evident in schools where the implementation of planning centers was rated high and where PATHS and SST implementation were rated medium or high.

LIMITATIONS OF THE RESEARCH

Research limitations included the small number of years analyzed and the use of self-reported data from principals to measure implementation quality. Also, although the CFL data are valid and reliable, other quantitative data are not necessarily so. Still, the data presented here suggest that CMSD is starting to create safe and supportive schools for its students, the majority of whom are students of color.

SUMMARY AND RECOMMENDATIONS FOR POLICY/PRACTICE

Many members of Cleveland's education community believe the challenges they face are so extensive that a proactive preventive approach cannot take place in their schools or district. However, CMSD provides an example of what is possible, even in hard times and under less-than-perfect conditions, by implementing student-centered policies. Fortunately, the promise in Cleveland is growing. The chief academic officer who led the humanware efforts is now the school system's chief executive officer. He, the mayor, and the president of the Cleveland Teachers Union have succeeded in passing the first tax levy for education in 17 years. Furthermore, Cleveland has secured support from a local philanthropy, the NoVo Foundation, to support its humanware efforts.

Cleveland continues to move forward in strengthening the initiatives described in this chapter. For example, CMSD is now surveying students about conditions for learning three times a year so that its school planning teams can use the disaggregated data to continually improve quality. It also is expanding its humanware efforts by implementing SEL standards; using a student-driven, evidence-based computer SEL program (Ripple Effects) in the planning centers; and holding class meetings in high schools districtwide.

Based on our research findings, we make the following six policy and practice recommendations. These are also grounded in lessons learned from the larger body of research and professional literature, as well as our work with school districts and schools. Children and youth require safe, supportive schools and communities to succeed and thrive, and these six recommendations can help districts in realizing these essential conditions.

Recommendation 1: Assess factors contributing to disparities in school safety and discipline. Conducting audits and using them to identify assets, as well as areas of need and factors contributing to poor discipline and violence, can facilitate a more efficient use of public resources. It also can identify the causes of discipline-related disparities. Audits should be methodologically sound and provide an independent, external perspective. The CMSD audit, which was the basis for its humanware efforts, exemplifies this.

Recommendation 2: Develop school capacities to reduce disciplinary disparities. Low-quality implementation of SEL and school-based supports, along with cultural disconnects between and among students, families, and educators, can contribute to disciplinary disparities. It is essential to collect and disaggregate data for student populations with particular characteristics associated with disparities. This should include English language learner, disability, and poverty status; gender identity (not just biological sex since some students might express their gender in ways that do not align with expectations based on their sex); race/ethnicity; and sexual orientation. An increasing body of research points to the importance of implementation quality and capacity (Durlak & DuPre, 2008; Myers, Durlak, & Wandersman, 2012), as well as educators' cultural competence (Osher et al., 2012; Poirier, 2012). Policy and practice should support the development of individual and organizational capacity to reduce disparities while building safe, orderly schools with strong conditions for learning.

Recommendation 3: Expand the collection and use of data on nonacademic conditions in schools. Data on a school's conditions for learning—academic challenge, physical and emotional safety, student social and emotional skills, and student support—can facilitate continuous improvement, performance management, and accountability. These data should be examined to understand the general conditions in districts and schools, and should be disaggregated by subgroups to support data-informed decisions about interventions and strategies to address disparities and identified areas of need.

Recommendation 4: Apply tiered approaches. Trauma and mental health challenges and disorders can contribute to and exacerbate academic and behavioral problems. Tiered approaches to preventing and addressing these disorders can ensure that more concentrated support is delivered to the students who need it. These approaches can also provide a foundation that minimizes problems, and their associated costs to individuals and districts, while making early intervention easier. (Models for implementing this approach are available; see Osher et al., 2004.)

Recommendation 5: Implement evidence-based social and emotional learning. Developing students' abilities to understand and manage emotions and relationships is critical to creating safe and productive learning environments. SEL can promote social competence while reducing antisocial behavior (Durlak, Weissberg, Dymnicki, Taylor, & Schellinger, 2011). Districts can address discipline-related concerns more proactively by building adults' and students' social and emotional competence through training and the effective implementation of SEL.

Recommendation 6: Broaden investment in humanware. Although it is changing, federal and state policy has incentivized schools to push out problem students and invest in hardware (e.g., metal detectors) and policing. We recommend providing schools with incentives to invest in humanware that are equal to or greater than incentives for adding hardware and policing. Federal policy has supported hiring police to protect schools and investing in hardware, but it has not done the same for humanware, other than through competitive grant programs. Cleveland was able to spend $2.5 million on metal detectors, taken from a $3.3 million fund for state capital improvements.

REFERENCES

Borum, R., Cornell, D., Modzeleski, W., & Jimerson, S. (2010). What can be done about school shootings? A review of the evidence. *Educational Researcher, 39,* 27–37. Retrieved from http://scholar commons.usf.edu/cgi/viewcontent.cgi?article=1533&context=mhlp_facpub

Cornell, D. G., & Mayer, M. J. (2010). Why does school order and safety matter? *Educational Researcher, 39*(1), 7–15.

Durlak, J. A., & DuPre, E. P. (2008). Implementation matters: A review of research on the influence of implementation on program outcomes and the factors affecting implementation. *American Journal of Community Psychology, 41*(3-4), 327–350.

Durlak, J. A., Weissberg, R. P., Dymnicki, A. B., Taylor, R. D., & Schellinger, K. B. (2011). The impact of enhancing students' social and emotional learning: A meta-analysis of school-based universal interventions. *Child Development, 82*(1), 405–432.

Dwyer, K., Osher, D., & Warger, C. (1998). *Early warning, timely response: A guide to safe schools.* Washington, DC: U.S. Department of Education.

Dwyer, K., & Osher, D. (2000). *Safeguarding our children: An action guide.* Washington, DC: U.S. Department of Education and U.S. Department of Justice, American Institutes for Research.

Elias, M. J., Zins, J. E., Weissberg, R. P., Frey, K. S., Greenberg, M. T., Haynes, N. M., . . . Shriver, T. P. (1997). *Promoting social and emotional learning: Guidelines for educators.* Alexandria, VA: Association for Supervision and Curriculum Development.

Faria, A. M., Kendziora, K., Brown, L., & Osher, D. (2012). *PATHS implementation and outcome study in the Cleveland Metropolitan School District: Final report.* Washington, DC: American Institutes for Research.

Gregory, A., Skiba, R. J., & Noguera, P. A. (2010). The achievement gap and the discipline gap: Two sides of the same coin? *Educational Researcher, 39*(1), 59–68.

Kendziora, K., & Osher, D. (2009). *Starting to turn schools around: The academic outcomes of the Safe Schools, Successful Students Initiative.* Washington, DC: American Institutes for Research.

Meyers, D. C., Durlak, J. A., & Wandersman, A. (2012). The quality implementation framework: A synthesis of critical steps in the implementation process. *American Journal of Community Psychology, 50*(3–4), 462–480.

Osher, D., Bear, G., Sprague, J., & Doyle, W. (2010) How to improve school discipline. *Educational Researcher, 39*(1), 48–58.

Osher, D., Coggshall, J., Colombi, G., Woodruff, D., Francois, S., & Osher, T. (2012). Building school and teacher capacity to eliminate the school-to-prison pipeline. *Teacher Education and Special Education, 35*(4), 284–295.

Osher, D., Dwyer, K. P., Jimerson, S. R., & Brown, J. (2012). Developing safe, supportive, and effective schools: Facilitating student success to reduce school violence. In S. R. Jimerson, A. B. Nickerson, M. J. Mayer, & M. J. Furlong (Eds.), *Handbook of school violence and safety: International research and practice* (2nd ed., pp. 27–44). New York, NY: Taylor & Francis.

Osher, D., & Kendziora, K. (2010). Building conditions for learning and healthy adolescent development: Strategic approaches. In B. Doll, W. Pfohl, & J. Yoon (Eds.), *Handbook of youth prevention science* (pp. 121–140). New York, NY: Routledge.

Osher, D., Poirier, J. M., Dwyer, K. P., Hicks, R., Brown, L. J., Lampron, S., & Rodriguez, C. (2008). *Cleveland Metropolitan School District human ware audit: Findings and recommendations.* Washington, DC: American Institutes for Research. Retrieved from http://www.air.org/files/ AIR_Cleveland_8-20-0821.pdf

Osher, D., Poirier, J. M., Jarjoura, G. R., Brown, R., & Kendziora, K. (2013). *Avoid simple solutions and quick fixes: Lessons learned from a comprehensive districtwide approach to improving conditions for learning.* Washington, DC: American Institutes for Research. Retrieved from http://civilrights project.ucla.edu/resources/projects/center-for-civil-rights-remedies/school-to-prison-folder/ state-reports/

Osher, D., Sandler, S., & Nelson, C. (2001). The best approach to safety is to fix schools and support children and staff. *New Directions in Youth Development, 92,* 127–154.

Osher, D., Sprague, J., Weissberg, R. P., Axelrod, J., Keenan, S., Kendziora, K., & Zins, J. E. (2007). A comprehensive approach to promoting social, emotional, and academic growth in contemporary schools. In J. Grimes & A. Thomas (Eds.), *Best practices in school psychology V* (pp. 1263–1278). Bethesda, MD: National Association of School Psychologists.

Osher, D., VanAker, R., Morrison, G., Gable, R., Dwyer, K., & Quinn, M. (2004). Warning signs of problems in schools: Ecological perspectives and effective practices for combating school aggression and violence. *Journal of School Violence, 2/3,* 13–37.

Poirier, J. M. (2012). Fostering safe, welcoming, and supportive schools for LGBT youth. In S. K. Fisher, J. M. Poirier, & G. M. Blau (Eds.), *Improving emotional & behavioral outcomes for LGBT youth: A guide for professionals* (pp. 159–172). Baltimore, MD: Brookes.

Skiba, R. J., & Horner, R. H. (2011). Race is not neutral: A national investigation of African American and Latino disproportionality in school discipline. *School Psychology Review, 40*(1), 85–107.

Wright, A., Lamont, A., Wandersman, A., & Osher, D. (in press). Accountability and social emotional learning programs: The getting to outcomes approach. In J. Durlak, T. Gullota, & R. Weissberg (Eds.), *Handbook of social emotional learning.* New York, NY: Taylor Francis.

Effectiveness of Schoolwide Positive Behavior Interventions and Supports in Reducing Racially Inequitable Disciplinary Exclusion

Claudia G. Vincent, Jeffrey R. Sprague,
CHiXapkaid (Michael Pavel), Tary J. Tobin, and Jeff M. Gau

Researchers have consistently documented racially inequitable disciplinary exclusion and concomitant disparities in academic achievement (Aud, Fox, & Kewal-Ramani, 2010; Skiba et al., 2011). Because schoolwide positive behavior interventions and supports (SWPBIS) is widely adopted to reduce overall disciplinary incidents (Sugai & Simonsen, 2012), our goal was to examine its capacity to reduce inequitable disciplinary exclusions, as well as how it might need to be modified to do so more effectively.

According to nationally representative data collected by the U.S. Department of Education's Office of Civil Rights in 2009–2010, about 7.4% of all students enrolled in U.S. public schools were suspended at least once that year. Disaggregated by students' race/ethnicity, disturbing disparities emerge: 17% of all Black, 8% of all American Indian,[1] and 7% of all Latino students were suspended at least once, compared to 5% of all White students (Losen & Gillespie, 2012). And these disparities widen at the secondary level, and even more when the data are further disaggregated by disability status (see Chapter 6).

Black and American Indian students tend to be most affected by disciplinary disparities. Black students tend to be not only excluded at higher rates but also subject to more severe disciplinary consequences, including suspensions, than White students for similar violations (Skiba, Michael, Nardo, & Peterson, 2002; Skiba & Peterson, 2000). They also are more likely than their White peers to be suspended for subjectively interpretable violations, such as disrespect or noncompliance (Skiba et al., 2011). American Indian students are also suspended at a higher rate than their White peers (Aud et al., 2010). In addition, American Indian students tend to be truant at a much higher rate than White students (Aud et al., 2012).

Disparities in disciplinary out-of-school suspensions increase at higher grade levels (see Losen's introduction to this book). Not surprisingly, racial disparities in disciplinary exclusion are paralleled by racial disparities in academic outcomes. Based on the 2009 National Assessment of Educational Progress (NAEP) in reading at the 4th-grade level, American Indian students scored 26 points lower than their White peers, whereas Black and Latino students scored 25 points lower. Similar results occurred at the 8th-grade level: American Indian students trailed their White peers by 22 points, Black students by 27 points, and Latino students by 24 points (Aud et al., 2011). On the most recent NAEP 4th-grade reading assessment, conducted in 2013, Black students scored 24 points lower, Latino students 21 points lower, and American Indian students 19 points lower than their White peers.[2] Based on the most current data available, the average freshman graduation rate for American Indian students in 2009–2010 was 69%, compared to 83% of White students, 71% of Latino students, and 66% of Black students (Aud et al., 2013).

In sum, racial disparities in disciplinary exclusion have increased in recent decades; they are more pronounced in secondary than elementary schools and for students with disabilities; they affect Black and American Indian students most severely; and they are accompanied by disparities in academic performance and high school graduation rates. Because SWPBIS has been linked to overall reductions in disciplinary referrals, it presents itself as a potential remedy for disciplinary inequities.

SCHOOLWIDE POSITIVE BEHAVIOR INTERVENTIONS AND SUPPORTS

To provide an overview of SWPBIS, we briefly describe its key features, the extent to which it has been adopted by schools across the United States, its presence in educational policy, and the evidence-base linking its implementation to improved student outcomes.

Key Features

With its origin in positive behavioral interventions and supports (PBIS) strategies designed to include students with emotional and behavioral disability in general education classrooms (Carr et al., 2002; Colvin, Kame'enui, & Sugai, 1993), SWPBIS has evolved into a schoolwide approach to discipline that is intended to create safe, predictable, and positive school environments that are responsive to entire school populations' varying needs for certain types and levels of support (Sprague & Horner, 2006). The key SWPBIS practices are (a) clearly defining behavioral expectations valued by the school community, (b) proactively teaching what those expected behaviors look like in various school settings at least once a year, (c) frequently rewarding students who comply with behavioral expectations,

(d) administering a clearly defined continuum of consequences for behavioral violations, and (e) continuously collecting and analyzing data to assess students' responsiveness to the behavioral support provided.

The hallmark of SWPBIS is a focus on changing adult behavior, such as proactively teaching behavioral expectations, frequently rewarding students for engaging in appropriate behaviors, and making data-based decisions about students' support needs based on their behavioral performance. Implementation of SWPBIS is team based and driven by adults. A team whose members are representative of the school's demographics and that includes the school administrator and members of all school constituencies (e.g., general education teacher, special education teacher, parent, school psychologist, counselor, custodial staff) defines the school's behavioral expectations, develops lessons to teach these expected behaviors to all students at the beginning of the school year and as needed throughout the year, designs activities to acknowledge and celebrate students' behavioral successes, and reviews patterns of office discipline referral (ODR) data.

To accommodate students with differing needs, the implementation of SWPBIS follows the multitiered response-to-intervention logic. Universal support (tier 1) is provided to all students at all times; that is, all students are exposed to annual lessons in how to comply with behavioral expectations and are rewarded for doing so. Students who do not respond sufficiently to this universal tier receive additional support, often in the form of a check-in/check-out program (tier 2). This type of program gives students increased contact with adults. In the morning, students check in with a staff member who makes sure the student has all materials and is prepared for the day, and in the afternoon students check out with the same staff member, who provides praise and encouragement for the next day. Students also carry a "point card" they present to teachers throughout the day to get feedback on their behavioral performance, which enables teachers and schoolwide teams to monitor their behavioral progress frequently. Students who do not respond to the tier 2 program, or who clearly need more intensive interventions because they are students with significant behavioral challenges, receive intensive individualized or tertiary support (tier 3). The individualized support students receive in tier 3 is specified by a behavioral support team in a behavior support plan.

Adoption

Since its initial testing at select demonstration sites in the 1990s (Colvin & Fernandez, 2000; Taylor-Greene et al., 1997), SWPBIS has become a widely adopted disciplinary approach. Its dissemination in schools, districts, and state education agencies occurred largely through the Technical Assistance (TA) Center on PBIS, which has been funded by the U.S. Department of Education's Office of Special Education Programs since 1998. In 2008, the TA Center on PBIS assessed the extent to which SWPBIS has been adopted and found that 30 states and the District of Columbia had statewide PBIS initiatives, and 46 states plus the District of Columbia were implementing SWPBIS in some of their schools. A total of 8% of all U.S. schools had implemented SWPBIS (Spaulding, Horner, May, & Vincent, 2008). In 2012, the TA Center on PBIS reported that 16,000 school teams had been trained in SWPBIS implementation (Sugai & Simonsen, 2012).

Presence in Educational Policy

True to its origins in the inclusion movement (Carr et al., 2002), PBIS is now firmly embedded in special education law, as its widespread adoption and efforts to increase its political visibility (Sugai et al., 2010) brought SWPBIS to the attention of policymakers. The 1997 Amendments to the Individuals with Disabilities Education Act (IDEA) called for using PBIS to address inappropriate behavior among students receiving special education services. In the 2004 reauthorization of the IDEA, PBIS was retained as a strategy to support students with disability who exhibited challenging behavior.

In the wake of mounting evidence of racial disparities in disciplinary practices and an increased focus on finding ways to alleviate those disparities and associated disparities in academic outcomes, SWPBIS was proposed as a strategy to facilitate equity in student outcomes in a bill introduced in the U.S. Senate (S.1094, Strengthening America's School Act of 2013). Sections 1114–1116 of the bill, intended to help schools close the achievement gap and improve school environments, included SWPBIS among the recommended strategies to achieve those goals. These policy recommendations make good sense, given the focus in SWPBIS on establishing safe, predictable, and positive school environments, as well as the large base of evidence supporting its beneficial effect on student outcomes.

The Evidence Base for SWPBIS

Abundant evidence links SWPBIS to a reduction in office discipline referrals, primarily in elementary schools (Horner, Sugai, & Anderson, 2010). The results of two randomized controlled trials, the gold standard for scientific evidence, support the benefits of SWPBIS. Horner et al. (2009) conducted a randomized controlled trial with 60 elementary schools and found that the implementation of SWPBIS was functionally related to improvement in adults' perceptions of school safety and gains in students' reading performance.

Bradshaw, Mitchell, and Leaf (2010) conducted a randomized controlled trial with 37 elementary schools and found that schools implementing SWPBIS had a lower overall percentage of students receiving ODR. A reduction in time spent on disciplinary incidents translates into increased instructional time—thus SWPBIS has clear benefits for students' academic outcomes as well as their behavior.

To assess the extent to which SWPBIS can alleviate racial disparities in disciplinary outcomes, a number of studies have examined the relationship between the implementation of SWPBIS and disciplinary equity across students from various racial/ethnic backgrounds. It is important to keep in mind that disparities in disciplinary outcomes between racial groups can be expressed in different units of measurement. Rate differences indicate if the number of students affected by disciplinary events in one racial group is equivalent to the number of students affected by disciplinary events in another racial group. Odds ratios indicate if students of one racial group are more likely to be disciplined than students of another group. Ideally, both comparisons should be reported to arrive at a balanced interpretation of existing disparities. Unfortunately, few studies report both.

Bradshaw, Mitchell, O'Brennan, and Leaf (2010) examined discipline data collected during 1 academic year in schools implementing SWPBIS and found that Black students had significantly greater odds of being referred to the office than White students. Kaufman et al. (2010) examined discipline data collected during 1 academic year in schools engaged in the implementation of SWPBIS and found that African American students had higher rates of ODR than their peers. On the other hand, Vincent and colleagues (Vincent, Tobin, Swain-Bradway, & May, 2011) compared 3 years of discipline data collected in elementary schools that implemented SWPBIS with discipline data collected in elementary schools that did not implement SWPBIS. In all schools, Black students were referred to the office at a higher rate than White students. In the schools that implemented SWPBIS, the disparity in the rates of Black and White students referred to the office was smaller at each time point and stayed approximately the same across the 3 years. In the schools that did not implement SWPBIS, the disparity in the rates of Black and White students referred to the office was larger at each time point and increased slightly across the 3 years. Examining equity in the multitiered continuum of supports provided through SWPBIS, Vincent, Tobin, Hawken, and Frank (2012) found that at the elementary level Black students had higher rates of discipline referrals than their peers and higher odds of receiving secondary support (tier 2) in the form of a check-in/check-out program than White students. At the middle school level, Black students had more significantly higher rates of disciplinary referrals compared to their peers but lower odds of receiving secondary support than White students.

In sum, the extent to which SWPBIS is effective in reducing racial disparities in disciplinary exclusion is currently unclear, particularly at the secondary level, where racial disparities are most pronounced (Losen & Martinez, 2013). Though there are some promising outcomes, SWPBIS in its current form might not be sufficient to improve disciplinary equity; thus, modifications might need to be considered (Drakeford, 2004; Vincent, Randall, Cartledge, Tobin, & Swain-Bradway, 2011).

Because Oregon has a strong statewide PBIS initiative, and because racial disparities in disciplinary exclusion are greater and perhaps most consequential for the long-term success of non-White students at the middle school level, our research focused on examining whether SWPBIS in its current form has an impact on racial disparities in discipline in middle schools in Oregon. Furthermore, because American Indian students have very poor disciplinary outcomes and are often excluded from large-scale analyses due to their overall low numbers, and because Oregon has the 10th largest American Indian enrollment in the nation, we examined practices in schools with few disparities in disciplinary outcomes between American Indian and White students to see how those practices might guide necessary modifications to SWPBIS.

SWPBIS AND DISCIPLINARY DISPARITIES IN MIDDLE SCHOOLS

To assess the relationship between implementation of SWPBIS at the middle school level and changes in racial disparities in discipline, we provide a brief overview of our research project, its primary goals, and its outcomes.

Overview of the Research

We merged data from a randomized controlled trial designed to test whether SWPBIS can be implemented with fidelity in middle schools with data on disciplinary exclusion collected by the Oregon Department of Education. The fidelity of SWPBIS implementation was measured with the Prevention Practices Assessment (Institute on Violence and Destructive Behavior, 2008). The Oregon Department of Education's disciplinary data included in-school suspension (ISS), out-of-school suspension (OSS), expulsion (EXP), and truancy (TRU). The number of ISS, OSS, and EXPs were recorded as well as the duration of each exclusionary incident. Duration was measured in half-days; for example, a student could be suspended out of school for half a day, 1 day, 1 and a half days, and so on.

Our sample consisted of 35 middle schools in Oregon, which ranged in locale and size from rural schools with 65 students to suburban/urban schools with over 1,100 students. On average, the schools' enrollment was predominantly White (70%), followed by Latino (20%), American Indian (5%), Asian (3%), and Black (2%). Schools were randomly assigned to a treatment condition (full SWPBIS training schedule with ongoing coaching) or control condition (1-day annual workshop or consultation on SWPBIS). The racial distribution of school enrollments was approximately equal in the treatment group and the control group.

To examine the impact SWPBIS had on equity in middle schools, we first used statistical tests to determine whether the method can be implemented with fidelity in these schools. Descriptive analyses of discipline data focused on rates of disciplinary events per 100 students per day, as well as the percentage of days of instruction lost, based on 170 annual school days multiplied by each racial group's enrollment in each condition. To follow up on descriptive outcomes, we examined differences in ISS rate, OSS rate, EXP rate, TRU rate, and "percentage of student days lost" for each racial/ethnic group across the treatment and control conditions.

Can SWPBIS Be Implemented in Middle Schools?

Data on implementation fidelity showed that treatment schools made larger over-all gains in the key SWPBIS practices across the 4 years of the project than the control schools. In treatment schools, the key practice "defining schoolwide behavioral expectations" increased from 23% implemented in year 1 to 66% implemented in year 4; "teaching behavioral expectations" increased from 17% implemented in year 1 to 70% implemented in year 4; and "reinforcement of expected behavior" increased from 10% implemented in year 1 to 49% implemented in year 4. Control schools increased their level of "defining schoolwide behavioral expectations" from 32% implemented in year 1 to 56% implemented in year 4, their practice of "teaching behavioral expectations" from 22% implemented in year 1 to 54% implemented in year 4, and "reinforcement of expected behaviors" from 16% implemented in year 1 to 26% implemented in year 4. According to our statistical tests, the differences in the implementation of SWPBIS between treatment schools and control schools was statistically significant.

Was SWPBIS Implementation Associated With Reduced Inequities in Disciplinary Exclusions?

Figure 14.1 provides an overview of disciplinary exclusion rates by racial/ethnic group across time and treatment condition. We focused on African American, Latino, and American Indian/Alaska Native (AI/AN) students because they tradi-tionally experience the poorest discipline outcomes, and we included White stu-dents as the comparison group. Panels 1 to 4 show the mean rates for ISS, OSS, EXP, and TRU for each racial group across conditions. Panel 5 shows the mean percentage of student days lost across racial/ethnic groups and condition.

Based on these outcomes, the implementation of SWPBIS in middle schools seems associated with (a) overall lower rates of ISS, the least severe form of disci-plinary exclusion; (b) overall high rates of truancy, especially for American Indian and Latino students; (c) some reduction in disciplinary exclusions for Latino and American Indian students, but few for African American students; and (4) fluc-tuations in the duration of disciplinary exclusions for African American students. Statistically significant interactions among time, condition, and race/ethnicity indicated that changes in disciplinary exclusion across time differed not only by condition but also by students' racial/ethnic backgrounds; that is, race remained a predictor of trends in disciplinary exclusion despite the implementation of SWPBIS. Effect sizes for the interaction terms were extremely small, ranging from = .059 to = .065. (For study details, see Vincent, Sprague, & Gau, 2013.)

Given the outcomes for American Indian students in our middle school sam-ple—especially their high truancy rates, which appear consistent with national findings—we followed up with a supplementary analysis of the extent to which schools in Oregon implement recommendations from the Native American

Figure 14.1. Mean Rates of EXP, ISS, OSS, TRU, and Mean Percentage of Student Days Lost Across Racial/Ethnic Groups and Conditions

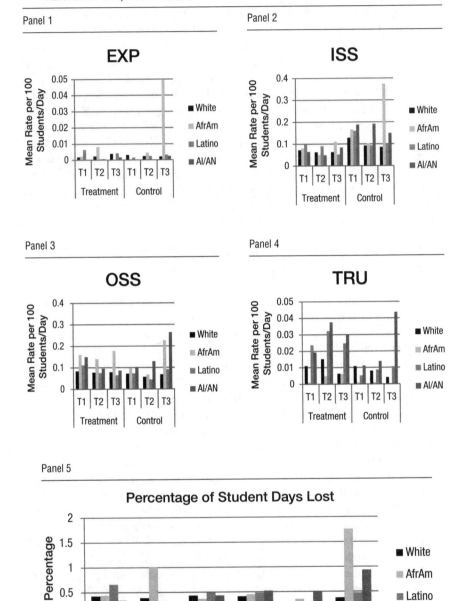

Community to reduce disciplinary exclusion and improve the academic achievement of American Indian students. If the Native American Community's recommendations translate into promising practices, they might provide guidance on how to modify SWPBIS to make it more responsive to the behavioral support needs of American Indian students in particular, and perhaps of non-White students in general.

RECOMMENDATIONS OF THE NATIVE COMMUNITY

To improve its students' school outcomes, the Native American Community recommends (a) improving teachers' cultural awareness through a focus on Native culture in preservice and inservice teacher training; (b) enhancing the relevance of the curriculum by incorporating tribal traditions, customs, and languages; and (c) increasing Native parents' participation in school events and local policymaking (Chavers, 2000; CHiXapkaid et al., 2008; NCAI/NIEA, 2010). Unfortunately, our research indicated that limited efforts had been made to implement these recommendations. However, we also found that, in schools containing grades K through 8 or K through 12 (K–8/12) in our sample, the discrepancy in suspension rates between American Indian and White students was only .02 percentage points. Based on these findings, we took a closer look at these schools' schoolwide support practices.

Promising Practices to Improve Disciplinary Equity for American Indian Students

One of the K–8/12 schools stood out with zero OSS for both American Indian and White students. In this school, teachers reported the highest use of Native culture in instruction and the greatest amount of staff development focused on American Indian issues. The school also had the highest number of teachers who identified as American Indian, and a Title VII Indian education coordinator. Parent involvement and strong community relationships were a feature shared by all schools with low OSS rates for American Indian and White students. One school actively involved parents by conducting an online survey asking them to rate whether their child's education was adequately challenging, whether homework assignments were meaningful, and whether they as parents felt well informed about school activities and felt welcome in the school.

The policies and practices of schools with low American Indian disciplinary exclusion rates seemed to emphasize the importance of relationships and how to nurture them carefully. Notably, two of the four schools with the lowest OSS rates for both American Indian and White students had implemented SWPBIS. Their behavioral expectations clearly reflected Native traditions, and their student handbooks emphasized exhibiting positive behaviors and parent involvement.

In sum, the schools with the lowest disparities in disciplinary exclusion between American Indian and White students clearly followed the recommendations of the Native American Community by focusing on staff development in cultural sensitivity, culturally relevant instruction, and strong school relationships with parents and families. In two schools, these practices were successfully merged with the SWPBIS model, which resulted in greater disciplinary equity. (For details of our study, see Vincent, CHiXapkaid, Sprague, & Tobin, 2013.)

Limitations of the Research

Because the samples for our studies were relatively small and data often violated the assumptions of the statistical tests, our outcomes should be interpreted as purely exploratory. Moreover, both studies were limited to schools in Oregon. Replication in schools located in other states might provide additional important information.

SUMMARY AND RECOMMENDATIONS FOR POLICY AND PRACTICE

There is little doubt that SWPBIS has substantial benefits for schools. Reductions in ODR translate into less chaotic classrooms, less time spent by teachers and administrators on disciplinary issues, and more time spent on teaching and learning. Moreover, implementation driven by local school teams requires few additional resources, and the wide adoption of SWPBIS speaks to its appeal to school personnel who are strapped for time and resources. Its current limited effectiveness in reducing racial/ethnic disparities in disciplinary exclusion suggests that, in its current form, SWPBIS might have to be supplemented with other practices or be modified to increase its capacity to reduce disciplinary inequity. SWPBIS was not specifically designed to address disciplinary inequities but to create safe, predictable, and positive school environments in which students can succeed behaviorally as well as academically. It was developed approximately 3 decades ago, when fewer non-White students attended U.S. schools and less attention was focused on equity in student outcomes. Although it is intended to meet the support needs of *all* students, its current limited attention to cultural differences in the student population and potential differences in cultural backgrounds between adults and students within a school make SWPBIS vulnerable to criticism for not sufficiently reducing racial/ethnic disparities in discipline outcomes. However, our studies show that practices that appear to produce desirable outcomes for American Indian students could guide us in modifying SWPBIS to be more responsive to the support needs of culturally diverse students in general. Based on our findings, we make the following policy recommendations for improving the effectiveness of SWPBIS in reducing inequities in discipline practices.

Increase Accountability for Cultural Awareness Within the SWPBIS Framework

Although the U.S. student population is becoming rapidly more diverse, the majority of school personnel are still White (Toldson, McGee, & Lemmons, 2013). This means that cultural discontinuities between students and teachers are becoming more common. Within the SWPBIS framework, these cultural discontinuities might affect the extent to which adult-driven behavioral support practices match students' support needs. To create greater cultural continuity between students and teachers, we recommend professional development that focuses on cultural awareness (Bradshaw, Mitchell, O'Brennan, & Leaf, 2010; Gregory, Allen, Mikami, Hafen, & Pianta, 2013). The implementation of SWPBIS could be modified to include systemic support for staff to increase their awareness of cultural differences, including professional development opportunities, internal coaching, or holding regular forums for problem solving and the discussion of discipline issues potentially related to cultural differences (Vincent, Randall et al., 2011). Incentives such as grants to schools to implement these additional staff supports might be useful in encouraging those implementing SWPBIS to enhance their accountability for cultural awareness.

Increase Accountability for Basing Support Decisions Within the SWPBIS Framework on Data Disaggregated by Student Race/Ethnicity

One hallmark of SWPBIS is data-based decisionmaking. Although fidelity in the implementation of SWPBIS is assessed according to the extent to which schools continuously collect and review discipline data, it is commonly not based on the extent to which those data are disaggregated by students' race/ethnicity. Based on 3 years (2005–2008) of ODR data collected using the Schoolwide Information System (SWIS), only 14% of SWIS users accessed the ethnicity report (Vincent, 2008).[3] Disaggregating discipline data should be a matter of course for SWPBIS implementers. Making implementation fidelity dependent on the use of discipline data disaggregated by student race/ethnicity for decisions regarding students' support needs might encourage schools to engage in this highly recommended practice.

Triangulate Data to Capture Multiple Perspectives of School Discipline

In its current form, SWPBIS implementation is heavily focused on ODR data. Though these data are a valid index of a school's overall behavioral health (Irvin, Tobin, Sprague, Sugai, & Vincent, 2004), they might not be sufficiently nuanced to capture differences in teachers' disciplinary practices, students' perceptions of the discipline process, or parents' perceptions of how students should be disciplined. As our study of behaviorally successful schools serving American Indian students has shown, collecting data on parents' perceptions can promote mutual trust and meaningful collaboration that appears to be beneficial in reducing disciplinary inequities.

Furthermore, ODR data focus exclusively on behavioral violations, whereas collecting data on the extent to which students engage in appropriate social skills might add a decisionmaking dimension that is better aligned with SWPBIS's focus on positive school environments. Currently, the federal government has set aside funds for grant applicants to receive support for implementing PBIS. Thus grantees could be given incentives, such as in the application evaluation criteria, to link data systems to yield more nuanced information. For example, linking discipline and academic performance data might provide important information on students' overall school success. Teacher-reported data on student behavior could be linked with student self-reported behaviors to assess the extent to which teacher and student perceptions converge. Linking teacher data to parent data might also add important information on how behavioral expectations in school align with behavioral expectations at home. This might encourage SWPBIS implementers to modify their practices to meet the support needs of culturally diverse students more effectively.

Merge SWPBIS Practices with Prevention-Oriented Student Codes of Conduct

Although SWPBIS relies on the proactive teaching of appropriate behavior and the frequent reinforcement of students who comply with behavioral expectations, research has shown that many schools that implement SWPBIS have student codes of conduct that are primarily punitive (Fenning et al., 2013). Student codes of conduct that focus on the consequences of behavioral violations appear to conflict with the overall prevention-oriented focus of SWPBIS.

Fenning and colleagues (2013) found that codes of conduct that prescribe disciplinary exclusion for relatively minor or subjective violations might produce racially inequitable discipline outcomes, given that non-White students tend to be disciplined disproportionately for such violations (Skiba et al., 2011). Simply removing the option of excluding students from school for these types of offenses might reduce disciplinary inequities (Fenning et al., 2003).

These recommended modifications clearly align with the current SWPBIS framework. They focus on expanding existing staff support systems to include an emphasis on cultural awareness, on actively using available tools to disaggregate data, on expanding data-based decisionmaking to include more nuanced information, and on redefining the severity of consequences for minor behavioral violations to prevent disciplinary exclusion. Taken together, these modifications could increase the effectiveness of SWPBIS in reducing racial disparities in disciplinary exclusion.

NOTES

The study was partially supported by Grant Number R01 DA019037 from The National Institute on Drug Abuse. Its contents are solely the responsibility of the authors and do not necessarily represent the official views of the Institute.

1. OCR's more recent estimates for 2009–2010 put American Indan suspension at 14%.

2. See http://nces.ed.gov/nationsreportcard/naepdata/report.aspx.

3. See www.swis.org. SWIS is a data-collection system used by many schools implementing SWPBIS. It has the capacity to produce an "ethnicity report" showing discipline data by student race/ethnicity.

REFERENCES

Aud, S., Fox, M. A. & Kewal-Ramani, A. (2010). *Status and trends in the education of racial and ethnic groups* (NCES 2010-015). Washington, DC: U.S. Government Printing Office.

Aud, S., Hussar, W., Johnson, F., Kena, G., Roth, E., Manning, E., . . . Zhang, J. (2012). *The condition of education 2012* (NCES 2012-045). Washington, DC: U.S. Department of Education, National Center for Education Statistics. Retrieved from http://nces.ed.gov/pubsearch

Aud, S., Hussar, W., Kena, G., Bianco, K., Frohlich, L., Kemp, J., & Tahan, K. (2011). *The condition of education 2011* (NCES 2011-033). Washington, DC: U.S. Government Printing Office.

Aud, S., Wilkinson-Flicker, S., Kristapovich, P., Rathbun, A., Wang, X., & Zhang, J. (2013). *The condition of education 2013* (NCES 2013-037). Washington, DC: U.S. Department of Education, National Center for Education Statistics. Retrieved from http://nces.ed.gov/pubsearch

Bradshaw, C. P., Mitchell, M. M., & Leaf, P. J. (2010). Examining the effects of school-wide positive behavioral interventions and supports on student outcomes. *Journal of Positive Behavior Interventions, 12,* 133–148.

Bradshaw, C. P., Mitchell, M. M., O'Brennan, L. M., & Leaf, P. J. (2010). Multilevel exploration of factors contributing to the overrepresentation of black students in office discipline referrals. *Journal of Educational Psychology, 102,* 508–520.

Carr, E. G., Dunlap, G., Horner, R. H., Koegel, R. L., Turnbull, A. P, Sailor, . . . Fox, L. (2002). Positive behavior support: Evolution of an applied science. *Journal of Positive Behavior Interventions, 4,* 4–16.

Chavers, D. (2000). Indian teachers and school improvement. *Journal of American Indian Education, 39*(2), 1–18.

CHiXapkaid, Banks-Joseph, S. R., Inglebret, E., McCubbin, L. Sievers, J., Bruna, L., . . . Sanya, N. (2008). *From where the sun rises: Addressing the educational achievement of Native Americans in Washington State.* Pullman, WA: Washington State University, Clearinghouse on Native Teaching and Learning.

Colvin, G., & Fernandez, E. (2000). Sustaining effective behavior support systems in an elementary school. *Journal of Positive Behavior Interventions, 2,* 251–253.

Colvin, G., Kame'enui, E. J., & Sugai, G. (1993). School-wide and classroom management: Reconceptualizing the integration and management of students with behavior problems in general education. *Education and Treatment of Children, 16,* 361–381.

Drakeford, W. (2004). *Racial disproportionality in school disciplinary practices* [Practitioner brief series]. Denver, CO: National Center for Culturally Responsive Educational Systems.

Fenning, P., Pigott, T., Engler, E., Bradshaw, K., Gamboney, E., Grunewald, S., . . . McGrath Kato, M. (2013). *A mixed methods approach examining disproportionality in school discipline.* Paper presented at the Closing the School Discipline Gap conference, Washington, DC.

Gregory, A., Allen, J., Mikami, A., Hafen, A., & Pianta, R. (2013, January 10). *The promise of a teacher professional development program in reducing the racial disparity in classroom exclusionary discipline.* Paper presented at the Closing the School Discipline Gap Conference, Washington, DC.

Horner, R. H., Sugai, G., & Anderson, C. M. (2010). Examining the evidence base for school-wide positive behavior support. *Focus on Exceptionality, 42*(8), 1–14.

Horner, R. H., Sugai, G., Smolkowski, K., Eber, L., Nakasato, J., Todd, A., et al. (2009). A randomized, waitlist-controlled effectiveness trial assessing school-wide positive behavior support in elementary schools. *Journal of Positive Behavior Interventions, 11*, 133–144.

Institute on Violence and Destructive Behavior. (2008). *Prevention practices assessment.* Eugene, OR: Author.

Irvin, L. K., Tobin, T. J., Sprague, J. R., Sugai, G., & Vincent, C. G. (2004). Validity of office discipline referral measures as indices of school-wide behavioral status and effects of school-wide behavioral interventions. *Journal of Positive Behavior Interventions, 6*, 131–147.

Kaufman, J. S., Jaser, S. S., Vaughan, E. L., Reynolds, J. S., Di Donato, J., Bernard, S. N. et al. (2010). Patterns in office discipline referral data by grade, race/ethnicity, and gender. *Journal of Positive Behavior Interventions, 12*, 44–54.

Losen, D., & Gillespie, J. (2012). *Opportunities suspended: The disparate impact of disciplinary exclusion from school.* Los Angeles, CA: University of California, the Center for Civil Rights Remedies at the Civil Rights Project.

Losen, D. J., & Martinez, T. E. (2013). *Out of school and off track: The overuse of suspension in American middle and high schools.* Los Angeles, CA: The Civil Rights Project at UCLA, the Center for Civil Rights Remedies.

National Congress of American Indians/National Indian Education Association. (2010). *National tribal priorities for Indian education.* Washington, DC: Author. Retrieved from http://www.niea.org/Policy.aspx

Skiba, R. J., Horner, R. H., Chung, C., Rausch, M. K., May, S., & Tobin, T. (2011). Race is not neutral: A national investigation of African American and Latino disproportionality in school discipline. *School Psychology Review, 40*, 85–107.

Skiba, R. J., Michael, R. S., Nardo, A. C., & Peterson, R. (2002). The color of discipline: Sources of racial and gender disproportionality in school punishment. *Urban Review, 34*, 317–342.

Skiba, R. J., & Peterson, R. L. (2000). School discipline at a crossroads: From zero tolerance to early response. *Exceptional Children, 66*, 335–347.

Spaulding, S., Horner, R., May, S., & Vincent, C. G. (2008). *Implementation of school-wide PBIS across the United States* [Evaluation brief]. Retrieved from http://pbis.org/evaluation/evaluation_briefs/nov_08_ (2).aspx

Sprague, J. R., & Horner, R. H. (2006). Schoolwide positive behavioral supports. In S. R. Jimerson & M. J. Furlong (Eds.), *The handbook of school violence and school safety* (pp. 413–427). Mahwah, NJ: Erlbaum.

Sugai, G., Horner, R. H., Algozzine, R., Barrett, S., Lewis, T., Anderson, C. . . . Simonsen, B. (2010). *School-wide positive behavior support: Implementers' blueprint and self-assessment.* Eugene, OR: University of Oregon.

Sugai, G., & Simonsen, B. (2012). *Positive behavioral interventions and supports: History, defining features, and misconceptions.* Available at http://pbis.org/school/pbis_revisited.aspx

Taylor-Greene, S., Brown, D., Nelson, L., Longton, J., Gassman, Cohen, J. . . . Hall, S. (1997). Schoolwide behavioral support: Starting the year off right. *Journal of Behavioral Education, 7*, 99–112.

Toldson, I., McGee, T., & Lemmons, B. (2013, January 10). *Reducing suspensions by improving academic engagement among school-age black males.* Paper presented at the Closing the School Discipline Gap Conference, Washington, DC.

Vincent, C. G. (2008). *Do schools using SWIS take advantage of the "school ethnicity report"?* [Evaluation brief]. Retrieved from http://pbis.org/evaluation/evaluation_briefs/default.aspx

Vincent, C. G., CHiXapkaid, Sprague, J. R., & Tobin, T. J. (2013, January 10). *Towards reducing disciplinary exclusions of American Indian/Alaska Native students.* Paper presented at the Closing the School Discipline Gap Conference, Washington, DC. Retrieved from http://civilrightsproject.ucla.edu/events/2013/closing-the-school-discipline-gap-conference-research-papers/closing-the-school-discipline-gap-research-to-practice

Vincent, C. G., Randall, C., Cartledge, G., Tobin, T. J., & Swain-Bradway, J. (2011). Towards a conceptual integration of cultural responsiveness and school-wide positive behavior support. *Journal of Positive Behavior Interventions, 13,* 219–229.

Vincent, C. G., Sprague, J. R., & Gau, J. (2013, January 10). *The effectiveness of school-wide positive behavior support in reducing disciplinary exclusions of students from non-White backgrounds in middle schools.* Paper presented at the Closing the School Discipline Gap Conference, Washington, DC. Retrieved from http://civilrightsproject.ucla.edu/events/2013/closing-the-school-discipline-gap-conference-research-papers/closing-the-school-discipline-gap-research-to-practice

Vincent, C. G., Tobin, T. J., Hawken, L., & Frank, J. (2012). Disciplinary referrals and access to secondary interventions: Patterns across students across African-American, Hispanic-American, and White backgrounds. *Education and Treatment of Children, 35,* 431–458.

Vincent, C. G., Tobin, T. J., Swain-Bradway, J., & May, S. (2011). Disciplinary referrals for culturally and linguistically diverse students with and without disabilities: Patterns resulting from school-wide positive behavior support. *Exceptionality, 19,* 175–190.

## CHAPTER 15

Reconsidering the Alternatives

The Relationship Among Suspension, Placement, Subsequent
Juvenile Detention, and the Salience of Race

Judi E. Vanderhaar, Joseph M. Petrosko,
and Marco A. Muñoz

The primary purpose of this research was to explore the relationships among suspension, removal to disciplinary alternative schools, subsequent juvenile detention, and race in a way that informs policy regarding investment in disciplinary alternative schools. The longitudinal nature of the research allowed us to track changes in students' event histories throughout their education careers to help determine who is being removed to alternative school and when, key predictors of removal, and the likelihood of subsequent juvenile detention for students with no prior juvenile justice involvement. The findings in this study raise serious questions about programs that isolate, concentrate, and exclude students deemed too disruptive or dangerous, and about whether school systems that lack systemic early intervention programs and invest in costly alternative schools contribute over time to the school-to-prison pipeline, particularly for students of color.

CONTEXT OF THE RESEARCH

Kentucky's Jefferson County Public School (JCPS) district served as the site of this research. It is important to note that Kentucky has the second highest rate in the nation of detaining youth charged with nonviolent offenses, which accounts for 20% of all youth detained for status and public offenses in the United States (DiLoreto & Grieshop-Goodwin, 2010). In the exact years of this study (1997–2006), Kentucky had the nation's seventh highest increase (15%) in the number of youth in juvenile facilities and a simultaneous 11% decrease in the number of violent offenses reported (Justice Policy Institute, 2009). Jefferson County, the largest county in Kentucky and one of the largest contributors to the state's juvenile incarceration rates, had the second highest juvenile arrest rate for offenses such as disorderly conduct and drunkenness (May & Chen, 2006).

JCPS is a large, ethnically diverse urban school district that serves approximately 100,000 students, 68% of whom receive free or reduced-price lunch. The district has 161 schools, including 26 alternative schools. The alternative schools serve several student populations, such as pregnant and parenting teenagers, over-age students, and students removed to youth psychiatric hospital units.

The disciplinary alternative schools in this study serve students whom the school and district administrators have determined to be either in violation of the student code of conduct, for which alternative school is a disciplinary option, or too disruptive or dangerous to remain in the regular school setting. Importantly, the district's zero expulsion policy sets the expectation that no student will be removed from the educational setting. However, any student who is assigned to a disciplinary alternative school but does not attend is prohibited from returning to any school in the district. The widespread implementation of zero-tolerance policies following the adoption of the state's Safe and Drug Free Schools and Community Act in 1994 resulted in an increase of the number of students removed to alternative schools, including younger children. In fact, due to an increase in the removal of elementary students, the disciplinary middle school expanded to serve students in 4th and 5th grades.

CHARACTERISTICS AND GROWTH OF ALTERNATIVE SCHOOLS

Alternative school settings for students who are identified as "disruptive" or "dangerous" are playing an increasingly prominent role in the world of public education, yet significant gaps in our understanding of their efficacy remain. Although the rapid expansion of alternative schools and our reliance on them is evident, the amount of research on alternative schools has not kept pace with their growth. In theory, alternative schools exist to provide optional learning environments for students who are struggling in traditional schools. Two basic subsets of alternative schools have emerged to serve students deemed at risk of failure: (a) one for students experiencing academic difficulty and at risk of dropping out, and (b) the other for students described as dangerous or disruptive.

In the early 1980s, based on the premise that schools could play a significant role in reducing youth crime (Barber, 1980), the U.S. Justice Department's Office of Juvenile Justice and Delinquency Prevention began promoting alternative schools for delinquent students. Alternative schools continue to be promoted today by education leaders and advocates as a promising strategy to reduce expulsion from school, provide alternative learning environments for students who are unsuccessful in regular schools, ensure a safe environment at mainstream schools, and reduce juvenile delinquency. However, the dearth of empirical evidence demonstrating that disciplinary alternative schools actually realize or support these objectives should temper the rush to employ the strategy.

National data reflect a rapid expansion in the last decade of alternative schools for at-risk students (Lehr, Soon Tan, & Ysseldyke, 2009). In 1998, the National Center for Education Statistics (NCES) indicated that there were 3,850 public alternative schools for at-risk students; by 2002, NCES identified 10,900 public alternative schools, although researchers looking at national data estimated that, in reality, there were more than 20,000 alternative schools and programs (Lange & Sletten, 2002).

The increase in alternative schools correlates with the mounting population of disenfranchised students, minority students, and students who live in poverty (Kim & Taylor, 2008; Verdugo & Glenn, 2006). The demand for alternative schools for disruptive or dangerous students outweighs the supply, particularly in urban districts, and such schools are increasingly serving elementary school–aged students (NCES, 2010). Urban school districts are relying on alternative schools at a far greater rate than rural and suburban districts in an attempt to decrease school crime, yet national school crime trends raise questions about their need and utility for serving this function. In the 2003 national school survey on crime and school safety, 70% of urban public schools cited a lack of alternative placements for disruptive students as the most common factor impeding efforts to reduce or prevent crime at school (NCES, 2007). Paradoxically, the report on indicators of school crime and safety showed a decrease in students reporting being victims of violent crime in schools from 10% to 6% between 1995 and 2001 (NCES, 2003) and is down to 4% in 2011 (NCES, 2012).

Some research highlighting best-practice alternative schools indicates the promise these schools hold for supporting excluded students (Quinn & Poirier, 2006), yet (a) the normalization of exclusion, (b) the high cost and wide variation in the quality of these schools, and (c) the lack of regulation and accountability at the state and district levels are causes for great concern. The literature on alternative schools shows their characteristics are associated with both positive and negative student outcomes. Positive characteristics such as small schools, low student–teacher ratios, flexible and understanding teachers, individualized instruction, student involvement in decisionmaking, and family/parent participation result in a more positive school climate and student outcomes (Cox, 1999). The alternative school characteristics deemed deleterious to student outcomes include racial isolation, punitive disciplinary focus, intensified social control, inadequate resources, lack of accountability, and unchallenging curriculum (Cox, 1999).

Research suggests that moving disruptive students to alternative schools has exacerbated inequities rooted in race, poverty, and special education status and heightened segregation by race and disability (Quinn & Rutherford, 1998). Also, there might be a lack of services for special education students in alternative school settings (Lehr & Lange, 2003; Verdugo & Glenn, 2006). Several decades of research document that exclusionary discipline is consistently applied disproportionately to Black students (Arnove & Strout, 1980; Losen & Gillespie, 2012; Wald & Losen, 2003) and that disciplinary alternative schools might be used increasingly for the punishment, exclusion, and tracking of African American students deemed too disruptive or dangerous (Dunbar, 2001; Lehr, Lanners, & Lange, 2003), which increases the likelihood of future incarceration (Shollenberger, 2013) and dropout (see Chapter 2).

Although many alternative schools provide a variety of services, there apparently is more collaboration with the juvenile justice system and the police than with agencies that can help students with life after school (Dunbar, 2001; Verdugo & Glenn, 2006). Kliner, Porch, and Ferris (2002) found that, in large districts and districts with high minority enrollment and concentrated poverty, 84% of the alternative schools collaborated with the juvenile justice system, 75% with mental health agencies, and 70% with police departments. The punitive nature of removal to disciplinary alternative schools, coupled with the lack of regulation and a strong law-enforcement presence in alternative schools, might create a pathway to juvenile detention. In some cases, disciplinary alternative schools might more closely resemble juvenile detention facilities than schools. A relatively recent study examining the relationship between alternative schools and delinquency suggests that, rather than helping to equalize the playing field for youth already at risk, alternative schools simply act as a sorting mechanism (Free, 2008).

OVERVIEW OF THE RESEARCH

The study sample consists of an entire cohort of 3rd-grade students (N = 7,668) enrolled in JCPS during the 1997–1998 school year, whose demographic characteristics reflected the overall district: 52% male and 48% female; 61% White, 35% Black, and 3.5% other ethnicities; 59.6% receiving free or reduced-price lunch; and approximately 23% identified as eligible for special education. Of all the students in the cohort, 1.3% had emotional-behavioral disability (EBD), and there was a racial gap among this population: 2.3% of all Blacks in the cohort were students with EBD, compared with 0.8% of the White population.

In order to determine whether and to what extent race and other student factors and experiences contributed to the likelihood of removal to alternative school and subsequent juvenile detention, we constructed a dataset allowing us to follow 3rd-grade students as they moved through the school system for 10 years, through 12th grade. Each variable and student movement between settings and grade level was tracked for each year.

The primary dependent variable, removal to alternative school, was determined based on individual records of students' entries into one of the JCPS disciplinary alternative schools at any point during a given school year. There were a large number of repeated entries into alternative schools for individual students, but to isolate the impact of a student's first removal to alternative school, only the first occurrence was used in the statistical modeling analysis. Similarly, the analysis considered only a juvenile detention event that occurred *after* a student was removed to an alternative school for students with no prior juvenile detention entries.

The predictor variables include student race, gender, free and reduced-price lunch status (used as a proxy for poverty), suspension (experienced out-of-school suspension), school mobility (the number of times a student moved from one school to another), school attendance, grade retention (repeating the same grade), disability status (EBD and LD), and Comprehensive Test of Basic Skills (CTBS) reading level. The racial groups were collapsed into two categories, minority and White, for purposes of the statistical modeling analysis.

We used a set of statistical procedures that allowed us to track risk of removal to alternative school and the impact of each variable on alternative school entry across the 10-year period. We used a second set of descriptive and statistical procedures to determine subsequent juvenile detention. With these longitudinal data we could thus ascertain the impact of race on the risk for juvenile detention while controlling for other variables. A comprehensive description of the methods and complete results of the discrete time hazard analysis are available online at http://tinyurl.com/JanCRPconference (Vanderhaar, Petrosko, & Muñoz, 2013).

Fundamentally, this study describes trends and raises questions but was not designed to determine whether alternative schooling causes higher rates of juvenile justice involvement. Although the study was not designed to determine whether alternative schooling *causes* higher rates of juvenile justice involvement and thus did not include a control group, the literature asserts that alternative schools are ideally tools to help struggling students and prevent future delinquency. Thus, one marker of success would be low rates of subsequent detention for students who attend the alternative schools.

RESULTS

Of the 7,668 3rd-grade students in the study cohort, only 4,758 (62.1%) remained through grade 12. Over the course of 10 years, 2,910 students (37.9%) left school and/or were withdrawn from the cohort due to various other factors, including dropout, transfer to another school district, home schooling, and death.

Suspension Rates and Race

Confirming nearly decades of research on school suspensions, the overrepresentation of minority and poor children in out-of-school suspensions was evident in this study and is consistent with the longitudinal findings described in Chapters 1 and 2. As shown in Table 15.1, the cohort suspension rate for poor minority students is nearly twice that of all other groups across time. Interestingly, poverty

Table 15.1. Suspension Rates for Entire Cohort by Level

N		Elementary			Middle			High		
		$N = 7,668^a$ Suspensions	Rate	N	$N = 6,656^a$ Suspensions	Rate	N	$N = 5,893^a$ Suspensions	Rate	
White	Nonpoor	2,626	29	1.1%	2,400	462	19.3%	2255	529	23.5%
	Poor	2,057	119	5.8%	1,514	723	47.8%	1201	482	40.1%
Minority	Nonpoor	471	12	2.5%	542	215	39.7%	596	379	63.6%
	Poor	2,514	282	11.2%	2,200	1,644	74.7%	1841	1,265	68.7%

^{a}N differences at each level reflect loss of sample across time due to withdrawals from the district due to dropout, transfer to another school district, home schooling, and death.

appears related to a greater risk for suspension for both minority and White students up until high school. In high school, poor White students have almost double the suspension risk (40.1%) of nonpoor White students (23.5%), but the suspension risk for poor minority students (68.7%) is similar to that of nonpoor minority students (63.6%).

What Is the Risk of Removal to a Disciplinary Alternative School?

A 1-year snapshot of disciplinary alternative school enrollments in JCPS might lead one to believe that a very small percentage (between 1% and 2%) of students ever experience removal to these schools. However, tracking individual students over 10 consecutive years reveals a far higher risk of removal, especially for Black students. Specifically, over the course of 10 years, 544 members of the original 3rd-grade cohort were removed at least once by 12th grade. Thus the total percentage of students who were removed to a disciplinary school between 3rd and 12th grade was 7.1%, or 1 in 15 students. Further, 356 (13.1%) of the 2,715 Black 3rd-grade cohort were removed to an alternative school, compared to 178 (3.8%) of the 4,638 White members, a gap of over 9 percentage points. As shown in Figure 15.1, the removal rate to disciplinary alternative school is at least three times higher for Black students than for White students at every level (i.e., elementary, middle, and high).

Importantly, although many students experienced repeat entry to an alternative school over the 10 years they were tracked, these percentages reflect only the first time a student was removed to an alternative school. In other words, the percentages are based on the unduplicated count of students from the cohort who were removed to alternative school at least once, and not on the number of removals. For all students, regardless of race, the risk of first removal to alternative school is highest in 7th grade.

Figure 15.1: Racial Difference in the Risk of Removal to Alternative School Over Time

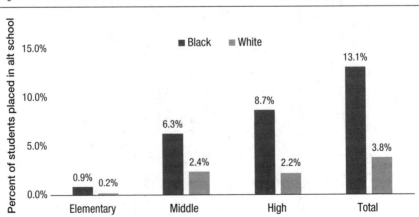

What Are the Key Predictors of Removal to Disciplinary Alternative School?

Race. The statistical models demonstrate the significant impact of race, even when controlling for the effects of poverty. Regardless of which grade a student entered a disciplinary school, the estimated odds of removal were three times higher for minority students than for White students.[1] Coupled with the descriptive results illustrated in Table 15.1, this indicates that poor minority students are most at risk of removal to a disciplinary school.

Emotional-Behavioral Disability. Students diagnosed as having EBD are at great risk of being removed to an alternative school; in fact, their odds of removal are more than eight times higher than for students without EBD.[2] Research has illustrated the vastly disproportionate suspension of students with EBD nationwide, particularly of Black students (Osher et al., 2004). When controlling for the effects of prior suspension, the odds of removal to alternative school are still almost three times higher for students with EBD. During the 8th-grade year of this study, 14% of all Black students with EBD were removed to a disciplinary alternative school, compared to 4% of their White counterparts.

School Mobility. The data reveal that students who change schools once within the school year are 6.5 times more likely to be removed to alternative schools than students who do not move, and students who attend two or more different schools within the same year are 19 times more likely to be removed to disciplinary alternative schools than students who don't move.[3] Studies show that student mobility is strongly correlated with low achievement and disengagement and poverty (Rumberger, 2003). The heightened risk for disciplinary removal to alternative school observed here raises questions as to whether students who move schools frequently are getting adequate support in their new school environment, especially considering the multitude of mobility-linked stress factors that might diminish a student's social and emotional health.

Grade Retention. Regardless of the grade(s) in which removal takes place, students who experience grade retention at least once are over 4.5 times more likely to be removed to a disciplinary alternative school than their peers who were not retained.[4] Grade retention typically indicates that the student is struggling academically and/or socially, that intervention is either lacking or ineffective, and that the student is not prepared to move to the next grade level.

Learning Disability. Unlike grade retention, having been identified as having a specific learning disability (SLD) does not appear to be systematically related to removal to a disciplinary alternative school.[5] Interestingly, the descriptive statistics reveal that students who score below average in the CTBS in reading are overrepresented among those removed to disciplinary alternative schools.[6] One possible explanation for this pattern is that a delayed diagnosis of a learning disability that might require additional, targeted academic support is often associated with ongoing academic failure. Thus, though students might be retained due to academic struggles, they might also not be receiving a critical diagnosis or getting the intervention services they need to make academic progress. In other words, it is possible that the high risk of removal to an alternative school among low-performing students reflects a systemic failure to identify and provide needed special education supports and services to students with specific learning disabilities.

These significant findings shed light on the fact that students being removed to disciplinary alternative schools have multiple risk factors for school failure that they cannot control, but some of which a school could mitigate. Research suggests there is a lack of early interventions to address the needs of students who are later excluded for being deemed too dangerous or disruptive (Dunlap et al., 2006).

The Cyclical Nature and High Cost of Removals to Alternative School

One noteworthy finding that arose during the course of this study was the high incidence of repeat entries into disciplinary alternative schools. For example, while in 7th grade, 186 cohort students registered 266 removals to disciplinary alternative schools within that school year. This suggests that the first removal did not deter behavior warranting a subsequent removal once students returned to a mainstream school. However, it also points to a lack of formal transition planning that has been identified in alternative school research as a chief drawback of alternative schools. Ensuring systemic support for students as they return to the regular school is critical. Jones (1999) found that successful student transition back to the regular school environment necessitates the existence of formal transition programs inherent in both the alternative and mainstream schools.

Another disturbing finding revealed a high incidence of cyclical placements in foster care school settings (district schools situated within foster care residential facilities) among students who have been removed to alternative schools, and to district schools that are situated within psychiatric hospital facilities. An internal evaluation conducted on the district's middle and high disciplinary alternative schools at the end of this study showed that, of the students enrolled in one disciplinary high school, 30% had attended a disciplinary alternative middle school and, disturbingly, 50% had previously attended a special school located in a psychiatric facility (Vanderhaar & Chang, 2007). This raises serious concerns about the cyclical nature of removing students experiencing emotional, mental, and behavioral difficulties to segregated settings.

The capacity of disciplinary alternative schools, including staffing and program decisions, to address the root causes of students' challenges should be seriously examined, especially in light of the human and financial costs of providing disciplinary alternative schools. The exorbitant cost of removing students to disciplinary alternative schools cannot be understated: In Jefferson County in 2012, the average district cost per student in regular schools was $13,312; in the disciplinary alternative schools it was $40,720.

What Is the Likelihood of Subsequent Juvenile Detention After the First Alternative School Placement?

Of the 544 cohort students who were removed to alternative schools, a total of 215 (39.5%), or 4 in 10 students, experienced juvenile detention at some point between when they were removed to an alternative school the first time and 12th grade.[7] Among students removed to alternative elementary schools, the risk was even higher, with 52.9% experiencing juvenile detention before 12th grade.

What Is the Relationship Between Race and Subsequent Juvenile Detention?

A greater number of Black students were detained as juveniles after being removed to an alternative school in elementary, middle, or high school. Of those removed to alternative school, 38% ($n = 135$) of the Black students and 29% ($n = 52$) of the White students subsequently wound up in juvenile detention. The racial gap was largest in middle school, where there was a nearly 18% gap between Black and White students in the rate of subsequent detention: 50% ($n = 76$) of the 153 Black students removed to the disciplinary alternative school in grades 6 through 8 were eventually detained, compared with 32% ($n = 30$) of the 94 White students.

When combining the risk of being removed to an alternative school and subsequently being put in juvenile detention, we find that 5% of all Black 3rd-graders and 1.1% of all White 3rd-graders in the cohort had this combined set of experiences. This means that among the cohort whose progress we tracked for 10 years, Black children in Jefferson County were nearly five times more likely than White children to follow a path to detention that began with removal to a disciplinary alternative school.

SUMMARY AND RECOMMENDATIONS FOR POLICY AND PRACTICE

The findings of this research suggest that relying on suspensions as a disciplinary strategy increases the likelihood of eventual removal to a costly alternative school, recidivism, and subsequent involvement with the juvenile justice system. The relationships and propensities described in this study are best understood in the broader context of Jefferson County, which has the second highest rate of juvenile detention in the state of Kentucky, and of Kentucky, which ranks among the top in the nation in terms of incarcerating juveniles for nonviolent offences (DiLoreto

& Grieshop-Goodwin, 2010). In other words, Jefferson County's rate of removal to alternative disciplinary schools—13% of Black students and 4% of White students—and higher than average youth incarceration rates are cause for great concern. Moreover, the fact that such high percentages of Black students and White students sent to an alternative school ostensibly designed to mitigate their problematic behavior subsequently wound up in juvenile detention facilities raises the question of whether Jefferson County's alternative disciplinary schools are instead contributing to the unusually high number of school-age youth, especially Black youth, who flow from school to prison.

Proponents of disciplinary alternative schools might argue that the number of youth in the juvenile justice system in Jefferson County would be even higher if not for the frequent removal from the mainstream. We believe that argument might hold water if the data on this county and this state did not rank them among the nation's highest in terms of juvenile incarceration. This study instead reveals that alternative schools are part of a high-suspending district's investment in an exclusionary practice that is disproportionately experienced by Black students in poverty, students in special education, and students with social-emotional and mental health needs. Although this study, being limited to one district, and with no control for comparison, cannot prove that disciplinary alternative schools are increasing the number of students who wind up in the juvenile justice system, the data do raise critical questions about their utility.

The peak of removal occurs in 7th grade, which points to a need to address the dynamics of middle school removals. The high likelihood that students removed to alternative disciplinary schools will subsequently experience juvenile detention is distressing, particularly among Black youth. Enacting policies to ensure that equal levels of accountability and oversight are maintained in both alternative and mainstream schools is imperative. Furthermore, policymakers should consider the ramifications of the erosion of traditional boundaries between the juvenile justice system and the educational system (Hirschfield, 2008) through the heavy police presence and school disciplinary policies that might be unintentionally merging the two systems.

Importantly, the level of accountability for states and districts that rely on disciplinary alternative schools must be strengthened to ensure system-wide implementation of sound policies around removal decisions, research-based practices that promote positive student outcomes, accommodations for special education students, and transition planning.

The financial costs associated with exclusionary discipline (Chapter 4, this book) cannot be understated, particularly with alternative schools. Though initially more time-consuming, schoolwide social–emotional programs, positive behavior intervention supports, and restorative justice practices are proving to be more cost effective, promising alternatives that have short- and long-term implications for students, schools, and their communities (Chapter 13, this book). Policies that support early intervention for students should far outweigh any that support exclusion. Restorative practices and threat assessment also have been demonstrated to be useful tools for ensuring safety while reducing the unnecessary and repeated exclusion of students deemed dangerous (Chapter 12, this book; Schiff, 2013).

Although what has been proven to work to reduce juvenile detention was beyond the scope of this study, it is demonstrated through the data that students who were removed to alternative schools had risk factors at an early age, and that earlier, preventive, and nonpunitive interventions are a better long-term investment if the goal is to keep children in school and out of the juvenile justice system. Thus the implementation of an early-warning program to identify students in trouble that is linked to research-based interventions would enable systematic intervention with young students and could reduce the number of students removed to disciplinary alternative schools (Chapters 1 and 13, this book).

In the current context in which costly disciplinary alternative school demand outweighs supply, policymakers would be wise to support reduction on the demand side by considering the following recommendations:

1. Revise the district code of conduct so that restorative measures are the primary response to offenses, and ensure these measures are implemented with fidelity and accountability across schools; also, ensure that offenses are clearly defined to reduce the practice of miscoding behavioral incidences into offenses that lead to alternative placement.
2. Develop and tighten systematic links of risk factor identification through student-level data by matching interventions to individual students to address root causes of behaviors.
3. Ensure system-wide training occurs for all administrators and staff on de-escalation skills, implementing restorative practices in the classroom, cultural responsiveness, the impact of trauma and toxic stress on behavior, and schoolwide mentoring programs.
4. Reassign, repurpose, and balance security guards, school police, and disciplinary administrators to increase staff dedicated to student social and emotional support and mentoring.
5. Develop, build capacity, develop and support a system-wide framework to facilitate districtwide, whole-school implementation of social–emotional learning approaches, cultural responsiveness, trauma-informed practices, restorative practices, and positive behavioral intervention programs.

CONCLUSION

The findings of this research suggest a need to reconsider the efficacy and the deleterious ramifications of out-of-school suspension and removal to disciplinary alternative school. The fundamentally flawed approach of removing students from environments for behavioral incidences if the root of the behavior goes unaddressed should be seriously deliberated. In addition to being cost ineffective for budget-strapped school systems, the removal of students to disciplinary alternative schools mirrors and reinforces to all students an acceptance of our nation's mass incarceration approach, an approach demonstrated to be ineffective at deterring future occurrences of crime and disproportionately affecting those in poverty and people of color and the combination.

In addition to promoting and supporting policies and practices aimed at early proactive intervention as opposed to exclusionary approaches, a simultaneous focus on strengthening alternative school standards and accountability at district, state, and federal levels is a vital necessity to systematically ensure the success of the nation's most vulnerable children. Specifically, standards should address staffing requirements that include high-quality teachers with special education certification for students with emotional and behavioral issues; staff training on the impact of trauma and toxic stress on student behavior; and policies that focus on addressing the root causes of the incident or behavior that led to removal, including early prevention and support, low student-to-counselor ratios, full-time mental health support, restorative practice, strengths-based individual student-learning growth plans, and—critically—intentional transition programming between the mainstream and alternative schools.

The findings of this longitudinal study should be cause for an abundance of caution and reconsideration among advocates and policymakers alike who may promote disciplinary alternative schools as a way to keep disruptive students in school. The early schooling experiences and trajectories of students removed to alternative schools raise considerable doubts about the efficacy of a system that relies on out-of-school suspensions and disciplinary alternative schools as strategies to reduce delinquency and to provide support for children deemed too disruptive or dangerous. More systemic, high-quality supports with an intentional focus on early intervention would produce better and more equitable outcomes than exclusionary discipline practices and policies.

NOTES

1. The estimated coefficient for race is .692 ($p = .001$), yielding an odds ratio (exp) of 1.99.

2. The estimated coefficient for EBD is 2.135 ($p = .000$), yielding an odds ratio (exp) of 8.46.

3. The estimated coefficient for mobility is 2.081 ($p = .000$). The antilog of this parameter estimate yields an odds ratio (exp) of 7.52. The probability for students in alternative schools compared with the cohort for one school move (.195 and .030 respectively) and two or more moves (.077 and .004, respectively).

4. The estimated coefficient for retention is 1.511 ($p = .000$), yielding an odds ratio (exp) of 4.53.

5. The estimated coefficient for LD is .447 (p = .504).

6. A large percentage of students in the alternative school sample did not have a CTBS score. This speaks to missing accountability for academic testing. In 3rd grade, 29 (85%) had missing scores, in 6th grade 149 (41%) had missing scores, and 160 (62%) had missing scores on CTBS reading in 9th

grade. Due to the large amount of missing CTBS data, this variable was removed from the discrete-time hazard analyses. The unusually high number of missing scores raises the issue of whether removal to alternative schools was used somehow to skirt school-based, test-driven accountability, but that question is beyond the scope of this study.

7. Incidences of detention are conservative because (a) the data system captures only detentions that occur during the school year and not in the summer, and (b) in high school, students might be detained in the regular local jail, which is not entered into the district data warehouse.

REFERENCES

Arnove, R. F., & Strout, T. (1980). Alternative schools for disruptive youth. *Educational Forum, 44,* 453–471.

Barber, R. (1980). *Alternative education to address student behavior concerns.* Frankfort, KY: Kentucky State Department of Education.

Cox, S. (1999). An assessment of an alternative education program for at-risk delinquent youth. *Journal of Research on Crime and Delinquency, 36,* 323–336.

DiLoreto, R., & Grieshop-Goodwin, T. (2010). *Reducing the use of incarceration for status offenses in Kentucky: Blueprint for Kentucky's children.* Retrieved from http://fatlip.leoweekly.com/wp-con tent/uploads/2010/11/10brief_statusoffenses.pdf

Dunbar, C. (2001). *Alternative schooling for African American youth: Does anyone know we're here?* New York, NY: Peter Lang.

Dunlap, G., Strain, P. S., Fox, J., Carta, J. J., Conroy, M., Smith, B. J., . . . Sowell, C. (2006). Prevention and intervention with young children behavior: Perspective regarding current knowledge. *Behavior Disorders, 32,* 29–45.

Free, J. L. (2008). *First step, or last chance? At-risk youth, alternative schooling and juvenile delinquen-cy.* (Unpublished doctoral dissertation). Northeastern University, Boston, MA. Retrieved from http://iris.lib.neu.edu/cgi/viewcontent.cgi?article=1001&context=soc_diss

Hirschfield, P. J. (2008). Preparing for prison: The criminalization of school discipline in the USA. *Theoretical Criminology, 12*(1), 79–101

Jones, I. (1999). *Case studies of students transitioning from an alternative school back into high school.* (Unpublished doctoral dissertation). Virginia Polytech State University, Falls Church, Virginia.

Justice Policy Institute. (2009). *The costs of confinement: Why good juvenile justice pol-icies make good fiscal sense.* Retrieved from http://www.justicepolicy.org/images/ upload/09_05_rep_costsofconfinement_jj_ps.pdf

Kim, J. H., & Taylor, K. A. (2008). Rethinking alternative education to break the cycle of educational inequality and inequity. *The Journal of Educational Research, 101,* 207–219.

Kliner, B., Porch, R., & Farris, E. (2002). *Public alternative schools and programs for students at risk of educational failure: 2000–2001.* Washington, DC: National Center for Educational Statistics.

Lange, C. M., & Sletten, S. J. (2002). *Alternative education: A brief history and research synthesis.* Alexandria, VA: National Association of State Directors of Special Education. Retrieved from http://www.nasdse.org/DesktopModules/DNNspot-Store/ProductFiles/115_0fb117db-a3df-4427-bae7-3226541d3e34.pdf

Lehr, C., Soon Tan, C., & Ysseldyke, J. (2009). Alternative schools: A synthesis of state-level policy and research. *Remedial and Special Education, 30*(1), 19–32.

Lehr, C. A., & Lange, C. M. (2003). Alternative schools serving students with and without disabilities. *Preventing School Failure, 47*(2), 59–66.

Lehr, C. A., Lanners, E. J., & Lange, C. M. (2003, October). *Alternative schools: Policy and legislation across the United States* (Research report no. 1). Minneapolis, MN: University of Minnesota, Institute on Community Integration.

Losen, D., & Gillespie, J. (2012). *Opportunities suspended: The disparate impact of disciplinary exclusion from school.* Retrieved from http://civilrightsproject.ucla.edu

May, D., & Chen, Y. (2006) *Kentucky juvenile crime analysis: 2006.* Retrieved from http://www.jjab.ky.gov/NR/rdonlyres/EE16300F-20EC-4981-A304-B4CD01A01DEE/199938/KYJuvenileCrimeAnalysis2006.pdf

National Center for Education Statistics. (2003). *Indicators of school crime and safety: 2002.* (NCES 2003-009/NCJ 196753.) Washington, DC: U.S. Departments of Education and Justice

National Center for Education Statistics. (2010). *Alternative schools and programs for public school students at risk of educational failure: 2007–08.* Retrieved from http://nces.ed.gov/pubsearch/pubsinfo.asp?pubid=2010026

National Center for Education Statistics. (2012). *Indicators of school crime and safety: 2011.* (NCES 2012-002/NCJ 236021). Washington, DC: National Center for Education Statistics, U.S. Department of Education, and Bureau of Justice Statistics, Office of Justice Programs, U.S. Department of Justice.

Osher, D., Cartledge, G., Oswald, D., Sutherland, K., Artiles, A. J., & Coutinho, M. (2004). Cultural and linguistic competency and disproportionate representation. In R. B. Rutherford Jr., M. M. Quinn, & S. R. Mathur (Eds.), *Handbook of research in emotional and behavioral disorders* (pp. 54–77). New York, NY: Guilford Press.

Quinn, M. M., & Poirier, J. M. (2006). *Study of effective alternative education programs: Final grant report.* Washington, DC: American Institutes for Research.

Quinn, M. M., & Rutherford, R. B. (1998). *Alternative programs for students with social, emotional, and behavioral problems.* Reston, VA: Council for Children with Behavioral Disorders.

Rumberger, R. W. (2003). The causes and consequences of student mobility. *Journal of Negro Education, 72*(1), 6–21.

Schiff, M. (2013). *Dignity, disparities and desistance: Effective restorative justice strategies to plug the "school to prison pipeline."* Retrieved from http://civilrightsproject.ucla.edu

Vanderhaar, J., & Chang, F. (2007). *Program evaluation alternative schools.* Retrieved from http://www.jefferson.k12.ky.us/Departments/Planning/ProgramEvaluation/WebMASTER_Updates_July2011/AltSchools_JV.pdf

Vanderhaar, J., Petrosko, J., & Muñoz, M. (2013). *Reconsidering the alternatives.* (Unpublished manuscript). Retrieved from http://civilrightsproject.ucla.edu/resources/projects/center-for-civil-rights-remedies/school-to-prison-folder/state-reports/copy4_of_dignity-disparity-and-desistance-effective-restorative-justice-strategies-to-plug-the-201cschool-to-prison-pipeline

Verdugo, R., & Glenn, B. (2006). *Race and alternative schools: The new tracking.* Washington, DC: Hamilton Fish Institute on School and Community Violence.

Wald, J., & Losen, D. (Eds.). (2003). *Deconstructing the school to prison pipeline: New directions for youth development.* Hoboken, NJ: Jossey-Bass.

## CHAPTER 16

Personal Perspective on School Discipline Issues and Remedies

Interview With Karen Webber-Ndour, Executive Director of
Student Support and Safety for Baltimore City Schools

Interviewed by Daniel J. Losen

*Often policymakers and practitioners who are prepared to reject the status quo
would like to embark on a path toward change but hesitate. Some might meet
with resistance from segments of the school community who predict reducing
suspension will reap havoc on the learning environment. Others might feel they
are on shaky ground because they do not know any other administrators in
districts like their own who have successfully pursued policies aimed at reducing
suspensions. For this reason we have infused a few personal narratives in this
volume. Among the most powerful voices of those pursuing reforms is that of
Karen Webber-Ndour, who is currently the executive director of Student Support
and Safety for Baltimore City Schools.*

*The National Justice Summit provided this description of her work history
and current job functions. "Ms. Webber-Ndour served as the dynamic principal of
the National Academy Foundation (NAF) School in Baltimore, Maryland. Under
Webber-Ndour's leadership, the NAF School doubled in size (absorbing the Dunbar
Middle School in 2009); saw a dramatic increase in test scores; and attained one
of the city's highest graduation rates. Webber-Ndour's current role as the Executive
Director of Student Support and Safety for Baltimore City Schools utilizes her prior
work experiences in a role in which she oversees Suspension Services, Baltimore
School Police, School Health, and other departments which directly affect various
aspect of school climate. In School Year 2012/2013 Webber-Ndour commenced a
school climate initiative that resulted in the reduction of out-of-school suspensions
by 24% in a one-year period"[1]*

*Karen Webber-Ndour's voice, her story, expresses the empathy of one who
understands the challenges faced by school administrators as well as those faced by*

poor urban youth and their families. Her discussion of her successful efforts and her ongoing approach to reducing disciplinary exclusion from school in Baltimore lends a personal perspective on many of the issues and remedies represented in the chapters of this book.[2]

DL: Why is reducing the use of suspensions important to your work in Baltimore?

Because when we send kids out of the schoolhouse door, we are sending them into a tough city, and into neighborhoods that have very serious crime and violence issues. What are we hoping to gain if we send them packing? The greatest likelihood is they return with the same problems that are amplified by the time missed on classwork, and many suspended students fall easy prey into the juvenile justice system.

If we use suspensions as a first response, we have missed an opportunity to build a relationship with the student and parent that a simple inquiry or conference would help create. Frequent suspensions often exacerbate problems and ultimately detract from our overall school climate. Many students have experienced or witnessed serious violence, incarceration, sexual abuse, hunger, or abandonment. If we acknowledge the problems of the majority of our students, it becomes a moral imperative for the adults to go the extra mile and approach students with respect, forbearance, and some measure of kindness. I give the same advice to school leaders regarding their treatment of the adults in the school community.

[Webber-Ndour next explained how her own teaching experience informs her understanding about what needs to change.]

For example, an honor student I had while teaching was suddenly absent for 3 solid weeks. I found out that she had not been ill. I asked in a harsh tone, "What's going on with you?" The girl had no answer. Later that day she pulled me aside and said, "We were evicted and lost most of our possessions . . . now I take three buses to school." She went on about how her younger siblings would not have a real Christmas this year. . . . My own stereotypes blinded me to the fact that an *honor* student was suffering from the same harsh conditions as her peers who were acting out. Had I not stopped myself and listened to her story, I might have referred her to the office for discipline. If educators were provided cultural sensitivity and trauma-informed teacher education training before entering urban classrooms, we would be much better prepared to avoid making potentially harmful assumptions about children's behaviors.

So, as teachers and administrators, we easily assume when we see a misbehaving, defiant, rude, inattentive, or chronically absent student that the student doesn't care about school, doesn't respect adults, and doesn't want to learn. But until we know the perils of urban life and until we as teachers and administrators have a better sense of the challenges these students face, they won't believe in our system of advancement through school. If we are not in tune with their lives, if we are not really listening to their voices, not paying attention to their struggles, they are not going to listen to us, or trust that we really will help them, and going to school will not seem like an opportunity for a better life.

DL: Baltimore had already begun a reform of school discipline under Superintendent Alonso. What did you find when you arrived, and how have you furthered the mission in Baltimore?

One of the first reform efforts [under former Superintendent Alonso] was a massive overhaul of the existing code of conduct, and that overhaul led to a dramatic decrease in out-of-school suspensions in Baltimore City Schools. Over time, the messaging and training around the code waned, and the numbers of out-of-school suspensions began to creep up.

When I began in this position 2 years ago, it was clear to me that we needed training on the code of conduct, the application of alternatives to suspension, and consistent messaging about building positive school climates. To that end I began a week-long intensive summer training with a cohort of 32 schools in each of these areas. Each group consisted of the school leader, select teachers, and the assigned school police officer. The message that was clearly articulated is that all adults in the school building are responsible for purposefully creating a positive school climate.

School climate was defined for the district as those elements in a school that encompass teaching and learning, school environment (how the school looks and feels), safety (both physical and mental), and most important, positive relationships in the school (including adult-to-student, student-to-student, and adult-to-adult relationships). We also provided school administrators with weekly data reports that enabled them to track the number, type, and location of their suspensions and thereby create actionable solutions to school climate issues.

As a result of these and other efforts, out-of-school suspensions declined by 24% in a 1-year period, and those schools that received the climate training experienced even further reductions in suspensions. For the same recorded period of time, the graduation rates continued to rise.

DL: What are the obstacles to creating positive school climates in Baltimore, and how do you overcome them?

There are numerous obstacles to creating positive school climates. What we're attempting to do in Baltimore is not done in most districts. By establishing a common definition and providing in-depth training on school climate, we help school leaders identify climate problem areas and create solutions to address those problems. Everyone has the capacity to improve their school climate given the proper tools and support.

Adult attitudes also create barriers to improving school climate. Principals often justify the use of suspensions with statements such as "I needed to send a message that this behavior will not be tolerated," whereas others proclaim they are protecting the "safety and well-being" of their school communities (by sending the bad kids away). The problem with these sentiments is that they label children as either "bad" or "good." We need a more realistic concept in which we perceive children as developing beings that require guidance—not only academically but behaviorally as well.

In Baltimore City, I'm messaging that the adult attitude toward students needs to be restorative rather than punitive. Adult responses need to invoke the student's voice and determine why the student misbehaved. The adult also needs to take measures to restore the school community and bring the student back into the safety that the school offers. This requires a huge shift in the average educator's mindset, but it is a mental shift that I have seen work miracles over and over again.

When I discuss these matters with principals, I often receive huge pushback and disbelief in my climate theories, but at the end of the day principals realize that I've walked in their shoes and that I understand the pressures they are under in Baltimore City. Based on my experiences, I feel comfortable about insisting that school leaders go the extra mile to *establish* the best school climate imaginable and take the time necessary to listen to the voices of their students.

When I became a principal in Baltimore City, students were initially incredibly defiant. I was disrespected on a regular basis for the first few weeks, but it seemed like an eternity! I might have overutilized suspensions at first under the "sending a message" theory of action, but I soon learned that talking and conferencing with parents and students, though exhausting, brought about true change and mutual understanding. I insisted on respectful behavior toward the adults in the school, but I also demonstrated the respect I sought to students, parents, and teachers alike.

As the high school became more successful, I was asked by the superintendent to expand our student enrollment and adopt a failing middle school. I saw this expansion as an incredible opportunity to determine whether the transformation in the high school could be repeated in another school environment. We successfully re-created a positive school climate in the middle school by employing the same practices of mutual respect, invoking and empowering the voices of the students and modeling the behavior we sought to create.[3]

NOTES

1. Daniel Losen interviewed Karen Webber-Ndour on February 28, 2014.

2. Available at http://school-justicesummit.org/presentations/data/B.2.E.%20Webber-Ndour-Sundius-PPT.pdf

3. For more information on some of the tools and processes referenced herein, please refer to www.baltimorecityschools.org/climate.

Conclusion

Daniel J. Losen

On February 27, 2014, President Obama announced My Brother's Keeper, his new initiative designed to call attention to what he called the "outrageous inequities" experienced by boys and young men of color and his commitment to ending the school-to-prison pipeline (Obama, 2014). He urged Americans to focus on

> building on what works, it means looking at the actual evidence of what works. There are a lot of programs out there that sound good . . . but they're not actually having an impact. We don't have enough money or time or resources to invest in things that don't work . . . if something's not working, let's stop doing it. Let's do things that work" (Obama, 2014, para. 20).

This book aims not only to help policymakers understand the folly of relying on excluding students from school to create healthy learning environments but to point out the benefits of alternative approaches. Though many of the remedies described in this book do require additional resources, Marchbanks's economic study in Chapter 4 establishes that more effective school policies would also be more efficient economically. The fact that a lack of resources is an obstacle to change, despite predictable net economic gains, is a reflection of a policy disconnect rather than a true shortage of resources. If states and localities could take projected savings from having lower delinquency and transfer them to their education budget, the remedies could likely pay for themselves (Osher, Quinn, Poirier, & Rutherford, 2003).

This book began with research describing the frequent removal of students from educational opportunity on disciplinary grounds. Some of the strongest empirical findings demonstrate that school policies and practices, rather than variances in student misbehavior, are what lead to a high volume of suspensions (see Chapter 9). Higher suspensions, in turn, lead to higher rates of dropping out and involvement in the juvenile justice system (see Chapters 1 and 2). Frequent suspensions are not only counterproductive but burden some subgroups of students far more than others. This is a detrimental and potentially unlawful approach to creating safe and productive schools. Simply put, educators should stop relying on suspensions as a primary response to minor misbehavior because that approach isn't working.

Some bad policies just need to stop, and such changes are cost-free. For example, without spending additional money, educators can eliminate harsh disciplinary responses to violations of school codes. Do schools really need to suspend students who are truant or tardy, use cellphones in class, or break the dress code? Many successful, safe schools allow the use of phones and have no dress code, but schools that do feel the need for strict rules should not need to enforce them with removal from school. As we learned in Chapter 8, even among schools serving children from the highest-crime neighborhoods, the sense of safety was higher in schools with strong teacher–student and teacher–parent relationships. Such schools, it turns out, also suspended fewer children.

Moreover, in several of the chapters focusing on specific remedies, researchers pointed to the benefits of revising the school code, which has been happening in many districts around the country (Fenning et al., 2013). For example, under Superintendent Andres Alonso, Baltimore City Schools cut suspensions by thousands and, as Karen Webber-Ndour has pointed out, the city is working hard to further reduce their suspension rates (Alonso, 2013). And in 2013, to a "roomful of cheers" Los Angeles's school board voted to stop making vague minor offenses such as defiance or disruption grounds for suspension (Watanabe, 2013). There are no obvious costs incurred if school codes follow the recent recommendations of the Academy of American Pediatrics[1] and limit the use of suspensions to only the most serious offenses.

Although new resources are important to bring to bear on this problem, policymakers need not be paralyzed by lack of new resources. Some remedies might entail shifting funds to support more effective policies. As described in Chapter 6, school district leaders may shift federal IDEA funds to improve the capacity of teachers to address behavioral issues. Further, increasing efficiency would not require additional funds. For example, based on research Finn and Servoss present in Chapter 3 and Osher et al. in Chapter 13, policymakers could shift some of the scarce funds, currently allocated in school budgets to security hardware and school policing, to support more school counselors, social and emotional learning initiatives, and more effective support services for students with special needs. At the national level, the new federal grants offered in response to the murders at Sandy Hook Elementary will allow applicants to request funds to add counselors *or* school resource officers (The White House, 2013). Based on the research findings presented in this book, most schools would be better off investing in the former.

Some of the most important research-based conclusions are highlighted by Skiba et al. in Chapter 9, in which they demonstrate that stark differences in the use of suspension are caused by differences in school policy, school leadership, and other factors that educators can control. Though poverty and other factors do appear to contribute to the high use of suspension, most of the chapters describing findings that controlled for differences in student behavior, race, and poverty support Skiba et al.'s finding that school-controlled factors are the strongest predictors of both frequency and disproportionality in the use of suspension.

One thing is clear—there are numerous factors that contribute to high suspension rates, and the chapters in this book help us to understand many of them. Of course there are other factors that are beyond the scope of this book, such as the pressure of high-stakes testing, inequities in state funding and distribution of resources, and intentional discrimination. Moreover, many of the chapters touch on the likely contributions of implicit or unconscious racial bias, gender bias, and bias against students with disabilities. Also beyond the scope of the research in this volume are the disparities experienced by LGBT students, how biases affect LGBT students, and related remedies.[2] Although research on the contributions of unintended bias to disparate discipline rates and how to remedy such influences is being developed, the rising attention to disparities in discipline will expand the opportunities to find effective practices in this area.[3]

We know that the problems schools face are complex, that the remedies are imperfect, and that more study is needed. However, two important common elements are within control of educators: the need to improve student engagement, and the quality of relationships and trust among all members of the school community. Progress in these areas will require teacher training, as Gregory et al. demonstrate in Chapter 11; leadership training, as suggested by Skiba et al.'s findings on the attitudes of school principals in Chapter 9; multicultural sensitivity, as suggested by Toldson et al. in Chapter 7 and Vincent et al. in Chapter 14; and community involvement, as González suggests in Chapter 10.

Fostering major improvement in these areas in the longer term will certainly require additional resources. However, as Balfanz et al. note in Chapter 1, efforts that focus exclusively on reducing suspensions are not sufficient to address the dropout crisis. Similarly, Toldson et al.'s findings in Chapter 7 suggest a strong connection between the academic engagement of Black males and their success in avoiding disciplinary exclusion. Thus it is critically important that policymakers, who might be reluctant to target funds solely for the purpose of reducing suspensions, understand the connections. For example, the teacher training to improve student engagement described in Chapter 11 was presented as a remedy to disparate discipline, but the explicit focus of the program was on imp   ʼ˥ˠ student engagement, not on reducing suspensions.

The fact is that efforts to improve student academic outcom' some approaches that can help reduce frequency of suspension a disparities commonly found in the use of suspension. Moreo suspensions mean that more students are receiving classroo/ grams that emphasize reducing suspensions to improve the o' such as restorative practices, can also be expected to impr' graduation rates. The most promising remedies highlighted in this book have a relatively broad anticipated impact. It is worth repeating that, during a period of systemic adoption of restorative practices in Denver (see Chapter 10), achievement scores rose every year at nearly every grade level for every racial and ethnic group in every subject tested.

TOWARD A POLICY CONSENSUS ON SUSPENSION REDUCTION

Fortunately, even without a definitive or singular theory on why we have such large disparities in suspensions, we are approaching a consensus that the status quo of frequently relying on exclusionary discipline is not acceptable and that discipline policy and practice, and related factors educators can control directly, are among the primary factors contributing to the high volume and large disparities observed. Achieving consensus is no accident: As a matter of policy, the federal government responded to the growing empirical evidence (including a comprehensive report from the Council of State Government's Justice Center depicting high rates of disciplinary exclusion across the state of Texas [Fabelo et al., 2011] and in 2011 began the Supportive School Discipline Initiative (U.S. Department of Education, 2013).

One of the most important developments stemming from the federal government's SSDI concerns was the Departments of Justice and Education's jointly released guidance to schools and districts regarding excessive school discipline (Departments of Justice & Education, 2014). The 2014 guidance focused on racial disparities, but the same principles apply to disparities by disability status and gender. The guidance explains that if an educational policy or practice is either unjustified or there are less discriminatory alternatives, and if the policy or practice burdens one racial or ethnic group more than others, it is potentially a violation of Title VI of the Civil Rights Act of 1964 pursuant to a "disparate impact analysis" (Departments of Justice & Education, 2014). The remedies described in this book that reduced racial disparities and overall suspensions are additional proof that less discriminatory alternatives to suspension are available and viable.

Another SSDI development is the School Discipline Consensus Project, which is called the "cornerstone of the initiative" (U.S. Department of Education, 2013). The consensus project ended with a report issued in 2014. This book's research-based recommendations for policymakers are consistent with the recommendations in the consensus report, which reflect contributions from practitioners in the fields of education, juvenile justice, behavioral health, and law enforcement, as well as state and local policymakers, advocates, researchers, students, and parents. According to the final School Discipline Consensus Report, released on June 3, 2014, "Leaders [from the fields of education, health, law enforcement, and juvenile justice] agree that local and state governments must not only help schools reduce the number of students suspended, expelled and arrested, but must also provide the conditions for learning wherein all students feel safe, welcome and supported" (Morgan, Salomon, Plotkin, & Cohen, 2014, p. 3).

Equally important to the policy implications of the remedies this book describes is that many needed policies might be in place already. Though most school districts could do more to reduce suspensions and problematic disparities, many can and do create orderly, safe, and productive learning environments without excessive disciplinary exclusion. An analysis of high- and low-suspending secondary schools suggests that 60% of schools employ more effective alternatives (Losen & Martinez, 2013). For example, in 2009, approximately 8,000 secondary schools in nearly 4,000 districts suspended fewer than 10% of every major student subgroup enrolled (Losen, Hewitt, & Toldson, 2014).

Educator awareness is already leading to changes in policy and practice and to significant reductions in suspensions. California's data on counts of suspensions per 100 students, for example, show a slight decline in the use of suspension for every racial/ethnic group between 2011–2012 and 2012–2013, although too many students are still being suspended each day. For White students the OSS count declined by 1 per 100 and for Blacks there was a decline in absolute terms of 3 per 100. Though it is hard to trumpet these numbers as success, the very large racial discipline gap did appear to narrow.[5] (Losen, Martinez, & Okelola, 2014).

Greater gains appear to have been realized in other states, including Maryland, Wisconsin, and Connecticut, where ongoing state or large district efforts appear to be working. In each of these states, reports based on data collected from the 2011–2012 (and in some cases 2012–2013) school year show declining suspension rates for all students, although most acknowledge that the rates and disparities are still too high.[6] Each of these states, or large school districts in them, have made policy changes calling for a substantial reduction in the use of out-of-school suspensions.

MORE SUBSTANTIAL CHANGES ARE NEEDED

The recent important policy changes are neither sweeping nor permanent. With the building consensus should come a sea change in policy and practice, but that will require more than privately funded initiatives such as My Brother's Keeper, and more than stronger federal civil rights enforcement policy, which by its very nature is more reactive than proactive.

What is needed are policy changes that expand and replicate what works and terminate what doesn't. To serve that important goal, we grouped recommendations for policymakers derived from the research in this volume into three overarching recommendations for policy action at the federal and state levels: (1) Improve data use, (2) add accountability, and (3) target support to replicate what works.

IMPROVE DATA USE

There is no question that we need good data (Morgan et al., 2014). We need to improve the flow of information about effective school discipline, and find and eradicate the counterproductive overreliance on removing students from class to maintain an environment conducive to learning. Since the No Child Left Behind Act (NCLB) was passed in 2002, every public school and district annually collects and publicly reports disaggregated data on achievement by subject and enrollment demographics. Parents feel they have a right to this information, and federal law requires extensive reporting of achievement scores in reading, mathematics, and science; thus in most states test results are publicized within a year of their administration. To calculate graduation rates, federal regulations were passed in 2008 to improve the requirement that states must annually track individual students from their entrance into grade 9 until they earn a diploma or exit for some other reason. Each year, high schools, districts, and states must publicly report their graduation rates, disaggregated by race, gender, English learner status, and disability status. Further, in response to incentives in federal competitive grant applications, many states have recently adopted annual individual teacher evaluations that rely extensively on student achievement data. When education policymakers decide information is important, they collect and publicly report it annually.

If school policymakers take one cue from the marketplace, it should be that businesses invest heavily in understanding their customers and finding ways to influence their behavior. Schools might never become as masterful as corporations in the collection and use of information about behavior, actions, and "likes" of customers, but they could do much more to understand whether their responses to bad behavior enhances or jeopardizes the productivity of the learning environment. What we specifically need in order to identify both problems and solutions are discipline data that are disaggregated by student subgroups down to the school level. These data need to be reported to the public annually.

Although Attorney General Eric Holder and Secretary of Education Arne Duncan have declared that reducing school discipline disparities is a federal priority, they have yet to call for legislation that requires states and districts to include discipline data in the annual report cards that federal law already says must be issued at the state, district, and school levels. Ironically, they shouldn't have to; federal law currently requires state level reporting of racially disaggregated discipline data for students with disabilities, pursuant to IDEA (U.S.C. Section 1418[a]). The law also calls for annual district-level comparisons of the discipline of students with disabilities to students without disabilities.[7] However, evidence indicates that only eight states are even approaching compliance with these federal reporting mandates (Losen, Martinez, & Okelola, 2014). To ensure that states fulfill their statutory obligation and make these comparisons, the federal government could require annual reporting on students without disabilities as well.

Biennial federal civil rights data collection, requiring every public school in the nation to report their data, is an important step in the right direction, albeit an incomplete one. The U.S. Department of Education can and does require many schools and districts to report disaggregated discipline data to the secretary through this survey known as the Civil Rights Data Collection. The survey includes data by race and gender for students with and without disabilities. In 2011–2012, and again in 2013–2014, every school and district in the nation was required to report its discipline data, and universal collection might also be required for 2014–2015. However, without a stronger permanent policy, the department could revert to less useful biennial data samples in the future. In fact, a new administration could decide to end the CRDC's discipline data collection in its entirety. The Office for Civil Rights is correct in calling the data an "opportunity gap data tool that is allowing citizens and schools nationwide to identify educational equity-related problems and their solutions."[8] In light of these critical benefits, many are frustrated that this tool is being used only every other year.

Given the federal mandates for annual report cards at the school, district, and state level, if annual collection and public reporting of discipline data remains optional, the strong federal recommendations in the new guidance for schools and districts to monitor suspensions and expulsions throughout each school year are unlikely to be realized. Ultimately, annual collection and public reporting is also more efficient because it increases the likelihood the data will be used and ensures that public awareness of disparities remains high.

Unfortunately, the data that are collected are not used effectively. The most glaring example concerns federal oversight and enforcement of the Individuals with Disabilities in Education Act (IDEA), particularly as it pertains to required responses to discipline disparities. Specifically, Section 1418(d) of the IDEA requires states to collect and examine data to determine if significant disproportionality in terms of race or ethnicity is occurring in state and local educational agencies (districts) with respect to the incidence, duration, and type of disciplinary actions, including suspensions and expulsions of 1 day or more. As described in detail in Chapter 6, this can lead to a shift in expenditures to a wide variety of preventive activities, including teacher training in behavior management and tiered intervention strategies such as positive behavior interventions and supports (PBIS). As the Department of Education recently acknowledged in a "request for information," most states have not identified any districts for racial disparities in discipline (Federal Register, 2014, p. 35155).

Although there are clear implementation problems, the President's My Brother's Keeper Initiative, the call for increased data use contained within the federal enforcement guidance, the recommendations of the SSDI's Consensus Report, and the policy changes at the state and district levels all seem to reflect a genuine awareness about and support for a need to reject the status quo and improve education policy.

The possibility for more sweeping and permanent changes might be before us, and with that positive outlook, we make the following research-based explicit data policy recommendations:

- Require states and districts to publicly report disaggregated data annually, including the number of students suspended, the number of suspensions, reasons for out-of-school suspensions, and days of lost instruction, at each school level (elementary, middle, and high). Ensure that the reported data are disaggregated by race/ethnicity, gender, English learner status, and disability status, and that the data are collected and reported in a manner that makes cross-sectional analysis (e.g., Black female students with disabilities) possible as well. Begin data collection on LGBT youth.
- Longitudinal and disaggregated data should be tracked and publicly reported for all students who become involved with the juvenile justice system, including specifics of the offense if school based and the transition back to school or the workforce.
- Annual reports should include more accurate data on security measures and school policing, including data on school-based arrests and referrals to law enforcement, as well as the number of police employed by schools and a comparison of security expenditures to funds dedicated to counseling, mental health, and special education.
- Ensure public reporting and better monitoring of the disciplinary provisions of the IDEA. Furthermore, federal policymakers should extend these statutory requirements to the Elementary and Secondary Education Act so that they apply to all students.

ADD ACCOUNTABILITY

Equally important is that school climate becomes a core component of education accountability systems to promote the use of evidenced-based practices over those driven by an attitude of intolerance.

Ultimately, until discipline data are incorporated into the broader account-ability rubrics used by states to evaluate schools and districts, it is unlikely we will witness comprehensive and lasting improvements in the area of school discipline. Some degree of accountability is now achieved by requiring public reports of the data, but we know that many districts do not comply with the required biennial civil rights data collection and that few states fully comply with the public report-ing obligations pursuant to the IDEA. Therefore, some measured consequence is needed to ensure that such noncompliance is eliminated rather than allowed to expand. Technical assistance should also be available to ensure all districts have the capacity to comply.

Beyond the accountability that comes from reporting data publicly, broader and more lasting policy change is unlikely until the data are used as part of our evaluation systems. Although federal and state accountability requirements are backing away from the most rigid and punitive measures that Congress legislated as part of the Elementary and Secondary Education Act (ESEA, also known as NCLB), these accountability requirements are still very much part of the federal education policy landscape, and most states have similar accountability systems in place. Most agree that when the ESEA is reauthorized, the accountability system will be revised considerably. Measures to report discipline levels and address disparities should be among the revisions to the extent that multiple indicators of academic progress are developed for school- and district-level accountability. The following additional policy recommendations could be adopted along these lines at the state or federal level to encourage the alignment of discipline policies with educational mission:

- Require schools and districts identified for improvement or turnaround measures under state and/or federal accountability provisions to adopt measures to improve teacher–student engagement and school climate and to limit the use of out-of-school suspensions to measures of last resort.
- Include suspension rates among the factors schools and districts use to measure the performance of secondary schools, and as early-warning systems to target supportive interventions for both schools and students.
- Improve the enforcement of the IDEA requirements that students with disabilities receive adequate behavioral supports and services and additional procedural protections to prevent unjust and unlawful suspensions.
- Hold disciplinary alternative schools accountable for improving student behavior and contributing to improved achievement and graduation rates at the district level.

TARGET SUPPORT TO REPLICATE WHAT WORKS

No volume of research for policymakers would be complete without a call for more research. Education reform efforts would no doubt be improved if we had a deeper understanding of why such disparities in discipline exist. And more information is needed on the experiences of LGBT youth. However, as this volume demonstrates, we already know a great deal about effective remedies. The following funding recommendations flow from those findings:

- Invest in remedies that reduce both suspensions and disparities in their use by targeting more funds for systemic improvements in nonpunitive approaches to school discipline, including restorative practices (see Chapter 10) and funding for tiered intervention protocols, such as the Virginia threat assessment guidelines described in Chapter 12.

- Leverage competitive grants to incentivize revisions of school discipline codes that make them align with effective and promising disciplinary practices, such as PBIS, social–emotional learning, and restorative practices.
- Provide support for teacher and principal training and preparation programs and for professional development aimed at promoting higher levels of student engagement and improved relationships between teachers and students (see Chapter 10). In particular, structure grant awards to give preference to research-supported programs. Attention to effective classroom management can also be included in standards for teacher-preparation programs and school leadership training and be required for state certification.
- Add safeguards to ensure that where federal and state dollars are used to create alternative schools, such schools are not fostering an approach that is counterproductive, as documented in Chapter 15.
- Require schools and districts seeking funds for policing and security to demonstrate that they have adequate resources in place for counseling, mental health support, and teacher training in classroom and behavior management.
- Add funds for federal and state civil rights enforcement agents to improve the quality of data reporting, to make discipline data collection and reporting annual, and to provide technical assistance to districts that have problematic disparities.

Whether the positive movement to improve discipline policies and practices under way will lead to sustained policy change is uncertain.

This book highlights just one area to which education reformers need to pay greater attention: school discipline. As this body of research demonstrates, discipline policy is about much more than codes of conduct, the use of suspension or expulsion, or alternative responses to misbehaving students. Effective discipline involves creating healthy and positive relationships among students and teachers, teachers and parents, and schools and communities. We argue that the quality of these relationships is something educators can control, and if that is indeed true, policymakers can create the systems, structures, incentives, and funding to help schools improve.

We have learned from the research findings presented in this book that school environments are often harsher for students in some subgroups than others and, just as important, that they do not need to be harsh at all.

NOTES

The recommendations of this concluding chapter are similar, or identical, to the recommendations of disparities in discipline research collaborative paper (Losen, Hewitt, & Toldson, 2014).

1. The Academy of American Pediatrics' (2013) recent statement put it bluntly when they concluded, "out-of-school suspension and expulsion are counterproductive to the intended goals, rarely if ever are necessary, and should not be considered as appropriate discipline in any but the most extreme and dangerous circumstances, as determined on an individual basis rather than as a blanket policy" (Council on School Health, 2013, p. 1005).

2. The research and remedies presented also did not adequately address the experiences of American Indian youth.

3. Research on implicit bias, and specifically a test developed by neuroscientists, shows that most people have implicit negative bias against Blacks (Akalis, Banaji, & Kosslyn, 2008). There is no reason to think teachers and administrators would be an exception. The most direct links we have about teachers are (a) Patricia Devine has been able to show that preservice teachers hold implicit bias; (b) that with intervention, it is possible to reduce this bias; and (c) that some students see bias in microaggressions (Devine, Forscher, Austin, & Cox, 2012). For summaries of the impact of implicit racial bias and school discipline see Wald, J., at http://www.indiana.edu/~atlantic/wp-content/uploads/2014/03/Implicit-Bias_031214.pdf and Staats (2014).

4. Compared National Estimates from OCR to recently released Civil Rights Data Collection Data Snapshot: School Discipline.

5. For example, Wisconsin's 2011–2012 reported data showed that compared to their 10-year peak in 2005–2006, suspension rates are lower by 1.73 percentage points for students without disabilities and 4.3 points lower for students with disabilities. Similarly, though Black/White disparities are disturbing in their size, they have been reduced slightly in Wisconsin since 2005–2006. The state of Wisconsin posts trend data on their website each year. See http://wisedash.dpi.wi.gov/Dashboard/portalHome.jsp. The disparity calculations were conducted by Daniel Losen. Analysis of the data reported by the state departments of education in California (2012–2013) and Maryland (2012–2013) indicates marginal declines as well. Both states post data on their websites on an annual basis. Maryland data can be found at http://marylandpublicschools.org/MSDE/divisions/planningresultstest/doc/20122013Student/susp13.pdf. The press has also reported lower suspension rates; see http://articles.baltimoresun.com/2014-01-27/news/bs-md-state-discipline-regs-20140127_1_discipline-policy-dale-rauenzahn-suspensions. In Connecticut, the state reports continued declines. Also see Lamback (2013).

6. At 20 U.S.C. Sec. 1418(a), the statute in the relevant parts reads as follows (emphasis added): "In general Each State that receives assistance under this subchapter, and the Secretary of the Interior, *shall provide data each year to the Secretary of Education and the public* on the following: (1) (D) The incidence and duration of disciplinary actions by race, ethnicity, limited English proficiency status, gender, and disability category, of children with disabilities, including suspensions of 1 day or more. . . . (E) The number and percentage of children with disabilities who are removed to alternative educational settings or expelled *as compared to children without disabilities* who are removed to alternative educational settings or expelled."

7. Remarks of U.S. Secretary of Education Arne Duncan at the Release of the Joint DOJ-ED School Discipline Guidance Package (Duncan, 2014, para. 4). See also, in its statement of support, Part A, OCR states that the transformed 2009–2010 CRDC "has been heralded as a first-of-its-kind opportunity gap data tool that is allowing citizens and schools nationwide to identify educational equity-related problems and their solutions" (Office for Civil Rights, 2012, p. 13).

8. The February 2013 GAO report, entitled *Individuals with Disabilities Education Act Standards Needed to Improve Identification of Racial and Ethnic Overrepresentation in Special Education,* addressed more generally the poor oversight of the enforcement of the provisions of 618 (d) regarding racial disproportionality in identification, placement, and discipline. The report focused on identification but is applicable to discipline (GAO, 2013).

REFERENCES

Akalis, S. A., Banaji, M. R., & Kosslyn, S. M. (2008). Crime alert! *Du Bois Review: Social Science Research on Race, 5*(02), 217–233. doi:10.1017/S1742058X08080181

Alonso, A. (2013). *School discipline and student achievement.* Retrieved from http://www.nycourts.gov/ip/justiceforchildren/PDF/NYS%20Summit-PPTs%20for%20Web/P3-Alonso.pdf

Council on School Health. (2013). Out-of-school suspension and expulsion. *Pediatrics, 131*(3), e1000–e1007. doi:10.1542/peds.2012-3932

Devine, P. G., Forscher, P. S., Austin, A. J., & Cox, W. T. L. (2012). Long-term reduction in implicit race bias: A prejudice habit-breaking intervention. *Journal of Experimental Social Psychology, 48*(6), 1267–1278. doi:http://dx.doi.org/10.1016/j.jesp.2012.06.003

Duncan, A. (2014). *Rethinking school discipline, 2014.* Retrieved from http://www.ed.gov/news/speeches/rethinking-school-discipline

Fabelo, T., Thompson, M. D., Plotkin, M., Carmichael, D., Marchbanks, M. P. III, & Booth, E. A. (2011). *Breaking schools' rules: A statewide study of how school discipline relates to students' success and juvenile justice involvement.* New York, NY, and College Station, TX: Council of State Governments Justice Center and Texas A&M University Public Policy Research Institute. http://www2.mysanantonio.com/PDFs/Breaking_Schools_Rules_embargo_final_report.pdf

Federal Register. (2014). *Notices, 2014.* Retrieved from http://www.gpo.gov/fdsys/pkg/FR-2014-06-19/pdf/2014-14388.pdf

Fenning, P., Pigott, T., Engler, E., Bradshaw, K., Gamboney, E., Grunewald, S., . . . McGrath Kato, M. (2013). *A mixed methods approach examining disproportionality in school discipline.* Paper presented at the Closing the School Discipline Gap conference, Washington, DC.

GAO. (2013). *Individuals with Disabilities Educational Act: Standards needed to improve identification of racial and ethnic overrepresentation in special education.* (GAO-13-137). Washington, DC: Author.

Lamback, L. C. (2013). *Suspensions down but imbalance persists.* Retrieved from http://www.ctpost.com/local/article/Suspensions-down-but-imbalance-persists-5046595.php

Losen, D. J., Hewitt, D., & Toldson, I. A. (2014). *Eliminating excessive and unfair exclusionary discipline in schools: Policy recommendations for reducing disparities.* Bloomington, IN: The Equity Project at Indiana University.

Losen, D. J., & Martinez, T. E. (2013). *Out of school and off track: The overuse of suspension in American middle and high schools.* Los Angeles, CA: The Civil Rights Project at UCLA, the Center for Civil Rights Remedies.

Losen, D. J., Martinez, T. E., & Okelola, V. (2014). *Keeping California's kids in school.* Los Angeles, CA: University of California.

Morgan, E., Salomon, N., Plotkin, M., & Cohen, R. (2014). *The school discipline consensus report: Strategies from the field to keep students engaged in school and out of the juvenile justice system.* New York, NY: Council of State Governments.

Obama, B. (2014, February 27). *Obama announces "My Brother's Keeper."* [Transcript.] Retrieved from http://www.cnn.com/2014/02/27/politics/obama-brothers-keeper-transcript

Osher, D. M., Quinn, M. M., Poirier, J. M., & Rutherford, R. B. (2003). Deconstructing the pipeline: Using efficacy, effectiveness, and cost-benefit data to reduce minority youth incarceration. *New Directions for Youth Development, 2003*(99), 91–120. doi:10.1002/yd.56

Staats, C. (2014). *Implicit racial bias and school discipline disparities.* Kirwan Institute Special Report, May 2014. Retrieved from http://kirwaninstitute.osu.edu/wp-content/uploads/2014/05/ki-ib-argument-piece03.pdf

U.S. Department of Education. (2013). *Supportive school discipline initiative.* Retrieved from http://www2.ed.gov/policy/gen/guid/school-discipline/appendix-3-overview.pdf

U.S. Departments of Education and Justice. (2014). *Nondiscriminatory administration of school discipline guidance.* Washington, DC: U.S. Departments of Justice and Education. Retrieved from http://www.justice.gov/crt/about/edu/documents/dcl.pdf

U.S. Department of Education Office for Civil Rights. (2012). *Helping to ensure equal access to education: Report to the president and secretary of education.* Retrieved from https://www2.ed.gov/about/reports/annual/ocr/report-to-president-2009-12.pdf

Watanabe, T. (2013, May 14). L.A. unified bans suspension for 'willful defiance'. *Los Angeles Times.* Retrieved from http://articles.latimes.com/2013/may/14/local/la-me-lausd-suspension-20130515

The White House. (2013). *Now is the time.* Retrieved from http://www.whitehouse.gov/sites/default/files/docs/wh_now_is_the_time_full.pdf

About the Editor and Contributors

Chapter 1

Robert Balfanz is a research professor at Johns Hopkins University, School of Education, and co-director of the Everyone Graduates Center. Vaughan Byrnes is a research associate and research methodologist at the Johns Hopkins Everyone Graduates Center. Joanna H. Fox is a senior policy analyst and program developer at the Johns Hopkins Everyone Graduates Center.

Chapter 2

Tracey Shollenberger is a Ph.D. candidate in sociology and social policy at Harvard University.

Chapter 3

Dr. Jeremy D. Finn is a distinguished professor and department chair at the University at Buffalo, SUNY. His extensive work on class size, student engagement, and dropping out has impacted research and policy nationally and internationally. Timothy J. Servoss is associate professor, Department of Psychology at Canisius College in Buffalo, New York.

Chapter 4

Dr. Miner P. Marchbanks III is an associate research scientist with the Public Policy Research Institute at Texas A&M University. His work focuses on the various predictors of exclusionary discipline and the ultimate results of this punishment. Jamilia J. Blake is an associate professor in the Department of Educational Psychology at Texas A&M University. Her research examines bullying and aggression and exclusionary discipline among Black females. Eric Booth is a research scientist with Gibson Consulting and the Public Policy Research Institute at Texas A&M University. His research focuses on advanced statistical methods for education program evaluation, particularly for at-risk and discipline involved students. Dottie Carmichael conducts applied research at the Public Policy Research Institute, Texas A&M University. Her studies have informed public policymaking in the areas of school discipline and juvenile justice. Allison Seibert is a senior research associate with the Public Policy Research Institute at Texas A&M University. She is responsible for managing large-scale research projects that monitor youth risk behaviors overtime. Dr. Tony Fabelo is the research director for the Council of State Governments Justice Center. He has been at the forefront of pushing data-driven decision-making in criminal justice matters and assisting governments in doing so.

Chapter 5

Jamilia J. Blake is an associate professor in the Department of Educational Psychology at Texas A&M University. Her research examines bullying and aggression and exclusionary discipline among Black females. **Bettie Ray Butler** is an assistant professor of Urban Education at the University of North Carolina, Charlotte. Her primary research interest is education policy, with a focus on issues of equity in the administration of school discipline. **Danielle Smith** is a doctoral student in School Psychology at Texas A&M University. Her research interests are punitive school discipline and juvenile delinquency prevention and intervention.

Chapter 6

Daniel J. Losen, J.D., M.Ed., is the director of the Center for Civil Rights Remedies (CCRR) at UCLA's Civil Rights Project/Proyecto Derechos Civiles, where his work has focused on racial disproportionality in special education, graduation rates, and school discipline since 1999. On these and related topics he conducts law and policy research, has testified before the U.S. Congress and the United Nations, helps draft model legislation, and provides guidance to policymakers, researchers, educators, and civil rights advocates. **Jongyeon Ee** is a graduate student researcher with the Civil Rights Project at UCLA, where she is also a doctoral student in the Graduate School of Education. **Cheri Hodson** is a doctoral student in the Graduate School of Education at UCLA. Her research interests include remedying disparities in school discipline and positive youth development. **Tia Martinez** is an independent consultant and co-author of "Suspended Education in California" with Dan Losen.

Chapter 7

Dr. Ivory A. Toldson is an associate professor at Howard University, senior research analyst for the Congressional Black Caucus Foundation, and current editor in chief of *The Journal of Negro Education*. **Tyne McGee** is a doctoral student in the Counseling Psychology program at Howard University. Her research interests focuses on non-cognitive factors that influence the educational tenure of African American youth. **Brianna P. Lemmons** is a doctoral degree candidate at Howard University in Washington, D.C. Her current research interests are related to the involvement of non-resident African American fathers in the lives of their children.

Chapter 8

Matthew P. Steinberg is assistant professor, Graduate School of Education, University of Pennsylvania. His research focuses on teacher evaluation, urban school reform, school finance and school discipline and safety. **Elaine Allensworth** is the director of the University of Chicago Consortium on Chicago School Research. She conducts research on school improvement and students' educational attainment. **David W. Johnson** is associate director of research and development at the University of Chicago's Urban Education Institute and senior research analyst at the Consortium on Chicago School Research.

Chapter 9

Russell Skiba, Ph.D. is a professor in school psychology and the director of the Equity Project at Indiana University. **Choong-Geun Chung** is a research associate at the Center for Evaluation and Education Policy at Indiana University, Bloomington. **Megan Trachok**, M.S.Ed., is a doctoral candidate in school psychology at Indiana University. **Timberly Baker** is a research associate at Indiana University Bloomington in the Center for Evaluation & Education Policy in The Equity Project. **Adam Sheya**, Ph.D., is an assistant professor in the department of psychology, University of Connecticut. **Robin L. Hughes**, Ph.D., is an associate professor in higher education student affairs in the School of Education at Indiana University.

Chapter 10

Thalia González is an assistant professor at Occidental College in the Department of Politics and Anderson Center of Public Policy. Her research engages the study of law from interdisciplinary and community-focused methodologies and perspectives.

Chapter 11

Anne Gregory is an associate professor at the Graduate School of Applied and Professional Psychology, Rutgers University. Her research aims to help schools reduce race and gender disparities in school discipline. **Joseph Allen** is the Hugh P. Kelly Professor of Psychology and Education at the University of Virginia. His research focuses on the predictors and long-term outcomes of social development processes from adolescence into adulthood. **Amori Yee Mikami** is associate professor, Department of Psychology, University of British Columbia. Her research focuses on parent and teacher interventions for the social problems of youth with externalizing behaviors. **Christopher A. Hafen** is a research scientist at the Center for Advanced Study of Teaching and Learning, University of Virginia. His work includes development of professional development interventions, as well as understanding the development of close relationships in adolescence. **Robert Pianta** is the dean of the Curry School of Education. His research and policy interests focus on the measurement and production of effective teaching in classrooms from preschool to high school.

Chapter 12

Dewey Cornell is Bunker Professor of Education at the University of Virginia and studies youth violence prevention and school safety. **Peter J. Lovegrove**, Ph.D., is a research associate at JBS International, Inc., specializing in youth development and program assessment/ evaluation.

Chapter 13

David Osher is vice president, institute fellow, and advisor to the Health and Social Development Program at American Institutes for Research. **Jeffrey Poirier** is a principal researcher at the American Institutes for Research, leading its LGBT practice area and applying research through training and technical assistance. **G. Roger Jarjoura** is a principal researcher at the American Institutes for Research. His research focuses on the use of mentoring to interrupt the school-to-prison pipeline. **Russell Brown** is the chief accountability officer for Baltimore County Schools, where he works to improve children's lives through education.

Chapter 14

Claudia G. Vincent is a senior research assistant in the College of Education at the University of Oregon. **Jeffrey R. Sprague** is professor of special education and directs research projects on school safety at the University of Oregon. **CHiXapkaid (D. Michael Pavel)** is professor of Native American Studies, Department of Education Studies at the University of Oregon. **Tary J. Tobin**, Ph.D., is a research associate in special education and clinical services at the University of Oregon. **Jeff Gau** is senior analyst at Oregon Research Institute. His quantitative interests are clustered randomized trials and mixed effects models.

Chapter 15

Judi E. Vanderhaar is an evaluation specialist with the Jefferson County Public Schools, Department of Data Management, Planning, and Program Evaluation. **Joseph M. Petrosko** is professor emeritus at the University of Louisville College of Education and Human Development. **Marco A. Muñoz** is an evaluation specialist with the Jefferson County Public Schools Department of Data Management, Planning and Program Evaluation and adjunct faculty at the University of Louisville.

Index

Aber, M. S., 134
Absence from school
  chronic, 26–29
  effect of SWPBIS implementation
    on, 213, 214f, 215
Academic achievement/outcomes
  restorative justice and, 164
  school climate and, 243–244
  school safety and, 124–125
  suspensions and, 17, 22, 23f, 24t, 36,
    37t, 38, 39t, 140, 143, 164
  truancy and, 114
Academic engagement. See Student engagement
Academic Excellence Indicator
    System (AEIS), 62–63
Academy of American Pediatrics, 9, 242, 242n1
Accountability, 217
  federal funding and, 59–60
  within SWPBIS framework, 217
Accountability frameworks/systems
  integrating disciplinary measures into, 41–42
  revision of, need for, 248–249
Achievement gap, 1, 36
Achilles, G. M., 108
Acoca, L., 85
Addington, L. A., 54
Advancement Project/Civil Rights Project, 134
Aggressive behavior. See also Physical assault
  academic disengagement and, 112
  attitudinal offenses vs., 108
Ahmed, D., 84
Akalis, S. A., 243n3
Algozzine, R., 210
Alienation, 55, 60
Allen, J., 169, 217
Allen, J. P., 166–169, 171, 243
Allen, K., 183, 189
Allensworth, E., 32, 118–120, 125
Alonso, Andres, 242
Alternative approaches to discipline, 222–234
  disciplinary exclusion vs., 41, 241

economic costs associated with, 70–71
high- vs. low-suspending schools and, 245
incentives and support for, 41
Alternative schools. See Disciplinary
  alternative schools
Alvarez, L., 142
Alvarez, R., 64–65
American Civil Liberties Union, 112
American Indian youth
  disciplinary disparity and,
    207–208, 243, 243n2
  improving disciplinary equity for, 215–216
  recommendations and, 215–216
  SWPBIS impact on, 213, 214f, 215
American Institutes for Research (AIR), 193, 195
American Psychological Association Zero
    Tolerance Task Force, 32, 129, 175, 180, 188
American School Counselor Association, 85
Anderson, C., 210
Anderson, C. M., 210
Anderson, G., 60
Anderson, G. E., 108
Andree, A., 167
Anthony, S., 91, 108, 134
Arnove, R. F., 225
Aronson, J., 176
Arrest, 32
  suspensions and, 36, 37t, 38, 39t
Artiles, A. J., 229
Arum, R., 32
Aster, R. A., 120
Attendance rates
  following intervention
    implementation, 198–199
  suspensions and, 26
Attitude
  offenses involving, aggressive behavior vs.,
    108
  of school leaders, as predictor for
    disciplinary exclusion,
    9, 134

259

270

Index